THE REFERENCE SHELF   VOLUME 43 NUMBER 2

LAND USE
IN THE UNITED STATES

EXPLOITATION OR CONSERVATION

EDITED BY

GRANT S. McCLELLAN

Editor, Current Magazine

THE H. W. WILSON COMPANY
NEW YORK   1971

THE REFERENCE SHELF

The books in this series contain reprints of articles, excerpts from books, and addresses on current issues and social trends in the United States and other countries. There are six separately bound numbers in each volume, all of which are generally published in the same calendar year. One number is a collection of recent speeches; each of the others is devoted to a single subject and gives background information and discussion from various points of view, concluding with a comprehensive bibliography. Books in the series may be purchased individually or on subscription.

LAND USE IN THE UNITED STATES

Copyright © 1971
By The H. W. Wilson Company

International Standard Book Number 0-8242-0447-6
Library of Congress Catalog Card Number 76-159161

PRINTED IN THE UNITED STATES OF AMERICA

PREFACE

One of the authors quoted in this book points out that our land is an integral part of all life and its resources remain part of the environment. And it is in these terms that this compilation has been envisaged. Today, for the first time in two hundred years, the nation is beginning to grapple with new overall policies regarding our national, or public, lands. Many of the issues of public land policy relate to environmental problems. At the same time contemporary awareness of the varied pollution crises we face has led many to realize that our use of private as well as public lands requires urgent reassessment.

We appear, in fact, to be on the verge of national action respecting land use policy in general, as we overhaul our public lands policies. Interest in the latter has been sparked by a Congressional Committee report called "One Third of the Nation's Land," issued in the summer of 1970 by the Public Land Law Review Commission (PLLRC). Concern about air pollution, water pollution, disposal of solid wastes, and other environmental needs directs attention almost immediately to land use policy—both public and private.

The future of our resources—forests, mines, water, and recreation areas—is locked up with the land in more than a mere semantic sense. Where and how we live—in cities or rural areas, in denser cities or entirely new towns and cities—directly affects our land resources. They are also affected by our modes of travel and where we park our cars and build our airports, as we can see from the increasing paving over of great stretches of land across the country, around and through our cities, and at the supermarkets, and the widespread resistance to the building of new airports.

As these topics are so intimately interrelated, this compilation treats them in the broad ecological situation the

3

country now confronts. The first section touches on our emerging land use policies. Section II, A Land To Live In, briefly raises the issue of a new urban-rural balance and the building or rebuilding of our cities. Questions of conservation and proper use of our water, forest, and mining resources are dealt with in Section III. Brief reference in Section IV is made to our national parks, wilderness areas, and other scenic lands. Last, the important new report of the Public Land Law Review Commission is given in digest form with several critiques appended.

The editor wishes to thank the authors and the publishers of the selections which follow for permission to reprint them in this compilation.

GRANT S. MCCLELLAN

April 1971

A NOTE TO THE READER

The reader's attention is directed to earlier Reference Shelf compilations dealing with related aspects of the problem: *The Water Crisis* (Volume 38, Number 6), edited by George A. Nikolaieff and published in 1967; *Protecting Our Environment* (Volume 42, Number 1), edited by Grant S. McClellan and published in 1970.

CONTENTS

PREFACE 3

I. TOWARD NEW LAND USE POLICIES

Editor's Introduction 9
Henry M. Jackson. Toward a National Land Use Policy   10
Robert E. Bergstrom. Emerging Land Use Problems ...
.... Science   16
John Fischer. Planning a Second America ....
.... Harper's Magazine   19
Judith T. Younger. A New "Domesday Book"? ....
.... Nation   31
Gaylord A. Nelson. Toward a Total Ecological Program
.... Playboy   36

II. A LAND TO LIVE IN

Editor's Introduction 45
Orville L. Freeman. Toward an Urban-Rural Balance ..
.... Minnesota Law Review   46
Frank L. Hope, Jr. Building Entirely New Cities ......
.... Washington Post   55
Wolf Von Eckardt. Rebuilding the Cities We Have ....
.... Washington Post   58
William H. Whyte. A Case for Higher Density Cities ...   62
Helen Leavitt. Highway Networks and Our Lands .....
.... Reader's Digest   74
League of Women Voters of the United States. Zoning
and Proper Land Use   80
Martha Fisher. Cemeteries and Land Use ....
.... Journal of Housing   93

III.   Our Land and Its Resources

Editor's Introduction 99

James Nathan Miller and Robert Simmons. Crisis on
    Our Rivers .... Reader's Digest 100

David W. Hacker. A Storm Roils the Mississippi ......
    .... National Observer 108

William S. Beller. Coastal Areas and Seashores ....
    .... Current History 113

Michael Frome. Forest Lands .... Current History 123

Dale A. Burk. "Mining" the National Forests .. Nation 136

Terri Aaronson. Problems Underfoot .... Environment 144

Luther J. Carter. Land Use and Power Plants .. Science 155

The Evils of Strip-Mining .... New York Times 162

David E. Rosenbaum. Developing Alaskan Lands .....
    .... New York Times 163

IV.   Our Land and Recreation

Editor's Introduction 169

The National Park Service .... Current Biography 169

Kenneth P. Davis. Caring for Our Wilderness Areas ....
    .... Current History 174

John Noble Wilford. For a Prairie National Park ......
    .... New York Times 182

William E. Burrows. Nature's Nurseries ....
    .... Wall Street Journal 188

Burt Schore. Saving the Scenery ... Wall Street Journal 194

V.   Toward a New Public Lands Policy

Editor's Introduction 199

Gladwin Hill. Revising U.S. Lands Policy ....
    .... New York Times 200

Public Land Law Review Commission Recommendations on Public Land Use 206

Donald Jackson. The Conflict Over Public Lands .... Life 216

Angus McDonald. A Blueprint for Corporate Takeover .... Not Man Apart 223

Michael Frome. A Critique of the Public Land Law Report .... Field & Stream 229

Michael Frome. New Goals for Public Land Policy .... Field & Stream 233

Richard M. Nixon. The President Speaks Out .... Congressional Record 238

BIBLIOGRAPHY 245

I. TOWARD NEW LAND USE POLICIES
EDITOR'S INTRODUCTION

Indications that we, as a nation, are moving toward the elaboration of new land use policies—not only for our public lands—are shown by the articles in this opening section. Senator Henry M. Jackson leads off with what in his view is the next logical step in our efforts to maintain a quality environment—the enactment of a national land use policy by the Federal Government. Senator Jackson plans to introduce such legislation in Congress.

A short note follows on some of the present land use conflicts which are now receiving national attention.

John Fischer, former editor of *Harper's Magazine* and author of *Master Plan: U.S.A.*, writes about the "Second America" which will emerge by the end of the century. However difficult it is to grasp, current growth trends indicate that this country can expect *to double* the physical plant of all its cities. Mr. Fischer refers to several recent national Government reports, all of which deal with various facets of this staggering development in store. Needless to say, land use is a core problem here.

In the next article, Judith T. Younger, a former assistant attorney general of New York State, citing William the Conqueror's "Domesday Book," suggests that a similar land census is now needed in the United States.

In the final selection, Gaylord A. Nelson, the Democratic senator from Wisconsin and the state's former governor, outlines a total ecological program for the nation, broader than that undertaken by any national Administration to date, including legislation on economic growth, land use, transportation, population, and other environmental factors.

TOWARD A NATIONAL LAND USE POLICY [1]

Fortunately, we are now making some progress towards the development of intelligent long-range environmental policies, most recently in connection with the enactment of the National Environmental Policy Act.

Many of the environmental aspirations and desires of the American people were written into law in the Environmental Policy Act which the President signed as his first official act of 1970. This measure provides a congressional declaration of national goals and policies to guide *all* Federal actions which have an impact on the quality of man's environment. The act makes a concern for environmental values and amenities a part of the charter of every agency of the Federal Government. It establishes a high level overview agency, the Council on Environmental Quality patterned after the Council of Economic Advisers—in the executive office of the President. The Council's mandate is to identify the basic policy issues and alternatives for environmental administration. Finally, the Act calls for an annual report on the quality of the environment. This report will provide, for the first time, periodic baseline information on the state of the nation's environment.

The most important feature of the Act, however, and, I might add, the least recognized, is that it establishes new decision-making procedures for all agencies of the Federal Government. Some of these procedures are designed to establish checks and balances to insure that potential environmental problems will be identified and dealt with early in the decision-making process and not after irrevocable commitments have been made.

Full implementation of the goals and policies declared by the Act will require additional specific Acts of Congress.

[1] From "A View From Capitol Hill," by Senator Henry M. Jackson (Democrat, Washington), a speech at a conference on Ecology and Politics in America's Environmental Crisis held at the Center of International Studies, Princeton University. August 1970. (Policy Memorandum No 37) Princeton University. Center of International Studies. Corwin Hall. Princeton, N.J. 08540. '70. p 30-40. Copyright 1970 by Center of International Studies. Reprinted by permission.

A National Land Use Policy

A National Land Use Policy is, in my view, a next logical step in our effort to maintain a quality environment.

Land use planning is an essential tool of environmental management for the future. Most existing problems of population density, pollution, and congestion are directly attributable to past shortcomings of land use management—to poor selections among alternative uses of land.

Regulation and control of the land in the larger public interest is essential if real progress is to be made in achieving a quality environment. It is essential because the land is the key to insuring that *all* future development is in harmony with sound ecological principles and environmental guidelines. The problems of the present look relatively insignificant when they are compared with the problems we will have in ten, twenty, thirty years *if* we accept supinely the ultimate consequences of some current projections of future requirements.

Listen to these statistics which are thrown at us by Government prognosticators:

By 1975 our park and recreation areas, many of which are already overcrowded, will receive twice as many visits as today, perhaps ten times as many by the year 2000.

We must construct 26 million new housing units by 1978. This is equivalent to building 2.5 cities the size of the San Francisco-Oakland metropolitan area every year.

Each decade, new urban growth will absorb 5 million acres, an area equivalent to the state of New Jersey.

Demands for electrical energy double every ten years; by 1990 demands will increase by 284 per cent.

In the face of these and similar projections the Federal Government has done little to plan for and deal with the problem of accommodating future growth in a manner that is compatible with a quality environment. We have instead created conditions which encourage haphazard growth and compound environmental problems. These are some of the problems I see:

Public administration is oriented to an annual budget cycle which distorts resource allocation decisions in favor of short-term considerations.

Where long-range planning is undertaken, it is most often intended to meet the problems posed by projected trends. It is seldom directed toward achieving desirable goals.

Public policies are too often defined and carried out in fragmented, narrow-scope programs by mission-oriented agencies.

Because of these and other deficiencies in public administration, the alternatives available are narrowly limited when crises become immediate. Largely they consist of efforts to reclaim a small portion of what is being lost in the growing tides of environmental change.

Planning and Controls Needed

The pressures upon our finite land resource cannot be accommodated without better planning and more effective control. Our land resources must be inventoried and classified. The nation's needs must be cataloged, and the alternatives must be evaluated in a systematic manner.

These and other concerns can only be met if governmental institutions have the power, the resources and the will to enter into effective land use planning, if plans at all levels of government are coordinated, and if public decisions on land use are backed up with effective controls in the form of zoning and taxing policies.

I have introduced legislation in the Senate to establish a National Land Use Policy. While this measure does not purport to be the final answer, it does provide a focal point for analysis and for consideration of alternatives. As introduced, the bill has three major provisions. First, it establishes a grant-in-aid program to assist state and local governments in improving their land use planning and management capability. Second, states are encouraged to exercise states' rights and develop and implement a statewide Environmental, Recreational and Industrial Land Use Plan. Third, the Federal Government's responsibility for coordinating Federal land use planning activities, for improving Federal-state relations, and for developing data on land use trends and projections is enlarged and centralized.

The land use policy bill I have proposed carries with it a big stick, because a big stick is needed. The bill would authorize the President to reduce, at a rate of 20 per cent a year, Federal grant-in-aid programs which have potentially adverse environmental impacts *if* a state should fail to comply with the requirements of the bill.

The programs I have in mind are Federal Highway Trust funds, water resource projects, funds for airports and other public-works-oriented projects. It is my view that it is grossly irresponsible for the Federal Government to pay 90 per cent of the cost of a state transportation system unless the states have: (1) inventoried their land resource base; (2) identified areas for development and preservation; (3) related transportation plans to an overall design for the future; (4) implemented land use controls to protect lakes, ocean beaches, and units of the National Park and Forest system.

One of the recurring and most complex problems of land use decision making today is that existing legal and institutional arrangements are in many respects archaic. They weren't designed to deal with contemporary problems. Industry, for example, is unable to get effective decisions on plant siting and location without, in some cases, running an interminable gauntlet of local zoning hearings, injunctions, and legal appeals. In other cases, industry is welcomed into areas which should be dedicated to other uses under the banner of "broadening the tax base." Often this really means higher taxes, fewer amenities and more problems.

The land use policy bill I have proposed would require the establishment of industrial, conservation, and recreational sanctuaries. These sanctuaries would be established in advance of their need and on the basis of projected demands. Industrial sites would be located so that transportation and environmental problems would be minimized.

Developing New Towns

Another essential element of the bill is the planning and development of new towns. In the next decades, population growth will cause the growth of new communities all over the country. Whether this growth is haphazard and ill-planned or organized and directed depends on our willingness to act decisively now to formulate a new-towns policy. The planned location and development of new towns can relieve pressures on existing cities and avert potential environmental degradation in new areas before it occurs.

As chairman of the Senate Interior Committee, I am particularly interested in the potential of the public lands for new-town development and the Committee will be exploring this subject during the present [Ninety-First] Congress. . . .

Public interest in the environmental crisis has in recent months gathered remarkable momentum, producing an abundance of good intentions. I would remind you, however, as Princeton's Professor Marion Levy is fond of saying, that "good intentions randomize behavior."

To give physical expression to the manifest concern of legislators, students, conservation groups, lawyers and millions of citizens, an adequate level of national investment in a coordinated, systematic and long-range program of environmental administration is needed. We must be prepared to pay for those best things in life that used to be free, including the land, air and water that sustain life itself.

Paying for Quality

It is far easier to gain a consensus that we must pay for environmental quality than to reach agreement on the proper sources of funds. State and local governments, taxpayers and corporate executives, like Uncle Sam, frequently have arms too short to reach their pockets.

Industry's contribution to the "effluent" society has been so important that many feel it must be forced to pay the costs associated with new and higher standards of environmental protection. Unfortunately, many of the industries whose contribution to the deterioration of our environment is greatest are also industries furnishing necessities with a highly inelastic demand; fuels, power of all sorts, transportation and agriculture. In these cases the costs will be passed on to the consumer in a way that may be just as regressive as, say, the general sales tax.

User taxes give the appearance of a kind of roughhewn justice that is often deceptive. If they are carefully designed to exclude necessities, it may be possible, at least partially, to avoid the regressive aspects of some taxes and some programs forcing consumer-borne industry price increases. This method, unfortunately, provides little incentive for innovative controls by industry aimed at stopping pollution as opposed to costly remedial programs to cope with it when it becomes manifest.

The difficulty of arriving at fair and proper methods for generating the considerable capital resources that environmental quality will require is inherent in a society with millions of poor people and, more generally, an uneven distribution of income.

It is all very well for affluent middle class Americans—public officials, college students, politicians, even corporate officers—to demand that the factories be shut down, that a no-growth policy be adopted, that we adopt a new national life style which rejects the materialistic consumptive philosophy we have held dear for so long. But I would add a word of caution. The 26 million people in this country classified as being below the poverty line don't share this view. Poor people, black and white, do not espouse it. They want jobs. They want material goods. They want to be able to send their children to college. They don't want to be the first to suffer under a state-backed program of spartan rigor. Their attitude is that they neither created the environmental mess nor profited from the exploitation of common resources. I must say I find myself in sympathy with their point of view. A real commitment to restoring the quality of the environment means new priorities; this in turn means that housing, poverty, education and other programs must compete with environment for the tax dollar.

Dealing with the environmental problems we face will require some basic value judgments about the quality of life we desire and how it is to be attained. The great universities have many important roles to play in the days ahead in making these judgments. Some of our central environmental problems—such as the problem of air pollution—are vitally dependent on research and development that ought to be going on here and now. Economists can do much to bring to light the burden-sharing implications of alternative methods of financing environmental programs. Systems analysts can do much to illuminate the implications of choice under conditions of uncertainty. Agronomists and chemists can search for better methods of increasing agricultural production without reliance on chemicals that also pollute our land and water.

EMERGING LAND USE PROBLEMS [2]

The patterns of society and economy today foster land use conflicts. The population is growing rapidly. A larger ratio of the population is congregating in urban and suburban complexes. The demand for man's necessities and comforts for an affluent society creates the need for ever-increasing production of foodstuffs, materials, and energy. A highly mobile society energetically intent on recreation assaults our nearby playgrounds and the farthest reaches of our open spaces. When these patterns are combined with a heritage of personal freedom, conflicts in the use of land are inevitable.

[2] From "Land-Use Problems in Illinois," by Robert E. Bergstrom, Illinois State Geological Survey, Urbana, Illinois; a note for a symposium held by the American Association for the Advancement of Science, Chicago, Illinois, December 30, 1970. *Science.* 169:1003-4. S. 4, '70. Copyright 1970 by the American Association for the Advancement of Science. Reprinted by permission.

Furthermore, man, by building, manufacturing, mining, and farming, willfully or unwittingly brings about massive changes—many of them impairments—in his physical environment. These activities affect his fellow man and heighten conflict. Land uses that have deleterious side effects have always aroused the opposition of neighboring property owners, but today large segments of the general public are becoming concerned with certain land uses or practices detrimental to environmental quality. Sometimes this concern is expressed as wrath that may force precipitous action rather than a long-range solution.

The solution to land use conflict presumably should come as a result of fact-finding, planning, and management. Many of the planning agencies today perform only the first two functions and have no effective means of proceeding from a plan to its implementation. Some of the large Government agencies such as the United States Army Corps of Engineers, the Bureau of Reclamation, and the Soil Conservation Service have, in addition to planning functions, specific responsibilities in implementing land and water development and conservation programs. The trend toward broadening the scope of their programs has not always resulted in the gratification of greater portions of society, and conflicts over many of the projects of these agencies are still common.

Much planning is concerned with metropolitan areas and services that are required for concentrations of people and industry, but still conflicts arise when subdivisions willy-nilly overrun choice farmland, when suburbanites are annoyed by local gravel or quarrying operations, or when cities are alarmed by the construction of a nearby nuclear power station.

Industry commonly adds to the land use problems of the metropolitan area because it plans with goals that do not mesh with all the interests of society. To yield profit, industry must produce efficiently and maintain an uninterrupted flow of goods to the consumer. Efficiency sometimes results in the expedient venting of wastes at the factory site, to the detriment of the environment. Today's type of production leads to a further problem at the delivery point—the generation of solid waste. The technology of packaging and delivering "consumer" goods is highly advanced; yet the technology of collecting used or waste products and returning them to disposal points—enormous tasks in our large cities—is very primitive.

The disposal of solid waste is a land use problem inasmuch as a common practice today is to truck the waste into convenient places at the fringes of our cities, usually to the dismay of neighboring property owners. Some cities have more enlightened projects to sequester the solid waste under favorable natural conditions or engineered controls, sometimes with reclamtion or sequential-use benefits, but basically the state of solid-refuse disposal today is one of improvisation rather than thoughtful management.

Agriculture and Mining

Away from the cities, land uses of the open spaces—agriculture and mining—are beset with a number of old problems but are also under new attack by environmentalists. For example, agriculture comes in conflict with surface mining, highway construction, reservoirs, and cities and is also being berated for increasing nitrates and phosphates in our water sources and certain chemicals in our foods. Yet agricultural specialists claim that food production for an expanding population probably will require the most advanced crop-producing technology and that a return to a less sophisticated technology, with fewer chemicals, would require an increase in acres needed to produce food, with consequent utilization of the more marginal lands.

Surface mining of minerals brings on a rash of conflicts. In Illinois the mining of coal, rock, and sand and gravel has raised complaints of noise, dust, heavy vehicle movement, ravaging of land, and impairment of environmental amenities. In many urban areas, the common reaction to surface mining is to prohibit it or to restrict it by zoning ordinances.

In rural areas, it competes with agriculture for land on the basis of dollar return to the landowner.

As a result of legislation and regulation and the mining companies' interest in leaving a usable landscape rather than a wasteland after mining, there has been progress in mining methods and in the reclamation of mining lands for other purposes such as recreation, farming, industrial parks, subdivisions, and controlled solid-waste disposal. Carefully planned and controlled development of mineral resources rather than arbitrary prohibition or restriction of mining is a more logical policy for the future inasmuch as mineral resources are finite in quantity and limited in distribution.

Illinois provides an appropriate setting for illustrating these problems. It is an agricultural as well as a manufacturing state; it has a substantial mining industry; its downstate prairies create some special problems in the development of water resources; and it contains the metropolitan giant of Chicago, situated on one of the Great Lakes. Furthermore, it has experienced widespread public dissatisfaction with the state of its environment, wth the result that this year it combined the functions of several previously existing state agencies to form a new Environmental Protection Agency and created a full-time Pollution Control Board.

PLANNING A SECOND AMERICA [3]

If General Electric expected to double its plant capacity and office space within the next thirty years, you can be sure it would assign a platoon of its ablest executives to figure out the best way to do it. In fact, General Electric almost certainly is doing that right now. I have talked to some of its planning officers, who were (for obvious reasons) discreet about their specific projects, but they were candid enough about

[3] From "The Easy Chair—Planning for the Second America," by John Fischer, former editor of *Harper's Magazine* and author of *Master Plan: U.S.A. Harper's Magazine.* 239:21-5. N. '69. Copyright © 1969 by Minneapolis Star and Tribune Co., Inc. Reprinted from the November, 1969 issue of *Harper's Magazine* by permission of the author.

their operations in general. Their job is to answer questions about the future. . . .

In such long-range planning, General Electric is not remarkable. It is simply following sound business practice. Every enterprise of any consequence has a professional staff at work on its plans for future growth. Every enterprise, that is, except the United States of America.

Within the next thirty years, this country can expect to double the physical plant of all its cities. To take care of the predicted growth in population, it needs to build a new house, school, and office building for every one that now exists. It will need twice as many parking lots, universities, bus lines, jails, garbage dumps, airports, and bars. For the number of Americans almost certainly will rise from about 200 million to 300 million before the end of the century; and virtually all of the new people will live in cities. Indeed, our long-dwindling rural population probably will shrink still further, as displaced farmers continue to move to the metropolises. This means that we face the job of building a Second America—of duplicating all of our man-made assets—within a single generation. What our forebears did in three hundred years, we have to do in thirty. Such is the inescapable arithmetic of the population explosion.

The task probably is not impossible. A nation which can explore the moon ought to be able to tend to its own housekeeping, if it sets its mind to it. The odd thing is that, up until now, we haven't. During the years when we were cheerfully spending $23 billion on outer space, we spent peanuts on the space we have to live in. Even today thousands of talented people are busy planning what to do on the moon, but no agency of Government is planning the Second America. Nowhere in Washington can you find anybody who is responsible for figuring out where those 100 million extra people are going to live, how they will get to work, or who will put roofs over their heads.

Many agencies—indeed, far too many—are fiddling with bits and pieces of the problem; but they work at cross purposes, because they have no common goal. Neither the White House nor Congress has set forth an overall policy to guide them. No one in authority has said, "Here is the blueprint. This is what we want the United States to look like thirty years from now. Every one of you bureaucrats, from the county farm agents to the Atomic Energy Commission, is hereby directed to work to this pattern. Your first responsibility is to make sure that we reach these national goals by the end of the century."

Plans Already Present

Such a blueprint actually exists. It is traced out, in considerable detail and with hundreds of pages of supporting data, in four recently published books. The goals they set are clear, sensible, and well within the country's capacity. They are proposed by some of the best minds in America, after many months of argument and grinding labor. So far, of course, the plan has not been accepted by either Congress or the President. . . . Under our habits of government, it cannot be accepted in Washington until it has been thoroughly discussed throughout the country, and has won a considerable degree of public assent. This process has not even started, because the four books are practically unknown to the public at large. So far as I know, not one of them has been reviewed by the New York *Times* or any other major newspaper, though they have had casual mention in a few news stories. But they will not be ignored forever; on the contrary, they are likely to become central texts for the political debate of the coming decade, because they deal with issues which will shape the lives of all of us, and our children.

The books which comprise The Plan were produced by a curious, and uniquely American, process. It would be an exaggeration to call them underground publications, but they were created so quietly that they almost look surreptitious.

Until quite recently, the American credo held that planning was just dandy for businessmen, but was forbidden to politicians and civil servants. *Public* planning was regarded as a sin, indulged in by godless Communists but unthinkable for any right-minded American. This dogma was formally proclaimed some thirty years ago, when President Roosevelt tried to set up a National Resources Planning Board, on the theory that it might be useful to know what assets we had and how they were being used. . . .

Many people in Government realized that some planning was necessary for the efficient conduct of the public business, just as it is for private enterprise. Their problem was how to go about it without attracting the malevolent attention of the Eastlands, Goldwaters, and House Un-American Activities Committee. A customary solution—imperfect, but better than none—is to work behind a political heat shield: a commission.

Almost anybody can set up a commission. Usually it is appointed by the White House, but on occasion it may be created by a Cabinet member, a congressional committee, a foundation, or by some convocation of mayors or governors. Its chairman is a more-or-less eminent citizen without political ambitions, and therefore not too nervous about criticism; his fellow commissioners ordinarily are obscure characters, vaguely described as "experts." Since it is a quasi-official body, it can be financed with tax money, or in a pinch by foundation grants—usually enough to hire a highly competent staff. Such a commission is directed to study some question—almost always a politically ticklish one—and to come up with recommendations. If these recommendations turn out to be palatable, they can be adopted, with hosannas, by the original sponsor. If not, they can be repudiated or ignored.

The Impact of Commissions

Occasionally a commission produces immediate results, as in the case of the Hoover Commission which led in 1949 to a useful overhaul of the executive branch. More often a commission's findings will sound so radical, or expensive, that neither legislators nor executive agencies will dare to touch them right away. Nevertheless the findings—and the thousands of pages of testimony and studies on which they are based—are now in the public domain. With luck, they will attract the attention of academics and maybe a few journalists; they will be referred to in books and congressional debates; and so their once-startling propositions gradually become familiar. At that point they may be ripe for political action. Thus, for example, President Nixon's recent recommendations for reform of the welfare system are the outgrowth of suggestions put forth years earlier in half a dozen commission reports.

So it is with the four books which outline a plan to accommodate the country's next 100 million people. They are reports of commissions (although one calls itself a committee). While these groups worked independently of each other, their ideas are remarkably similar; and the recommendations of each one tend to complement and reinforce the recommendations of all the others. Nobody intended that their reports should thus fit together to form a reasonably coherent scheme of action—but it isn't altogether coincidence, either. You might say that the pieces fell into that pattern because the spirit of the times demands it; or, more prosaically, that when intelligent men stare long enough at the same body of facts, they are likely to arrive at similar conclusions. As usual, most of the politicians who are aware of these conclusions have greeted them with wary, not to say stunned, silence. It will take a little time yet for them to become commonplaces of political discourse.

Only one of the reports is likely to be read in its original form by any substantial number of ordinary people. Entitled *The New City,* it is the product of the National Committee on Urban Growth Policy. It was brought out . . . August [1969] in an attractive format, with plenty of pictures, by a commercial publisher, Praeger . . . , and is available through bookstores; moreover, it was edited by Donald Canty, a professional writer-editor. The other three reports were published by the Government Printing Office in its usual drab style; they have to be ordered from the Superintendent of Documents; and they are written for the most part in the Late American Mandarin dialect which is now standard with bureaucrats and social scientists. Consequently their ideas are not likely to to reach many readers, aside from determined urbanologists, until they are available in translation.

More People in Old or New Cities?

All I can attempt in this space is to indicate the main thrust of their argument. Each of the commissions concluded independently that it would be a hideous—and expensive— mistake to force the next 100 million Americans to live in our present cities. Yet that is precisely where they will end up, if present trends are permitted to continue. Already two thirds of our population is living in some 230-odd metropolitan areas: cities of 50,000 and more, together with their suburbs. According to the Census Bureau projections mentioned earlier, virtually all of the anticipated increase will crowd into those same cities unless we so something to divert it elsewhere. Not because everybody wants to hive up that way. People are being pushed in that direction by Government policies of long standing—the farm program, the welfare system, the location of science centers, the obsolete rules for building public housing and insuring home mortgages, the way Government contracts are let. None of these policies was meant to shove people into the already clotted-up metropolitan centers. Each of them was originally devised for an entirely different, and well-intended, purpose. Only belatedly did it become apparent that they are, as an unexpected byproduct, influencing the direction of future growth—and that the cumulative result may well be a national disaster.

How this works is explained in two of the reports: one by the National Advisory Commission on Rural Poverty, the other by the Advisory Commission on Intergovernmental Relations. The first was a temporary *ad hoc* group appointed by President Johnson; he did not like its findings, presumably because they were critical of measures to which he was committed, such as the oil-depletion allowance and the subsidy of rich farmers. For months the report (*The People Left Behind*) lay buried in the White House and might never have been released, if it had not leaked inadvertently to the press. The other commission is a permanent body established ten years ago as a joint enterprise of Federal, state, and local governments. In its quiet way it has been doing some of the most hardheaded and farsighted planning ever undertaken in this country, and has issued more than forty reports, many of them highly technical. The most important of these (in my opinion, at least) appeared in 1968 under the title *Urban and Rural America: Policies for Future Growth*. It not only presents a reasoned criticism of the country's present policies—or nonpolicies—but also sets forth an array of alternatives. The fourth book, *Building the American City*, is better known as the Douglas Report, after Paul H. Douglas, former Senator [Democrat] from Illinois and chairman of the Commission on Urban Problems. It is the longest (more than 500 pages) and offers the most detailed diagnosis of the cities' ills, together with prescriptions for curing them.

Revolutionary Proposals

Anyone who reads the four reports together quickly realizes that they are revolutionary documents—perhaps as revolutionary as anything published in this country since *The Federalist* papers. They demand nothing less than a reshaping of American institutions—the whole web of local governments, the tax system, the labor unions, the welfare programs, and many another hallowed relic—and they make such a compelling case that the reader is likely to find he has become a revolutionist himself before he reaches the last page.

The most dramatic proposals are those designed to channel our growing population away from Megalopolis. This is a prime goal of all four commissions, although each of them approaches it in a different way.

The New City recommends the building of 110 new communities within the next thirty years, to provide homes and jobs for 20 million people. Ten of them would be cities of at least one million population; the rest would average about 100,000 each. The Rural Poverty Commission in its report, *The People Left Behind,* puts more emphasis on encouraging the growth of existing small towns, especially in those parts of the country such as Appalachia, the South, and the Midwest which have been sending the most migrants to the big cities. Many a shabby and discouraged village of, say, 5,000 people can be converted into a thriving and attractive community of 50,000 to 100,000 if the right steps are taken to bring in new industries.

Urban and Rural America: Policies for Future Growth endorses both of these strategies. They supplement each other, and both are clearly needed since the proposed new cities would take care of only a fifth of the added population. But this study, like the Douglas Report, also devotes considerable attention to the things which have to be done to make our present big cities livable and governable. All four recommend the setting up of a new and muscular arm of Government to handle the detailed planning for future growth, and to see that the plans are carried out. (Mr. Nixon's Council for Urban Affairs, [formerly] headed by Pat [Daniel P.] Moynihan, might well evolve into just such an agency.)

My first reaction to this Grand Design was skepticism. It sounds great, all right, but isn't it too grandiose to be practical? And how could the country ever pay for it?

As I prodded deeper into the assembled evidence, however, my skepticism began to erode. I ended up convinced not only that the plan is feasible, but that it probably will be achieved in large part before the end of the century. Moreover, this undertaking could turn out to be more exciting than the exploration of space—and far more likely to enlist the enthusiastic commitment of alienated young people.

Cost is not so big an obstacle as it might seem. The new cities should pay for themselves; indeed, they might actually return a profit to the public purse. And in any case, most of the capital would come from private investors rather than the taxpayers.

That is one of the lessons we have learned from Western Europe, where new cities are an old story. Great Britain, for instance, already has built fourteen of them, providing homes and close-at-hand jobs for half a million people. They have proved so successful, both socially and economically, that fourteen more are now in the works. The latest of these, announced . . . [in] January [1969], will be the most ambitious new city yet undertaken; eventually it alone will accommodate a half-million people, and the total population of the twenty-eight projects should reach three million. The experience of Finland, Sweden, and Holland with similar projects has been equally encouraging.

America's Once-New Cities

Our own experience has been encouraging too, although few people realize it. For new communities are also an old story in America—so old it has been largely forgotten. Every schoolchild learns that Washington, D.C., was designed from scratch by Major L'Enfant. But how many know that he also planned Paterson, New Jersey, in 1791 as a new city sponsored by the Society for Establishing Useful Manufactures? Or that Marietta, Ohio; Salt Lake City; Bethlehem, Pennsylvania; and Winston-Salem all originated as new towns, to mention only a sampling out of dozens of such ventures?

Most of these were started before the Civil War, when cheap land was plentiful, by private corporations or religious sects. A few more were built with Government money during the Depression years, when private capital was hard to come by: notably Norris, Tennessee, and three so-called "Greenbelt Towns" near Cincinnati, Milwaukee, and Washington, D.C. They served as proving grounds for new ideas in design —the superblock, cluster housing, the separation of auto and pedestrian traffic—which eventually were widely adopted by private developers. At the time, however, they brewed up a storm of irrational emotion. . . .

Only in the last decade has big business started to invest in new communities, on a scale far larger than is generally realized. Fifty-two such projects were under way in 1968, each of them covering at least a thousand acres and offering all the facilities needed for a community of three thousand or more residents. The most famous are Reston and Columbia, on opposite sides of Washington, D.C., but most of them are located in California, Florida, Arizona, and Colorado. The largest is California City, embracing more than 100,000 acres and designed to accommodate eventually 600,000 people; it is the brainchild of a rich young man named William M. White, Jr., the head of Great Western United Corporation. Other major corporations involved in building new communities are General Electric, Westinghouse, IT&T [International Telephone & Telegraph Corp.], Boise Cascade, and the Del E. Webb Company. All of them, and a dozen smaller firms in the same field, obviously expect to earn a profit.

Can Big Business Do the Job?

In that case, why shouldn't we depend on private enterprise to build all the new cities we need, with little or no help from Government? In theory, this sounds reasonable, because the financial arithmetic is enticing. All you have to do is buy a few thousand acres of farmland at, say, $500 an acre, build the nucleus of your town, and then sell off the land at perhaps ten times its original price, plus construction costs. The creation of a new population center is all it takes to send land values skyrocketing; witness what has happened in Rockland

County, New York, or in the new city of Columbia, Maryland.

In practice, alas, private enterprise can't do the job alone, for two reasons.

First, it is too hard to assemble large tracts of land in places where new communities are needed. Only a genius like James Rouse could have assembled at a reasonable cost the 14,000 acres needed for Columbia, in the fast-growing area between Washington and Baltimore, and he probably could not duplicate the feat today. Several of the new-town builders in the West avoided this problem, because they already owned huge expanses of farming land; examples are the Irvine Ranch and the acreage where Great Western United once raised sugar beets. But few such situations are left.

In the second place, a new town requires a lot of "patient capital" to finance the initial streets, sewers, water supply, and other community facilities. The investment is safe enough, but it cannot be fully repaid until the whole project is completed—which may be twenty or thirty years, or longer. Even the strongest corporations find it hard to raise that kind of capital, especially in a tight money market. That is the reason why Robert Simon, the original developer of Reston, Virginia, got into trouble and had to turn control of the management over to Gulf Oil.

If we are going to get the new cities we need, therefore, some arm of Government will have to help out in three ways: (1) it must assemble large blocks of land, without running up the price, by use of its powers of condemnation and eminent domain; (2) it must put up a good part of the "front-end money" for building community facilities, in the form of long-term loans; (3) it must take responsibility for the over-all planning, which no private corporation is capable of handling; only a public agency can, or should, select the sites for the 110 new communities, set standards for protection of the environment, and arrange inducements, when necessary, to create job opportunities. (This does *not* mean Government subsidy to business; usually all it takes to bring new industries into the desired location is provision of a good highway, a dependable water supply, and perhaps an industrial park, a Government installation, or a nearby university. Witness what happened when Route 128 was built as a ring highway around Boston.)

The rest of the job can confidently be left to private enterprise. Experience to date, both here and abroad, indicates that plenty of businessmen will be eager to flesh out the new community with homes and factories, once the skeleton is in place: that is, the basic plan and the infrastructure of streets and utilities.

It makes no sense to calculate the cost of building the Second America according to the four-book plan—or some variant—without also looking at the cost of the alternative. If we simply let our present cities double in size, in the chaotic and heedless way they are now growing, the cost will be infinitely greater. One reason is what economists call "diseconomies of scale." After a city reaches a certain size, the per capita cost of providing services—water, police protection, transport, and all the rest—begins to rise sharply. (Nobody knows for sure what the optimum size might be, because our political scientists have done surprisingly little research on this question; the most plausible estimates I have seen suggest that the desirable population ceiling may lie somewhere between 200,000 and one million.)

Far greater, however, are the social costs of urban elephantiasis, and tax costs which inevitably follow. The events of the last five years have made one thing unmistakably clear: when a city gets too big, it pays an enormous price in crime, drug addiction, spreading slums, decaying schools, and racial turmoil.

If he is interested in saving money, therefore, every true conservative ought to be a passionate advocate of The Plan. So should everybody who simply wants the country to be a decent place to live in. After all, why shouldn't we build the Second America in a sensible and humane fashion? If the British and the Finns can do it, why can't we?

ancial incentives to teach owners and local govern-
to think in terms of the public good. The educational
of these programs, judging from the ugly buildings,
roads, smog-covered cities and polluted waters which
nd us, has not been impressive. Despite the deteri-
g environment, few Americans would vote to scrap the
t system of local land use regulation. They doubt that
al or central controls would yield anything better. The
an experience supports them.

the Soviet Union land belongs to the state. The gov-
nt has absolute powers and public values are supposed
e precedence over private. Despite these advantages the
ans have hardly made perfect use of their land. Rich
and is allocated to housing and industry while nearby
tivated acreage lies overlooked. Industrial enterprises
and mine but fail to take protective measures or re-
tate the land. Thus, large areas of the country have
ruined through wind and water erosion and lost fertil-
rable land per capita declined sharply from 1.06 hectares
56 to .96 in 1966. The situation is worse in individual re-
cs. . . . Citizens farm their private plots intensively—
make up only 3 per cent of the country's total cultivated
but produce more than half its eggs and potatoes and
y half its meat and vegetables—to the neglect of less
ding obligations on state and collective farms. Others
rich on profits from illegal building, rentals and sales.

A New Domesday Book?

he Soviet government has responded with a "new"
me for determining priorities, allocating land and con-
ng its use. This plan, Draft Principles of Land Legisla-
as it is called, is based on an idea which came out of
man England 884 years ago. The Russians, concerned for
uture, have harked to William the Conqueror's "deep
h with his wise men" which resulted, according to W. F.
land, in "the mission, throughout all England of 'bar
'legates' or 'justices' charged with the duty of collecting'

A NEW "DOMESDAY BOOK"? [4]

There are, according to the latest United Nations count, 3.42 billion people in the world. Two hundred thirty-nine million or 7 per cent of them are in the Soviet Union and 200 million, or almost 6 per cent, are in the United States. The Soviets have one sixth of the world's total land area, or 8.7 million square miles, to romp in; the American national playpen is less than half that size, 3.6 million square miles. Soviet and American boundaries, barring conquest or moon colonies, are fixed, but inside them the populations expand. Thus the need for land multiplies, and ever-increasing numbers of Russians and Americans clamor for more room. Take, for example, three of modern life's greatest consumers of space.

Housing, Cars, and New Towns

Housing. More and more land is destined to be occupied by housing. The Soviet Union is the third most prolific housebuilder in the world. It has been filling up acreage at an annual rate of 10 new dwellings per 1,000 people, and last year completed 2.3 million new units. Despite this intensive building program, begun in the mid-fifties, available housing facilities still lag behind the demand. To meet future needs in urban areas alone, the Russian house-building rate will have to increase by more than 30 per cent in the next eleven years.

The United States boasts 342 dwelling units per 1,000 people as compared to 240 for the Soviet Union. It proposes, nevertheless, to build another 26 million homes in the next 10 years. Even if this fantastic goal is met, a trend toward two-house families foreshadows unlimited need. A Bureau of the Census Survey reports that 1.7 million households (one out of every 35) new have second homes and 300,000 more planned

[4] From "A Tip From the Conqueror," by Judith T. Younger, a former assistant attorney general of New York State and a former teacher of land use planning at New York University School of Law. *Nation.* 208:275-6. Mr. 3, '69. © 1969, The Nation Associates, Inc (The views expressed here are those of the author and do not represent the official policy of the Attorney General of New York.) Reprinted by permission.

to acquire them during the two years beginning in April 1967. As the number of dwelling units increases, so does their size. In the five years from 1960 to 1965, the average number of rooms per Russian dwelling went up from 2.8 to 3. There was a comparable rise in the United States, from 4.8 to 5.

Cars. A record 9.6 million cars were sold in the United States in 1968, with almost 73 million of known age already in use in 1967. Despite the almost 4 million miles of municipal and rural highway on which cars can travel, more land continues to be set aside for their use. Last year Congress added $14 billion to its already burgeoning highway construction fund, authorized 1,500 miles of "missing link" highways, launched a program by which the Federal Government will pay half the cost of demonstration parking lots built at the boundaries of business districts in cities of more than 50,000, and ordered the construction of the controversial Three Sisters Bridge and an eight-lane Potomac River Freeway in the District of Columbia.

If the Soviet Union now assigns less land to cars, it is only because it has fewer of them. Recent developments indicate that it is catching up fast. Next year, for the first time in its history, the Soviet government will allocate funds under a separate budget heading for gasoline stations, car wash facilities, repair shops, spare-parts suppliers, garages and other service associated with automobiles. Passenger car production —now about 250,000 a year—will increase fourfold when the $800 million Fiat plant in construction at Togliatti on the Volga River begins operations in the seventies. . . .

New Towns. In 40 years from 1926 to 1966, the urban population of the Soviet Union rose from 26.3 million to 124.8 million; the rural population decreased from 120.7 to 107.1 million. Fifty-four per cent of the population now lives in urban developments; by 1980, the figure will grow to 70 per cent. Determined to avoid the urban sprawl, characteristic of American cities, the Soviets, like the English, have adopted a policy of containing the growth of old communities and settling increasing numbers of the population in new

ones. Thus from 1917 through 1965, than 900 new towns, 400 on complete through the development and radica ing small settlements.

Despite similar long-term popula in the United States, unlike those of been strictly private affairs. No one k there are, estimates ranging from 2 Johnson's Advisory Commission on I tions expressed doubt that "new com porating significant residential, con features exceed fifty projects in all o its April 1968 report, it listed fifty-t struction, covering 879,913 acres in e ing in size from 1,000 acres (Oxmoor acres (California City, California) . number, new towns are likely to p given them its imprimatur, offering, guarantee bonds, debentures and note to undertake their development.

Other Demands on th

Houses, motor cars and new town tenders for available space. Advocate power plants, parks, universities, ate wildlife refuges, jogging trails, subwa trial complexes all want more land f are getting it, but not in the most suit it, but not in the most beautiful ways; as if the supply were inexhaustible. T America, where land development is dickering between private landowne local governments endowed with the p Owners are interested in profits; local ing those who elect them. In the last has passed a host of laws, ranging from Act of 1949 to the New Communities for the Conqueror, "from the verdicts of the shires, the hundreds and the vills, a *descriptio* of his new realm." In essence, the Soviet Draft Principle is the same thing as William's *descriptio* or "Domesday Book," as it came to be called. If the Russian plan, being discussed throughout the nation, is passed as expected, the central government will be charged with compiling a nationwide *descriptio* of the use, soil characteristics and economic value of every bit of land in the country. The ultimate product, a Domesday Book for the Soviet Union, will be the basis for rational classification, assignment and use of the land.   1597180

The idea of a land census . . . is a good one in these times of expanding population and diminishing open space. It seems particularly apt for America, where land development is becoming a profitable corporate venture. Companies which have never been in the field before are suddenly buying up land. They are acquiring large tracts, planning their use, and marketing to builders what J. W. Van Gorkom, president of Union Tank Car Company, calls a "complete package," including roads, utilities and zoning. This kind of program may be good for stockholders in Union Tank Car Company, Chrysler, Westinghouse, I.T.&T. [International Telephone & Telegraph Corp.], Gulf and Western and the other corporations that will join them in the land development business. The important question, however, is whether the rest of America can afford it. Large corporations are unlikely guardians for a dwindling natural resource. They are in business for profits. Land development, Van Gorkom freely admits, is expected to "yield ample rewards." Should big corporations be allowed to enjoy them? Perhaps. Corporate giants may produce better landscapes than do individual developers or national governments, and we may still have enough undeveloped land left to afford the experiment. But perhaps not. Corporate carelessness made a cesspool of the Connecticut River, defaced the Kentucky countryside and created the oil slick which . . . [killed] sea birds in the Santa Barbara Channel and . . . [threatened] ruin to California's finest beaches.

Whatever the decision, it should be an informed one. We ought to take a leaf from the Conqueror's book and arm ourselves, like the Soviet Union, with an up-to-date inventory of our land. Once we know what we have, we can perhaps agree how to use it.

TOWARD A TOTAL ECOLOGICAL PROGRAM [5]

If we are to achieve a decent, livable environment, we are going to have to adopt new policies of a kind that will interfere with what many have considered their right to use and abuse our air, water and land just because that is what we have done throughout our history. . . .

Many of the battles will be fought on the local and state levels. But as a United States senator, I am especially concerned about what can be done by the Federal Government. The following are what I consider the steps necessary to a minimal beginning:

A National Policy on American Growth

We must establish a national policy that reconciles our powerful drive for growth in quantity with the need to preserve and enhance the quality of life. Such a policy must include establishing far better measures of our progress than sheer numbers of consumer goods produced or the gross national product alone. As economist Robert Lekachman has noted, the present GNP goes up even when a new pulp mill pours wastes into a river and people downstream have to pay to treat the dirty water.

To establish a true measure of this country's actual growth, we must require that the costs of protecting the environment be made a part of doing business. As an example, we ought to consider Lekachman's proposal to require airlines to pay property owners for the right to route flights

[5] From "Cleansing the Environment," by Gaylord A. Nelson, former governor of and now Democratic senator from Wisconsin. *Playboy.* 18:147+. Ja. '71. Originally appeared in *Playboy* magazine; copyright © 1970 by HMH Publishing Co. Inc. Reprinted by permission of *Playboy* and the author.

over their land. We also ought to consider setting a luxury charge on electric power; the threatened brownouts and blackouts around the country from the power- and fuel-supply squeeze ought to be fair warning that we must begin to regulate American growth and resource use. As another example of building environmental costs into the balance sheet, we ought to impose prohibitive penalty charges and court injunctions immediately on the manufacturers of detergents, pesticides and other products who have consistently refused to take into account the environmental and health consequences of their goods.

The question of how much of the cost of the environmental cleanup should devolve upon the consumer is a difficult one. I don't think there's any doubt, for example, that the consumer would have to bear some of the cost of the expensive cooling systems we should be attaching to all nuclear power plants. Yet it is also true that the free-enterprise system that invented mass production surely must be capable of minimizing such cleanup costs. As an example, the country's power industry could be compelled to complete a national power grid that would shift energy from one coast to the other as peak requirements shifted. In the crucial matter of cleaner automobiles, we have a case where competition should work to the consumer's advantage: My guess is that such countries as Japan will be able to meet stiff Federal standards for auto pollution without tremendous price increases. If they can do so, Detroit will have to follow suit.

At the Federal level, the President's Council on Environmental Quality should have the power to hold up any Government project that threatens environmental destruction. The Government has been one of the worst offenders in encouraging America's pursuit of quantity without regard for the consequences.

The powerful tools of the Federal budget must also be used to encourage an environmentally sound distribution of investment, growth and population. Our cities must be revived in human terms; new towns must be opened in our neglected rural areas. The top priority must be the elimination of urban and rural slums, the worst environments in America. Any environmental effort that does not confront the intolerable way of life in the slum—the rats, poor housing, ill health, immobility, lack of parks and recreation, congestion, noise, pollution—is a cruel waste.

The idea that a new growth policy and environmental control are going to destroy our economy is a myth. Water- and air-pollution-control technology alone will be a several-billion-dollar-a-year business very soon—and a signficant addition to the GNP. Building the urban transit we so urgently need would create a huge demand for new technology, capital and jobs. And cleaning the environment will, as already pointed out, result in immense savings.

A National Land Use Policy

We must establish a national policy for land use with enough teeth to halt the kind of development for industry, commerce, highways and housing that is needlessly ravaging the countryside. We desperately need a tough Federal statute regulating and requiring restoration in the strip-mining that has already laid open lands equivalent to a lane 100 feet wide and 1.5 million miles long. We should enact comprehensive coastal-zone-management legislation—such measures have been proposed—and use the Army Corps of Engineers' powerful regulatory authority to halt the reckless dredging and filling that have obliterated 900 square miles of our vital coastal wet lands in the past twenty years and is cutting a key link in the life systems of the sea.

We must launch a massive program to buy up for the public or protect by easements the remaining ocean and Great Lakes shore lines. Already, 95 per cent of the recreationally useful shore line has been gobbled up for private homes. And we need a national lakes-restoration program to stop the poor development and waste-treatment practices that are destroying the Great Lakes and thousands of other inland lakes. We must set tough new controls, carried out with all the powers of Government, to regulate the laissez-faire urbanization that is devouring 420,000 acres of land a year, wiping out everything in its path and causing widespread visual blight. Achieving rational land use in this country will, of course, require new metropolitan and regional authorities that have the power to implement plans, to eliminate the conflicts among the thousands of state and local agencies and to veto programs that violate environmental guidelines.

A National Policy on Air and Water Quality

We must establish a policy with standards tough enough to result in the actual enhancement of the environment. Very simply, the standards must require every industry, municipality and Government facility to install immediately the best pollution-control equipment available. And as better waste-treatment systems are designed, they must be installed without delay. The penalties for violation of these pollution-control standards must be, again, prohibitive fines and court injunctions.

Because of the ever-increasing quantity and complexity of our wastes, the national goal in the near future must in most cases be treatment approaching 100 per cent effectiveness. Nothing short of a Federal-assistance program to municipalities on the gigantic scale of the Interstate Highway Program will achieve this objective. Further, we must immediately conduct a national industrial survey to determine the exact breakdown of the wastes from every plant in the country and vastly increase our monitoring-and-surveillance program. We must also set a national deadline of 1975 for a near-pollution-free engine in all new cars.

A National Policy on Recycling Solid Wastes

We must find new uses for wastepaper, bottles, cans, jars and other trash, turning them into valuable new resources.

There is really no alternative, for we produce seven pounds of waste per capita per day in the United States. That's 145 pounds annually for every man, woman and child in the world. It is estimated that by 1976, wastes from packaging alone will come to 661 pounds per year for every American; that's a grand total of more than 66 million tons.

A National Policy on Resource Management

We need a national policy to halt the plunder of our mineral, timber and public land resources. This rape of the earth is being carried out with utter disregard for recreation, wilderness and the preservation of the life-support systems on which our survival depends. We must declare a moratorium on the drilling of any new undersea oil wells on the outer continental shelf until we need the oil and have the technology to avoid Santa Barbara-type disasters. Each year, there are more than 10,000 spills of oil and other hazardous materials in the United States.

We must also maintain the policy of protecting our national forests in perpetuity. These are now threatened by intensified industry pressures to vastly increase national forest timber-cutting. And we should act immediately to implement the National Wilderness Act of 1964 to preserve the remaining shreds of America's wild lands, a program now bogged down in the Federal bureaucracy.

A National Oceans Policy

To avoid the greatest disaster of all, pollution of the sea, we must establish a national oceans policy outlawing the use of the oceans by cities, industries, vessels and the Federal Government as dumping grounds for everything from nerve gas to junked automobiles—a step I proposed last February in the first such legislation. Most marine scientists say that if we continue to use the sea as the trash can for the world, all edible and otherwise useful marine life will be destroyed in 25 to 50 years.

A National Policy of Technology Assessment

A new national policy also must be established declaring that pesticides, detergents, fuel additives, the SST—all the plethora of products turned out for a consumer society— will not be allowed in the market place until they are tested and meet both environmental and health standards. A national technology review board should be established immediately by Congress to formulate those standards. We must also take immediate steps to eliminate slow-degrading chlorinated hydrocarbon pesticides and find an environmentally safe alternative for the phosphate base in detergents.

A National Transportation Policy

We must establish a national policy that will offer mobility for Americans without the social and environmental consequences of the present emphasis on more and more automobiles and more and more highways. In order to preserve the flexibility and freedom provided by the automobile, it is essential that we have adequate mass-transportation systems to relieve the pressure; as a first step, we should earmark monies from the Highway Trust Fund for such a program.

A National Policy on Population

We should establish a national policy whose objective is stabilizing our population growth with a program of intensive research into all the means of effective and safe family planning, and a broad educational effort making this information available to all who desire it. In all likelihood, it will be impossible to preserve an environment of quality if world population continues to double and redouble every few decades. By any standard of environmental measurement, the United States is already overpopulated. If this country cannot manage the wastes produced by 205 million people, it will be catastrophic if we reach 300 million as is possible within the next thirty years.

A National Policy of Citizens' Environmental Rights

Finally, a national policy must be established that recognizes every person's right to a decent environment, that gives the citizen standing in court to protect this right against abuse by other individuals, by industry or by public agencies. As matters now stand, the individual often finds himself with no remedy in the face of the pollution of a lake that belongs to the public or the dirtying of the air he must breathe or the shattering din to which he is subjected. To strengthen every individual's hand, I propose amending the Constitution to read: "Every person has the inalienable right to a decent environment. The United States and every state shall guarantee this right."

These are the specific first steps that should be taken at the Federal level. But they can't possibly work without the great weight of public concern and commitment behind them. In the past few months, we've seen environmental action groups organizing nationwide, building from the local and state levels up, to launch a sustained environmental effort.

We should now declare an annual Earth Week, to be held the third week in April, as a time of assessment in which every community, every city, every state—and the nation as a whole—could spell out the specifics of the environmental performance gap. The environmental groups should take inventory of local and regional problems, testify at hearings for tough standards and enforcement and campaign for candidates who will take strong environmental stands.

Up to now, the decisions that have destroyed our environment have been made in the board rooms of giant corporations, in the thousands of Government-agency offices protected from public scrutiny by layers of bureaucracy—and even in the frequently closed committee rooms of Congress. Now the public is rightfully demanding that these matters be brought out into the open and insisting that environmental and consumer advocates be installed in the Federal agencies and on the corporation boards. To those who will say it can't be done because "profit" and "progress" as we know them may have to suffer, I say that the cost of not acting will be far greater than anything we have yet imagined.

II. A LAND TO LIVE IN

EDITOR'S INTRODUCTION

Ultimately concern for our land is concern for living space—for all Americans. It is here that many social and economic issues join those of environment and use of land. Some of these can, of course, only be hinted at in this compilation. Thus full consideration cannot be given to zoning problems in cities (a crucial real estate as well as ethnic and racial problem) nor to transportation facilities and their inroads on our land—to say nothing of the lands of American Indians, once held in tribal ownership and conserved with reverent care.

The question of what urban-rural balance we should seek is dealt with in the first selection by former Secretary of Agriculture Orville L. Freeman. The pros and cons of rebuilding our cities or building entirely new ones are debated in the next two articles by an urban planner, Frank L. Hope, and a Washington *Post* staff writer, Wolf Von Eckardt. Next, an authority on planning, William H. Whyte, presents a closely reasoned case for accepting high population densities as inevitable while making efficient arrangements to accommodate them.

Then follows an article on the folly of our highway system excerpted from Helen Leavitt's *Superhighway— Superhoax*. The use of zoning to effect proper land use is the subject of the next selection, taken from a League of Women Voters of the United States review of a 1968 summary report of the National Commission on Urban Problems.

A final article on cemeteries comes from Martha Fisher, senior editorial associate of the *Journal of Housing*. Two million acres of cemetery land exist in the United States, most of it in choice locations in or near cities. She points out how we can plan better use for such lands.

TOWARD AN URBAN-RURAL BALANCE [1]

During my service as Secretary of Agriculture, the need for nationwide action to correct detrimental trends in domestic population distribution (settlement patterns) became dramatically clear. What I call rural-urban balance —an easy relationship of people, land (space) and economic opportunity, with all the social consequences this involves —had been destroyed in much of the nation. Virtually every aspect of the urban crisis—poverty and welfare, employment, crime, housing and health—could be linked to a migration from rural America that resulted in too many people on too little space. . . .

At the beginning of the 1960s, no level of government and few Americans in the private sector had shown either understanding or the capacity to anticipate the impact of gross population movements. Historically, this is understandable, since basic to the tensions and frustrations of the latter one third of the twentieth century has been our failure as a nation, during the first two thirds of the century, to grasp the implications of the unprecedented technological and productive forces and the resulting change in population patterns that we unleashed. In the short period since World War II, our population has grown by 55 million—37 per cent. The value of goods and services we produce each year has increased from $280 billion to more than $800 billion. Three million farms have disappeared in a technological revolution that is still sweeping through agriculture. More than 20 million persons have abandoned the farms and small towns for the city. One third of the population has left the city for the suburbs.

[1] From "Towards a National Policy on Balanced Communities," by Orville L. Freeman, former Secretary of Agriculture. *Minnesota Law Review*. 53:1163-78. Je. '69. © 1969 Minnesota Law Review Foundation. Reprinted by permission.

We have been aware that our society is changing, of course, but there has never been any national recognition of what this pellmell change meant in terms of stresses on our communities, schools, governments, homes, churches, neighborhoods, and on ourselves. Just as untrammeled laissez-faire economics has long since proven inadequate to regulate the national economy, so have do-nothing policies regarding living space proven inadequate to meet twentieth century human needs. We have failed to plan for change—to develop public and private institutions and attitudes that would shape and control the technological revolution to serve the needs of society. The result has been a national crisis of environment—the relationship between the people and the land—and from this crisis others have erupted all around us. . . .

In terms of ability and training, the migrants from rural America to the metropolis have been primarily the best and the worst. The departure of the best sapped the strength and dulled the potential of rural America. The arrival of the worst compounded the problems of cities already sorely tried by problems of growth. . . .

The Need for a National Program

The first step is recognition of the fact that rural-urban balance is a nationwide challenge. It cannot be met by concentrating on city, suburb, or countryside alone, but only by moving on all three at once, and in the context of the whole nation. That means our planning must be based on nationwide physical, economic, social and cultural geography, not just political geography. We have space to spare if we use it. But we cannot use it properly if, in our planning, this space is constrained by the city limits, the county line or the state border. We need a national settlement policy on the geographic distribution of economic opportunity, jobs and people.

Until we have such a national policy the problems of city and countryside will remain insoluble. The interaction

between them will continue to compound the problem of
each. Only a common national policy with complementary
efforts in city, suburb, and countryside can restore balance
to America. It is past time that we recognize these facts and
create a national plan which will coordinate a total national effort, designed to use the combined resources of
government, business and industry—and 200 million-plus
people—to erase the undesirable effects of fifty years of unplanned growth, and to create a new land where Americans
can live at ease with each other and with their environment. . . .

To do this will be to mount a revolution—not the violent
kind, but one just as far-reaching, comprehensive, and per-
vasive as that of 1776, or the Jacksonian revolution of the
last century, or the social revolution of the thirties. . . .

There is a serious lack of research data on population
and resource shifts and their impact on communities and
regions. There is also a great shortage of trained planners
to guide economic and social adjustments and the development of local and regional plans. These institutes should
be funded, initially at least, by the Federal Government
because their benefits will cross state lines. Each regional
institute would bring together the cooperative efforts of
the several states of the region plus assistance from the
Federal Government in a consortium. Research, teaching
and training at the consortium would be coordinated with
other university efforts in research, training and consulting
on community problems.

These institutes, tuned to both national and local planning, could be the vehicles to make the necessary links
between the various levels of planning—national to regional,
regional to state, state to county, city, suburban and rural.
Through such institutions, it should be possible to break
the barriers of political boundaries—local, county and state
—that stifle the orderly development of the cities and suburbs and choke off the development of town and country
America.

Too often there is confusion between jurisdictions of means and ends which constricts the planning necessary to set the course for people who in reality are joined by the same social and economic circumstances but separated by political boundaries. We have, as a nation, wasted more political energy arguing about states' rights, local rights, private domains, and Federal prerogatives than we can afford. The issue today should be responsibility—not local jurisdictional rights. . . .

Under our Constitution, the Federal, state and local governments are interrelated parts of a single governmental system. Modern transportation and communication make that much more so today than when the Constitution was written. As our population increases and as our society progresses, the need for government services of increased quantity and quality grows in more than equal proportion. We have reached the point where no single level of government can assume the burden. Each level—Federal, state, county, city—must do what it can do best, and as a nation we must determine what each can do best. When it costs twice as much to put another person or automobile in a crowded metropolitan area than in the countryside, the simple arithmetic of the cost-benefit ratio makes it vividly clear that everyone would be better off if both person and car could be located accordingly. The regional institutes will help us to do that.

A Rural Development Bank

But plans and expertise are worth nothing without action. Action to develop rural America will require money. Therefore, a special financial institution which could, with the help of the Federal Government, help develop nonurban, town and country districts should be considered. Such a special Town and Country Development Bank for Rural America, similar to the National Urban Development Bank that has been suggested by many, could be financed through subscription of private funds. Federal underwriting of the unusual risk elements which will be involved in meeting development challenges would provide such a bank with the borrowing and lending authority to do the job. It will take billions of dollars each year.

An appropriation of Federal funds would get the bank started. The balance of the funds would come from bonds guaranteed by the Federal Government, to be sold by the bank to private investors. It would provide for equity participation in the bank's operations. Town and Country Bank funds would be available to both public and private borrowers for programs that cannot be financed through any other means, but which are essential to community development. These banks could: (a) Fund nonprofit community development corporations; (b) Guarantee loans, made through private lenders, for community and district-wide development; (c) Offer loans to small businessmen whose contribution to the economy of their communities is limited by lack of financing; (d) Fund semipublic housing development corporations; and (e) Provide technical management help in local planning and development. . . .

These, then, would be the basic tools for recreating rural America and restoring rural-urban balance—regional population and planning institutes, to help give direction to local initiative and to coordinate nationwide efforts to take the pressure off urban America, and Town and Country Banks to provide the necessary funds. There are some additional specific questions which also need to be examined. What specifically can be done to give people the chance to live and work outside the city—where the polls show more than 50 per cent want to live if they could find a decent job?

Revitalizing Town and Country

There are eight key elements in a total town and country development program. The first is obvious—jobs created by rural industrialization. National tax incentives and other means such as special location subsidies and assistance will help attract industry to the countryside. Clean air, clear water, elbow room and a willing work force, which already are there, can be powerful additional inducements. Increasing numbers of industrialists, weary of fighting urban problems, have moved into town and country America, usually in response to the overtures of local communities —those with dynamic local leaders who know what they have to offer and sell it. . . .

The second force for reviving town and country is completely in the hands of the Federal Government. It lies in the location of Government installations and in the awarding of Federal procurement contracts. Federal agencies should take the lead in decentralizing many of their operations to less congested areas. . . . In addition, the Federal Government should use its buying power and its contracting responsibilities to promote the development of nonmetropolitan growth centers as a part of a total national plan of quality development.

The third incentive rural America has is the use of the great outdoors—beautiful scenery and the unfrenetic life of the countryside which will promote growing tourism, thus providing income and generating attractive jobs that will keep its people and attract others.

Fourth, the anchor for the well-being of rural America must remain agriculture, which in truth is not only the anchor for the rural economy but vital to the well-being of industrial, metropolitan America as well. The basic concept of our current farm programs is sound. They should be strengthened and improved by adding meaningful farm bargaining power, a grain reserve, and more efficient integration of feeding programs for poor people to strengthen demand and maintain adequate farm prices.

The Role of Education

The fifth element basic to a revitalized town and country is education. The 1960 census showed that more than 19 million rural people had failed to complete high school; more than three million were classified as functional illiterates. Rural education has improved, but proportionately more rural than city youngsters drop out before completing high school and fewer of those who complete high school go to college.

Schools in rural areas still lag behind those in the cities in facilities, budgets and teacher pay. The percentage of urban teachers holding Master's degrees is about three times that of rural teachers. This rural educational gap not only handicaps millions of our young people in learning how to live successfully as human beings, but nearly ruins their ability to win the better jobs in a society where skills are at a premium. They are denied a chance to choose where to live and work because they are denied a chance to develop their full potential as human beings. No community can grow in this modern world without well-educated people with marketable skills. . . .

But more than an educated, stable work force is required to attract industry to rural America. This is the sixth requisite for rural renewal: an adequate supply of physical facilities and services. It will take Government loan assistance to provide rural communities with such things as basic central water and waste disposal systems and recreation areas. Without these no area can hope to attract industries or the people to work in them. Some 33,000 rural areas now lack modern central water systems, and 43,000 lack adequate waste disposal systems. They need financial and technical help to develop the public facilities and services they must have before they can even begin to plan for economic growth. The Federal Government can help in this area. It can also help extend electric power and efficient telephone service to those areas that would require prohibitive sums of private capital to reach. It can expand its program of helping local people develop and use natural resources wisely through watershed and resource conservation and development projects.

While working with and for existing communities in developing opportunity in rural America, our planners should consider moving ahead on the seventh concept for a new America: that of new towns. Columbia, Maryland, is such a town. Planned from the outset as a completely new city to accommodate some 100,000 people, it was designed for people and to serve people's needs. The natural landscape carefully preserved can be enjoyed by all. The basic public facilities are in place. Provisions have been made for schools, churches, libraries, theatres, hotels, medical services, shopping, and jobs. When completed, Columbia will consist of a series of interrelated neighborhoods and villages, each served by centrally located facilities of its own, and the whole city served by a town center where department stores, a concert hall, college, hospital and other appropriate facilities and institutions will be located.

There is room for many of these new towns in the new America, essentially self-contained communities linked to the larger centers by the high speed transit that we have the technology to develop if we will. Our planners might start out by considering where twelve such new towns might be located along the length of Appalachia. The Housing and Urban Development Act of 1968 provides technical assistance and generous Federal guarantees for such new towns. They should play a key role in the new plan for America.

These proposals are by no means exclusive. These and other creative ideas should be aimed at the future by our national planners to restore the balance of land and people by putting commerce, industry and agriculture in rural America on a sound footing. If we do that, tens of millions more Americans will be able to find the jobs they need so they can choose where they really want to live.

Balanced Community Development

This [is] a major part of the battle, but another part remains. I would refer one final point to our national planners. There are hundreds of thousands of men and women in rural America who need help now. Unprepared and untrained, unemployed or underemployed, many hungry, they cannot wait for actions that will help them in a few months or longer. They must have interim help now, immediately. For these people, needs are basic and urgent. This means an all-out effort to provide all Americans in need the basic necessities of food, clothing, shelter and health care. It means giving them access to training that will build their skills and, most important, give them hope, without which no development, community or human, is possible. It means an investment in humanity.

Experience has shown again and again that, beyond simple humanitarianism, rehabilitation of the poor and destitute is an investment with a payoff as high or higher than any other we can make. The recipients go off the relief rolls, onto the tax rolls and into the mainstream of the American economy for a full and productive life. The initial investment in the short run reduces the public burden and adds to the public product in the long run.

What I have set forth is but a rough outline of the course we must take if we are to restore rural-urban balance and cease being pawns of our own progress and slaves of our own technology. There are no simple responses to the problems that beset us, but I believe that the purposeful, planned use of the space and the resources of America, for the people and on a total national basis, holds the solution to the problems of our nation. To provide the jobs, the opportunities, the chance for a choice that the American people are demanding—in the knowledge that we have both the resources and the know-how to meet these demands—we must have balanced community development.

A balanced community, large or small, with an adequate economic base can maintain the requirements needed to keep itself viable. In somewhat simplified terms, this means that adequate education, health care, cultural facilities and community facilities maintain a citizenry capable of working, and working well. In turn, such a work force attracts an economic and tax base that can support education, health, cultural and other community services. A positive cycle is thereby created for the good of the whole people.

Again, most of our problems can be traced in the last analysis to community imbalance and faulty use of resources. At one extreme, we have cities so impacted with population that they cannot catch up on servicing that population. Their costs are climbing so fast that city after city is declaring itself virtually bankrupt. To put another person or another car in the city will cost twice as much as in the countryside. At the other extreme we have rural poverty where the economic base is too weak to support services that will equip the population for anything but menial jobs that continue to disappear in the onrush of technology.

This perpetuates a cycle of increasing depopulation as the rural poor are forced to the cities, increasing impaction as they arrive. This vicious circle can be cut. But it will take a total national effort. Everyone must participate. Only the President of the United States can successfully call this nation to such an effort. I hope he will do it soon.

BUILDING ENTIRELY NEW CITIES [2]

With a great deal less than the resources used to put two men on the moon, our nation could create a metropolis, or perhaps two or three, such as no one could even have dreamed of until very recently. Within the space we still

[2] "Let's Build New Cities Out Yonder," by Frank L. Hope, Jr., president of Frank L. Hope & Associates, a San Diego architectural and planning firm. From "The Future of American Cities: Two Views." Washington *Post*. p B 3. N. 8, '70. © 1970 The Washington Post. Reprinted by permission.

have in this country, we could select climates and landscapes to suit our needs.

Our population is growing at the rate of 2.6 million a
year. We are now creating new towns to wedge in the cracks
between existing cities. They will provide shelter but never
the stimulation, the excitement or the freedom of choice
that a true city can give.

Our spiraling population deserves an environment in
which people can create, where they can grow mentally and
culturally, where they can, by their interaction, create a
sense of destiny. When a significant proportion of the
residents of an urban area must travel an hour to enjoy
a symphony, to reach their recreation areas, see a ball game
or go to work, the limit has been exceeded.

Building new towns of 20,000 or 50,000 people, or even
100,000, in the shadows of existing metropolises, is necessary,
I am sure. They will provide pleasant middle-class living—
but at the expense of existing urban centers.

Some of President Nixon's advisers have recommended
that we build up to ten new communities a year, in the
75,000 to 100,000 population range. This is an incredible
task, and if these new cities are placed near existing urban
centers they will only add to the crushing burdens of supporting public services and utilities that already exist.

But if these cities are off by themselves, self-sustaining,
they would not be large enough. A town too small for
major cultural, sporting and recreational facilities or a
sufficient variety of economic and employment opportunities
may have its delights, but it is not a true city.

A true city requires a critical mass of people. This
mass must be able to attract and support the arts and the
sports. It must be able to supply the activities, economic
and otherwise, to offer challenge and opportunity to its
young men and women. Such a city should be large enough
to absorb a year's growth of the national population, not
much less than 2.6 million. It is on such a scale that a

city for the twenty-first century—less than thirty years away
—should be conceived.

Until our own time, the opportunity to build such a
city did not exist. In the past, cities were dependent on locations with natural or military advantages. They required
access to the sea, to rivers or to raw materials. Now,
modern transportation has reduced the economic penalty
of distance, and technology has reduced our dependence on
natural resources. Moreover, the United States has largely
become a service economy, only a minority of whose workers
are engaged in turning raw materials into goods.

Enterprise today looks to the availability of skill and
talent as the critical elements to be drawn from an environment. These are elements which can be nurtured by the
quality of the environment itself.

Building Earth City

There are dozens of sites that would serve for Earth
City in the spacious interior of our continent: the plains
of eastern Oregon; the highlands of northern New Mexico,
near magnificent mountain ranges; the rolling green country
of central Wisconsin; perhaps a new Phoenix, rising in the
high desert of central Nevada.

Building Earth City would require an effort less in
order of magnitude than reaching the moon, but the operation would be as complex. It would require a national commitment of billions of dollars and a gigantic commitment
of public interest and support not measurable in dollars. I
believe the money and the commitment would be returned
many fold, as Earth City came "on line" and shouldered
its share of our growth responsibilities.

Perhaps a nonprofit corporation formed by Government, industry, labor unions, universities and other institutions of vision would constitute the most likely entrepreneur
for such a project. This corporation would be formed with
a limited lifespan, contrived to pass on its assets and its authority to the public when the city has grown to maturity.

The cost of Earth City must be compared with the cost of alternate solutions—such as the creation of an East Coast, West Coast and central megalopolis with any reasonable degree of life quality, or the restructuring of our existing metropolitan areas for extensive growth.

The growth of Earth City could not be left to chance. An economic base would have to be assured by both Government and industry. The Government could favor industries which locate in the city with contracts and subsidize links with the nation's rail and air networks.

Planning Earth City would have to be designed for what we know of twenty-first century man. We might, for instance, realistically imagine that the American of 2050 will have more mechanical energy under his control, have more leisure and be just as insistent as we are on having his independent means of transportation. It has not been sufficiently recognized that we are becoming a nation of mechanical slave owners and, as a consequence, may well be evolving as the first mass aristocracy of history. Such an aristocracy will be more critical in its taste and less devoted to practical affairs than we are today if we may judge by the behavior of past aristocracies.

Inevitably, this proposal will be called impractical or utopian by skeptics. Yet I believe it to be one of the most practical solutions to the current and future problems of our expanding population. Earth City is not an ideal scheme for an ideal society; it offers only a framework in which a democratic community can grow.

REBUILDING THE CITIES WE HAVE [3]

What architect Frank L. Hope, Jr., calls Earth City I would call Cop-Out City. His proposal only evades the task of cleaning up the mess we have made of urban America

[3] "Let's Make Habitable the Cities We Have," by Wolf Von Eckardt, staff writer. From "The Future of American Cities: Two views." Washington *Post*. p B 3. N. 8, '70. © 1970 The Washington Post. Reprinted by permission.

by messing up "the plains of eastern Oregon, the highlands of northern New Mexico and the rolling green country of central Wisconsin" as well.

The idea of building huge instant cities in the wilderness has become quite fashionable lately. People are fascinated by artist-architect Paolo Soleri's "arcologies," for instance. Shown in various museums, these fantastic sculptures depict modern Towers of Babel, three miles high, where three million people are to live with a view of an unpolluted ecology.

Buckminster Fuller, along with a number of other distinguished people, is working on plans for an experimental city in Minnesota that is dear to former Vice President Hubert H. Humphrey's heart. But the present Vice President, Spiro T. Agnew, also welcomes such an "engagement with the future," or so he says in his introduction to *The New City,* the report of the National Committee on Urban Growth Policy. This committee of very respectable politicians, including governors, senators, congressmen and mayors, recommends "the creation of one hundred new communities averaging 100,000 population each and ten communities of at least one million population."

The rubbery word *community* fails to make an important distinction which Hope makes when he advocates "new cities" but disparages "new towns." The terms have been utterly confused by the promoters, starting way back on the old frontier where they would advertise any two stores, a saloon and a hitching post as "a city." And now that Reston and Columbia have met with public acclaim, the promoters put a swimming pool and a convenience store into their subdivision and call it, if not a "new city," at least a "new town."

Urban Romanticism

Well, according to Webster, a city is "any important town." What makes it important, according to Hope, is "a critical mass of people"—critical enough "to attract and support the arts and the sports." That, I would judge, takes at least half a million people. Any place smaller than that would be proud to call itself a town (it is a much more endearing term, anyway). A "new town," as Webster defines the ones in Great Britain, is designed to accommodate at least 20,000 people with "a planned ordering of residential, industrial and commercial development." It is also within the orbit of a large existing city and should therefore be called a satellite town.

Americans, or at least American intellectuals, used to hate cities. But lately there is a new, somewhat abstract and usually rather romantic fervor about urban life, especially among the young, as well as among architects, like Hope, and people who write about cities, like me. But even with the help of the kids, romantic architects and writers, I have not been able to stop the flight from the American city. Most of them are losing population. The population increase is taking place in suburbia, especially in the suburban areas along the Atlantic, Pacific and Great Lakes shores.

These are what the British call conurbations (spreading cities that are sort of fusing together), a phenomenon that the French geographer Jean Gottmann has called Megalopolis, and they offer a greater variety of better jobs and better educational and cultural opportunities than the less urbanized areas, so they keep attracting more and more people. And since ever more people settle in these areas, the variety and the economic, educational and cultural opportunities keep improving even more.

It will be very hard to start this upward spiral from scratch somewhere out in the plains or hills, as Hope proposes. He is right, of course, that manufacturing need no longer be located on the waterfront. But manufacturing is dependent on labor and labor is people and how are you going to get them to move out to the sticks? They won't come before there are schools and hospitals and TV stations and movie houses and restaurants and golf courses and all the rest. There is no sense in building schools and movies before you are sure there are going to be people to fill them. But—now here is the rub—there aren't really very many people in manufacturing any more. The predominant and still growing number of jobs is in the service industries. And services, of course, depend on a high concentration of people.

So how is Hope going to get his "critical mass?" With enough cash on hand he may persuade some hardy souls to come and build his "Earth City" and stick it out until his ball park and symphony hall are ready to open. It will take a long time, though. And he won't be able to persuade very many. The days of the pioneer are over.

Meanwhile, we must do something about the big cities and their sprawling suburbs and the deterioration of both. That is not a matter of liking cities or hating cities or believing there is an urban crisis or pooh-pooing the urban crisis. It is simply because, like Mount Everest, they are there. You can't *not* do something about them. Even to neglect them further is action—though very expensive and possibly explosive action.

The first thing we ought to do about them is to forget the notion that Megalopolis is "overcrowded," that there is no more space for all the people who want to live there. That's nonsense. As Bucky Fuller keeps saying, you can put the whole world population on the island of Manhattan and there would still be enough room to dance the twist. If you don't want to dance the twist you can efficiently organize the space or, as Hope puts it, "restructure our existing metropolitan areas for extensive growth."

Transit Is Vital

One way to start doing that is to build new towns or satellite towns around rapid transit stops right in Megalopolis where you don't need any rugged pioneers but where people are within a twenty-minute high-speed ride from existing universities, research centers, libraries, symphony halls, stadiums, delicatessen stores and any kind of action our civilization comes up with.

The satellite towns are part of a new system of cities, and to build that system is a tall order, too. But we have to spend money on accommodating the growing population anyway—money for housing, for roads, rails, schools and all the rest. And we might as well spend it efficiently so as to save the tremendous investment we made in our cities over the past three centuries or so.

A system of satellites will help the existing cities in many ways. By concentrating people they fill the fare box and make rapid rail transportation economical and thus reduce the number of automobiles that threaten to overrun the city. They help preserve open space. And far from providing just "pleasant middle-class living," new towns built with Government help will also provide low-cost housing close to new jobs for people who are now confined in the ghetto. As some of the people in the ghetto are able to move out, the inner city can be decongested, renovated and modernized.

In the end, making Megalopolis work—making it ecologically sound, socially just and economically productive—is really a far more exciting challenge to our technology and sense of destiny than earth cities in the sky.

A CASE FOR HIGHER DENSITY CITIES [4]

[My] thesis is that . . . [our metropolitan areas] are going to look much better, that they are going to be much better places to live in, and that one of the reasons they are is that a lot more people are going to be living in them.

[4] From *The Last Landscape,* by William H. Whyte, author of *The Organization Man* and a member of President Johnson's Task Force on Natural Beauty. Doubleday. '68. p 1-12, 375-93 passim. Copyright © 1968 by William H. Whyte. Reprinted by permission of Doubleday & Company, Inc.

Many thoughtful observers believe the opposite is true. They hold that not only is the landscape of our cities and suburbs a hideous mess, as indeed much of it is, but that it is bound to become much worse. The saturation point has been reached, they say, and unless growth and population trends are redirected, our metropolitan areas will become fouler yet. Some think they are beyond redemption already and that the only real hope is to start afresh, somewhere else, with new towns and cities.

But there is a good side to the mess. We needed it. It is disciplining us to do out of necessity what we refused to do by choice. We have been the most prodigal of people with land, and for years we wasted it with impunity. There was so much of it, and no matter how much we fouled it, there was always more over the next hill, or so it seemed. . . .

In filling out the metropolis . . . we treated land as though we were in fact on the frontier. With the great post-war expansion of suburbia in the forties and fifties, we carried this to the point of caricature. We were using five acres to do the work of one, and the result was not only bad economics but bad esthetics. People began to feel that if things looked this awful, something had gone wrong. At last we were having our noses rubbed in it. . . .

Others have a more apocalyptic vision. Some say that we are on the threshold of a postindustrial society—i.e. it's a whole new ball game now—and that entirely new forms of living must be devised. They see a breakthrough in environmental planning with teams of specialists applying systems analysis and computer technology to create the city of the future. A number of people have already begun jumping the gun, and in the recent upsurge of futurology have been devoting great energy and imagination to anticipating what forms these cities will take. Even the popular magazines are now full of pictures of megacities, stilt cities, linear cities, and such.

Some are to be located far, far away from any place. A Government-aided research project has just been launched for . . . an "Experimental City" to be located somewhere in Minnesota or the Great Plains. Dr. Athelstan Spilhaus, the prime mover of the project, visualizes a self-contained city with a population limit of 250,000 people. The city would test a host of technological advances. Many of its functions would be put underground and possibly a transparent dome two miles in diameter might be constructed. Dr. Spilhaus, who thinks present cities are something of a lost cause, believes that Experimental City can be the progenitor of many such settlements.

What is being fed into the machines is a set of rather questionable assumptions. What comes out is an extrapolation of the trends of the last twenty years—surging population, increasing affluence, and more leisure. Maybe these will continue. Maybe they will not. The very unanimity and assurance with which these projections are made should be enough to make one quite nervous. . . . But faith in the grand design is stronger than ever. . . .

Living with Higher Density

Designs can indeed help shape growth, but only when the designs and growth are going in the same direction. Most of the year 2000 plans are essentially centrifugal— that is, they would push everything outward away from the city, decentralize its functions, and reduce densities by spreading the population over a much greater land area. I think the evidence is staring us in the face that the basic growth trends are in the other direction; that they are toward higher rather than lower density.

There will be no brief here for letting the free market decide how we are going to grow, but where people and institutions are putting their money is a phenomenon worthy of respect, and planning which goes against the grain usually comes a cropper. The English, who have far more stringent land controls than we do, have been doing their best to constrain London, but the beast keeps growing. Most thinking Frenchmen agree that Paris is much too big in relation to the rest of the country, and Paris keeps growing. The Russians have been doing everything they can to curb Moscow, and it keeps on growing. . . .

I think that the bulk of the significant growth is going to take place within our present metropolitan areas. I think we are going to see a build-up, not a fragmentation, of the core cities. There will be a filling in of the bypassed land in the gray area between the cities and suburbia and a more intensive development—a redevelopment, if you will—of suburbia itself. New towns, yes, but I will wager that the ones which work out will not be self-contained and that they will not be somewhere off in the hinterland. We are, in sum, going to operate our metropolitan areas much closer to capacity and with more people living on a given amount of land. . . .

Our densities are not high at all. They are low. In some of the slum sections of the city, to be sure, there are too many people crowded together. But overcrowding—which is too many people per room—is not the same thing as high density. The residential density in most of our cities is quite reasonable.

So is the density of the metropolitan areas around them. By European standards they are enviably underpopulated. The densest in this country are the metropolitan areas along the Boston-New York-Washington axis; the 150 counties that make up this Atlantic urban region contain 67,690 square miles and 43 million people. If this region was developed to the same average density as the western Netherlands, the number of people would be tripled. The comparison is an extreme one perhaps, but so is the difference in appearance. Our areas *look* more filled up than the ones that really are. . . .

Our eyes are not a bad guide. The kind of land we find ugliest is not that which is overused but the land that is largely vacant or hardly used at all: worked out gravel pits, derelict waterfronts, obsolete freight yards, the scores of vacant lots, the rubbish-strewn areas underneath the high tension lines. (Probably the dreariest of all urban views is that of the Jersey flats, with its billboards all the more obscene for the emptiness around.) Almost as bad are the lands that are devoted to only one use, and only a fraction of the time at that. The great seas of asphalt around our shopping centers, for example, chew up enormous amounts of high-priced land, yet they are used to capacity only four days of each December.

But the very existence of this waste land means that our metropolitan areas have a great capacity for regeneration. The increased competition for land use is not a force for blight; it is a discipline for enforcing a much more economic use of land, and a more amenable one. Developers, for example, are now taking to a subdivision pattern that treats land much more sensitively and is far more attractive than the conventional pattern; they have been doing this not because planners and architects convinced them it was better —planners and architects have been trying to do that for years —but because land prices had finally gotten so high they had to adopt the new pattern to make money.

The same discipline is going to apply to open space as well as developed space. We should try to save all the big spaces we can get our hands on, but there are only so many left. From here on out we are going to have to work much more inventively with the smaller spaces, the overlooked odds and ends; we are going to have to rediscover the obsolescent rights-of-way that thread the metropolitan area. We must use all sorts of devices for conserving key features of the landscape that are in private hands. We must explore much more diligently the use of air rights, and of creating open spaces where none existed before. We must make the spaces more accessible to people—to their eyes most of all. To overstate the case, we will have to jam more people in and make them feel they are not jammed. . . .

The net of what I have been saying . . . is that we are going to have to work with a much tighter pattern of spaces and development, and that our environment may be the better for it. This somewhat optimistic view rests on the premise that densities are going to increase and that it is not altogether a bad thing that they do. It is a premise many would dispute. Our official land policy is dead set against higher densities. It is decentralist, like official policies in most other countries. The primary thrust of it is to move people outward; reduce densities, loosen up the metropolis, and reconstitute its parts in new enclaves on the fringe.

I do not think it is going to work out this way. Certainly, outward movement will continue, but if our population continues to grow, the best way to accommodate the growth will be by a more concentrated and efficient use of the land within the area. The big "if" is whether or not intensity of use will be coupled with efficiency of use. It may not be. But it can be. . . .

The Case for Crowding

The case for higher densities cannot rest on a shortage of land. There is none. It is true that top-grade agricultural lands are being overrun by urban expansion, that open space in the right places is increasingly difficult to save. The fact remains, however, that if we wish to go the expansion route, there is room for it. Expand the diameter of a metropolitan area by only a few miles and enough land will be encompassed to take care of a very large population increase. This may be a poor way to do it, but the option exists.

Nor are our cities running into each other. Metropolitan areas are being linked more tightly, but this is not the same thing as collision. Consider, for example, the great

belt of urban areas along the Eastern Seaboard from Boston
to Norfolk. It is well that we are paying more attention
to the continuities of this megalopolis, as Jean Gottmann
[geologist and author of the noted study *Megalopolis: The
Urbanized Northeastern Seaboard of The United States*]
has done so well, but to call it a strip city, as many are
doing, is misleading.

There is no such city, and the proposition can be easily
tested. Fly from Boston to Washington and look out the
window. Here and there one suburbia flows into another
—between Baltimore and Washington, for example—but the
cities retain their identities. This is especially apparent at
night when the lights beneath simplify the structure so
vividly: the brilliantly lit downtowns, the shopping centers,
the cloverleafs, the spine of freeways that connect it all. But
just as striking is what is dark—the forests of Massachusetts
and Connecticut, the pine barrens of New Jersey, the farm-
lands of the Eastern Shore, the tidewater of Virginia. For
many miles along the great urban route you can look down
and see only the scattered lights of farms and small towns.

Urbanized sectors in other parts of the country—except-
ing, always, Los Angeles—show much the same characteristics. They are systems of cities, tied by high-speed rail and
road networks, but they have not yet congealed into an
undifferentiated mass. There is room outside them for
expansion. There is room inside them. Whichever way is
best, a measure of choice is still open to us. . . .

The Future of Suburbia

Further out, densities will continue to be relatively low,
and on the outer edge of suburbia fairly large lots will
probably continue to be the rule for many years to come.
Overall, however, there is bound to be an increase in the
number of people housed in a given area, and much of
this increase will be concentrated in pockets of high-density
housing.

So far, cluster has not been used to increase density, but the efficiency with which it can house more people per acre is so great that inevitably it is going to be used for that purpose. Developers already have this in mind, as local governments are only too aware; their density zoning ordinances, roughly translated, mean no more density. For the moment developers are not pushing too hard to up the allowable quota of houses; they are getting enough in return in construction savings to be content. But this happy coincidence of self-interests is too good to last much longer. The next big drive of the developers will be cluster *and* more houses, and if the population increase continues they are going to win.

Another rich source of suburban controversy will be apartments. Most suburbs do not want them, and at rezoning hearings the opposition, often the best people in town, will offer statistical proof that apartment people breed too many children, get more out of community taxes than they pay, have little allegiance to the place, and are in general not the element one would want. But the apartments have been going up just the same. Too many people need apartments, and the pressures have been translated into land prices of compelling force. If a plot can be rezoned from one-family residential to garden apartments, the market price per acre vaults immediately, and if the change is to high rise, it can leap as much as $250,000 an acre. The possibility of this profit overspill will prompt other local citizens to argue that apartment people have to live somewhere; breed few children, move to houses when the children are school age, are above average in education and income, and are highly desirable in every respect.

But a zoning variance is almost always necessary. Despite the clear warning of the market place, most suburbs are not anticipating apartments; they have their zoning so set that no new apartments will ever get built without a zoning change. They are playing Canute. There will be changes, just as in the density zoning. All in all, suburban zoning boards are in for a rough time.

Using Unused Land

There are other ways to raise the carrying capacity of our urban land than having more people per acre. We can also increase the number of effective acres, and this can be done without pushing farther out into the country to find them. Within the metropolitan area there is a considerable amount of land that is not used at all, and an appalling amount that is used wastefully.

Parking space is the greatest wastage. Even with our present parking technology, backward as it is, we are allocating much more space for cars than is necessary. . . .

Industry is profligate too. The trend to the one-story, horizontal plant has good reasons behind it. Esthetically, the new plants are built to a considerably higher standard than most new subdivisions. But they, too, consume a great amount of space, and as with shopping centers more of it is given over to parking than to the primary activity. Industrial parks pool space more efficiently, and they require no more land for buffering or landscaping than one isolated plant. If industrial expansion continues, it would seem inevitable that land costs would induce more of this kind of concentration. But might there not also be something of a reversal in the trend to the horizontal? Within a decade we may be hearing of the revolutionary new concept of a vertical stacking of manufacturing space, with improved materials handling making it possible to have factories four and five stories high.

Another possibility is a high-rise shopping center. This would concentrate on one acre what now is spread over many. The goods and services would be grouped by category, stacked in floors one above the other, with vertical transportation systems tying in with mass transit lines underground. No cars or parking space would be necessary.

The entire complex would be enclosed and kept at constant temperature and humidity. It could be termed a department store.

Utility rights-of-way should be tightened up too. High tension lines are so unsightly our eye tends to blank them out, and few people realize what a considerable swath they cut through our urban land. This single purpose use of land is unnecessarily wasteful, and . . . the rights-of-way can be put to good use as connective and recreational space.

Nor does so much land have to be taken. The most striking thing about a utility map of an area is the duplication of effort by different kinds of utilities. Oil pipelines, water conduits, and electric lines angle this way and that along separate rights-of-way, except, as in the central city, where they have been forced into joint routes. Why could they not be pooled? Several new high voltage transmission lines have been laid down over railroad tracks. The kind of right-of-way that has been greediest of space, the super-highway, offers similar potentials. . . .

Bridges can be made to do more duty. Instead of putting up massive towers for a new river crossing, utilities can put electric lines, even oil pipelines, on the underside of existing bridges. Most bridges are forbidden to such uses, but where they have been permitted the lines or pipelines have proved compatible. The bridge authority gets revenue it otherwise would not, the utility saves a great deal by not having to build the towers, and the public does not have to look at them. . . .

Some kinds of underuse will not be so easily resolved. For planners, the most frustrating open spaces to contemplate are the cemeteries of the city. Together, they take up a large amount of space—in some areas, like Queens in New York, they form the bulk of the urban open space. Many a planner has toyed with the thought of all the good things that could be done with the land were there a relocation effort. Those who are wise have kept the idea to themselves.

Title problems are immense, and the whole subject politically explosive.

Reservoir and watershed lands of private and municipal
water companies are in many states restricted to any use
except the gathering of rain. Pressure for recreational use
has been mounting—particularly from sportsmen—and in
time it would seem inevitable that these lands will be
opened up to multiple use. The delaying action is strong,
however, and in one respect it has been quite beneficial. The
fact these lands have been unavailable as usable open space
has made it easier to get public support for acquisition of
other open space.

City-owned land has great capabilities too. In New York
City, for example, subway freight yards, together with railroad yards, total some 9,641 acres. These are probably the
dreariest acres to look at in the city, and development over
top of them could greatly improve the looks of the city as
well as its finances. A few starts have been made. Two new
public schools are being built over subway storage yards.
Since school buildings are customarily low and flat roofed,
in some cases it would make sense to go a step further and
lease the air rights over the schools for yet another structure.
In a project for one new high school in New York, part of
the air rights are to be used for the construction of an apartment tower. The lease payments will pay a substantial portion of the interest on the school construction bonds.

City-owned reservoirs can be decked over too. Philadelphia is now considering the proposal of a developer to build
a commercial and shopping complex over a city reservoir.
The city's planners and engineers like the idea; in addition
to the income, the structure would keep the sun off the water
in summer and there would be much less loss through
evaporation.

Expressways and streets are going to be exploited more
vigorously. . . .

There are problems, of course, in this kind of construction. An apartment project built several years ago atop the Manhattan approaches to the George Washington Bridge, for example, has run into difficulties because of the great amount of noise and air pollution the high concentration of cars beneath sends up. But the technical challenge is not too difficult. The real problem, as the New York *Times'* Ada Louise Huxtable has pointed out, is governmental. "In the city," she notes, "the municipal pipeline is jammed with simple projects unable to clear the hurdles of requests, reviews and multidepartmental jurisdiction." . . .

Coping with Population Growth

Let me turn from the techniques of compression to the matter of whether or not it is justified. In bespeaking a more intensive use of the land I have been accepting the fact of growth. But is it inevitable? And is it good? A number of ecologists and conservationists think not. They are horrified by the specter of a growing population devouring the resources we have left. . . .

Malthusians argue that planners can no longer make sensible plans unless they face up to the issue of population control, and as a minimum, demonstrate to the public the choices involved. They point out that in almost all of the alternative regional design plans growth is assumed; in the worst alternative presented, unplanned growth, the bad word is *unplanned*. Why not, critics ask, a planned no-growth alternative? The planners could say to people, look, we've shown you different ways we can handle a growing population; now we'd like to show you what a job we could do if the population doesn't grow. . . .

I wonder. On the face of it, it would seem easier for land planners to cope with growth if there were not any, or, at least, much less. But there is a challenge and response equation involved. When growth pressures were less we wasted land and abused it. And were there respite we might be as bad as ever. We are, of course, still enormously wasteful, but we are beginning to feel guilty enough about it to try and mend our ways a bit. . . . It is quite doubtful if we would be now adopting better land use measures except for the pressures of growth.

It is a shame so much land had to be sacrificed to force the recognition, but the blight seems a necessary stimulant (it is not by accident that so many of the new approaches have been tried first in California). We have to have our noses rubbed in it. Whether or not, as the Malthusians hope, the discipline leads us to the further step of population control, we are being goaded to a more effective use of space, now, and the process is hardly a palliative.

HIGHWAY NETWORKS AND OUR LANDS [5]

The red, white and blue shield of the National System of Interstate and Defense Highways is a familiar guidepost to American motorists. It is now posted along more than 30,000 miles of superhighways on a transcontinental network that will eventually stretch 42,500 miles. By any standard, the Interstate System is the largest public works project ever undertaken by modern man.

When proposed by President Eisenhower in 1954, it was to be a chain of roads to serve interstate traffic. It was to bypass cities, enabling the motorist to drive from one corner of the country to another at high speed without stopping for a traffic light. Spurs from cities would connect to the Interstates, but there would be no massive highway construction in our cities.

It hasn't worked out that way. Some 5,600 miles of "interstate" roads have already been built in cities, and 1,900 more such miles are scheduled to open by 1974. During off-peak hours these urban freeways can work relatively well. But

[5] "The Folly of Our Superhighway System," by Helen Leavitt, free lance writer and journalist. *Reader's Digest.* 50:61-5. F. '71. From *Superhighway—Superhoax,* by Helen Leavitt. Copyright © 1970 by Helen Leavitt and published by Doubleday & Co., Inc. As condensed in the February 1971 *Reader's Digest.* Reprinted by permission of Doubleday & Company, Inc.

from 7:30 to 9 A.M., and from 4:30 to 6:30 P.M., drivers are likely to whiz along them at no more than 6 to 12 mph. The horse and buggy did as well.

Serenely confident, however, that the solution to automobile congestion is more concrete, highway planners now advance schemes for double-decker lanes, tunnels, bridges and ever more miles of city-adjacent highway. In theory, additional facilities should alleviate traffic jams. In reality, the new roads fill up as fast as the concrete hardens; traffic simply rises to meet capacity.

Meanwhile, profits on public transit nosedive, rail and bus equipment deteriorates, and service is cut back. In fact, the Government's vast investment in freeways has virtually scuttled all forms of land and water transportation except the automobile. Thus it has become essential for every American to maintain his own private transportation system, although in an area as small as a city any other form of commuting system would be more economical and beneficial to the public.

How did we get on this course?

The original Eisenhower proposal envisaged mostly toll roads that would pay for themselves. The Highway Act as passed by Congress in 1956, however, provided that the system was to be financed through a Highway Trust Fund. All Federal taxes on motor vehicles, gasoline, oil and ancillary equipment would be channeled into this fund and devoted solely to highway construction. From this account, the Federal Government would pay for 90 per cent of the construction of interstate projects. States, collecting their own automobile-related taxes, would pay the rest.

The 90 per cent Federal financing proved to be an irresistible lure for politicians, contractors and state highway officials who wanted as much of the Federal pie as possible and concluded that the highways should actually enter our cities. Washington, D.C., is a good example of what happened as a result.

The Case of Washington, D.C.

In 1944, an engineering survey showed that an expansion of the efficient trolley system serving the city would be the most economical way to move large numbers of people. Expensive highways would not be required. But if nothing was done to improve mass transit, the survey concluded, people would return to the private automobile, "a trend that threatens to explode the city."

The report was ignored, and the engineers began promoting the expressway system. Other cities were planning them —why not Washington? By 1960, traffic congestion had grown so bad that House and Senate District committees declared that "any attempt to meet the area's transportation needs by highways and private automobiles alone will wreck the city." Yet, by 1965, the Washington area had received $500 million for major highway projects, and led the nation in freeway mileage per square mile and per capita. Its trolley system had received orders to dismantle.

As more and more freeways were constructed, population and retail sales in the city diminished. Taxable land dwindled as more than 60 per cent of the land in the central business district became devoted to the moving and storage of automobiles. The homes of thousands of residents were demolished, and monuments and parks were engulfed by freeways. And anyone who witnessed the mass exodus of panicked suburbanites from the District on the afternoon preceding the riots of April 5, 1968, and the ensuing traffic jams on every major artery in the city, had living, stalled proof that in emergencies the system cannot effectively serve national defense, which highway advocates claim is an essential purpose.

Why do we continue to pour billions of dollars into creating rivers of noise and exhaust gas sweeping into the hearts of our cities, eating up real estate, compressing people, cars and services into ever narrower confines? Because that's all the law allows. The money pours into the Highway Trust.

Fund in everincreasing amounts each year, and *must* be spent for highways. House and Senate Public Works committees simply agree on a bill to authorize expenditures to meet the Fund revenues, and Congress passes it.

Even when a city has the temerity and perseverance to reject a proposed urban highway—as San Francisco, in 1966, rejected an eight-lane double-decker system in favor of its own rapid-transit train system—the conversion of cash into concrete moves on apace. San Francisco's portion of the Federal highway funds simply reverted to California, and engineers planned more mileage for Los Angeles.

The 1956 Highway Act provided that public hearings should be held whenever an Interstate road was planned to bypass or go through a community. State highway departments are expected to measure public response and adapt their plans accordingly. But it hardly ever works out that way. Public hearings go unadvertised and unattended; or, if they are advertised, the voice of the people is largely ignored. For instance, after fighting highway interests and state and Federal bureaucracy for years, a weary Seattle citizenry suffered the construction of a "twelve-lane ditch" right through the city, wiping out 5,000 houses.

Politicians and engineers tend to dismiss citizens' objections to freeways as impractical, even crackpot. "The truth is," wrote a spokesman for the American Roadbuilders Association, "the local people are not entirely aware of their best interests."

The Public's Interest

The Bureau of Public Roads (BPR), an arm of the Department of Transportation, is charged with representing the public interest in Federal road building. The Bureau continually talks about human values and the need to "bring more compassion" into the program. Yet its administrative task is so enormous—20,000 projects are now in some stage of activity—that it does not begin to supervise them effectively. The Bureau carries out what Congress, pressured by a gigantic highway lobby (contractors, engineers, gasoline producers, automobile manufacturers, truckers, billboard firms), enacts into law.

A classic illustration of what can result is to be found in the North Expressway in San Antonio. There, in spite of formidable public opposition, a proposed freeway is to curve, thrust and ram its way through, by or around an Audubon bird sanctuary, Olmos Creek (which would become a concrete ditch), a recreation area (wiping out a Girl Scout day camp and nature trail), a college campus, an elementary school, the zoo, a public gymnasium and outdoor theatre, a residential area, a municipal golf course, and a wooded portion of the San Antonio River's natural watercourse. So much for human values.

Highway engineers justify urban expressways by noting that in America the automobile "is a way of life." True enough. But the fact is that the Government's massive commitment to highways has left Americans with little choice. A 1968 study, partially sponsored by the BPR, asked whether the contribution to society made by the automobile was worth the air pollution, traffic congestion, demolition of property and homes, and the loss of thousands of lives annually. Eighty-five per cent of the respondents answered yes. When asked *why* the automobile was worth all this, almost 50 per cent replied, *because it is the only form of transportation available*.

How much longer can we tolerate what has been done in the name of automobiles? Apparently there is no end to it. By 1966, the cost of the Interstate System had mushroomed from the original estimate of $27 billion to $46.8 billion. In 1968, a new act was passed, extending the life of the Highway Trust Fund and authorizing expenditure of an additional $21.5 billion in 1970-74. Now Congress is considering extending the Trust Fund and the deadline for completion of the system through 1978, at a total cost of $75 billion. If it follows through, neither the American people nor our representatives will be able to prevent Trust Fund money from being spent on highways—and on highways alone. Moreover, most of the money will be spent on urban freeways, the most expensive, destructive and inefficient segments of the system.

What Must Be Done?

What can we do to establish sane, sensible transportation? Clearly, these steps are "musts":

Citizens and communities must be allowed to retain some control over the number of automobiles they are willing to accommodate. In September 1969, officials at Yosemite National Park introduced a tramway bus service in the magnificent Mariposa Grove area and banned automobiles there in an effort to keep it from being ruined by smog and traffic jams. Now the ban has been extended to the eastern end of the park. Surely, if the need to ban automobiles in parkland can be recognized and dealt with intelligently, civilized urban man can respond in kind. Automobiles can be banned from specific areas of cities and limited in other areas. The carless street, successfully tried in Manhattan in recent months, is a first step. Direct rail lines to airports would be another. We can discourage automobile ownership by limiting the amount of city parking space, charging stiff bridge tolls, reserving existing lanes for speedy buses, and even taxing individual parking places.

Congress must take measures to curb the power of all those who try to influence highway legislation. These measures should include full financial disclosure by legislators, administrators and lobbyists, and strict conflict-of-interest laws to keep separate the interests of private groups and public officials.

Most important, the Highway Trust Fund—chief cause of the vast imbalance of our transportation situation—must be abolished. The highway lobby avows that gasoline taxes can logically be used only to build highways. It would be equally "logical" to put all liquor taxes into a trust fund to promote and expand the liquor industry. Since inception of the fund in 1956, we have spent a total of $195 billion on highways while spending only $32 billion on all other forms of transportation—including the Coast Guard.

Revenue should continue to be tapped from petroleum and tire taxes, but the money should go into the general treasury so that highways, for the first time in fourteen years, will have to compete with all other forms of transportation for funds. Then a state or community could request either a block grant from the Department of Transportation or appropriations for a specific project, and have some real chance to plan and buy a system appropriate to its needs.

The mass-transit bill signed into law last October—providing for $10 billion to be spent on urban mass transportation over the next twelve years—is merely a step in the right direction. As long as the Highway Trust Fund remains intact, financing $15 billion in concrete annually, we are ensuring mass-transit's financial failure. We must abolish the Fund and lend *meaningful* support to our sagging public transportation systems, if we are to have balanced transportation for our troubled cities.

ZONING AND PROPER LAND USE [6]

The purpose of [this review] is to explain the origins and use of zoning practices and to relate them to the limitations on available housing for lower-income families, particularly in the suburbs. Although zoning practices are not the only determinants of land use policies, they have had an important effect on the kinds of communities we have built. . . .

Most of the material . . . is derived from the December 1968 summary report of the National Commission on Urban Problems (the Douglas Commission). The Commission's studies were authorized by Section 301 of the Housing and

[6] From *Local Zoning Ordinances and Housing for Lower Income Families—Goals in Conflict?* (League of Women Voters of the United States. Current Review No. 8: Human Resources) The League. 1730 M St. N.W. Washington, D.C. 20036. '69. p 1-14. © 1969. Reprinted with permission.

Urban Development Act of 1965, which directed a national study of the structure and effects upon housing construction of state and local housing and building codes and standards; state and local zoning and land use laws, codes and regulations; and Federal, state and local tax policies. President Johnson charged the Commission, headed by former Senator Paul H. Douglas (Democrat, Illinois), to place special emphasis on means of increasing the supply of decent low-cost housing.

In its two-year study, the Commission conducted hearings in more than twenty cities and suburbs, taking testimony from nearly 350 witnesses. It commissioned an extensive technical research program. Virtually all experts agree that the Douglas Commission's documents constitute the most comprehensive and current source of data on the problem of the impact of zoning regulations upon housing opportunities. . . .

Over the next thirty years, some 18 million acres of land will come into urban use for the first time, according to estimates prepared by the National Commission on Urban Problems (Douglas Commission).

This is approximately equal to all the urbanized land now within the 228 SMSAs (standard metropolitan statistical areas) identified by the Census Bureau—or the equivalent of the total areas of the states of New Hampshire, Vermont, Massachusetts and Rhode Island!

This estimate of land use needs is based on a projected population increase of some 100 million persons between 1967 and 2000. Ninety per cent of these people will live in cities, and unless an extensive new-town building program is carried out, 75 to 80 per cent of the expected population growth will occur in present metropolitan areas. Some growth is expected in central cities, but the major population pressures will be felt in the suburbs and rural areas surrounding our cities—requiring conversion of vast acreage from nonurban, primarily agricultural uses, to urban purposes—to build additional housing and urban facilities equal to what now exists in every American city of 25,000 or more persons! ...

Suburbs Face Challenge of New Growth

Achieving equal housing opportunity depends not only on nondiscriminatory practices but upon availability of an adequate supply of housing priced within reach of low- and moderate-income families. The growing concentration of population in our great metropolitan areas and the prospect of their continued future growth makes the housing problem most acute in these areas, particularly in the suburbs. The typical pattern of concentration of poor families in inner cities ringed by more affluent suburbs, the lack of housing sites in the core cities, the growth of industry in suburban areas, the resulting shift of job opportunities from city to suburb—all pose great challenges to the direction of future growth in suburban areas and to metropolitan area housing and transportation policies. ...

The prime factor in boosting housing costs is the high cost of building sites. Raw land prices have increased at an average annual rate of 6.9 per cent over the past ten years, compared with annual increases of 1 per cent in the wholesale commodity price index or 1.8 per cent in consumer prices. The cost of acquiring the land and preparing the building site (providing streets, curbs, gutters, storm drainage, etc.) now accounts for between 15 and 32 per cent (varying by regions) of the cost to the consumer of the finished dwelling, whether single-family or multifamily.

This trend of rising land costs results largely from increased urbanization and rising population pressures, but a less widely recognized influence is local land use controls, particularly zoning. Where zoning reduces the supply of land available for residential development or restricts the number of dwellings that can be built on the available acreage, the effect—whether intended or by chance—is to raise the cost of land and thus to raise the cost of housing that can be built.

History of Zoning Controls

Health and safety were major concerns of early tenement laws, which limited the proportions of a site which a building could occupy and also limited building heights and land uses. Regulations emphasizing such minimum standards were adopted by several major cities in the late nineteenth and early twentieth centuries. These laws provided the initial base for a concept of limited land use control through zoning. The crusade for parks and the "City Beautiful" movement stimulated by the Chicago Exposition of 1893 also influenced development of zoning controls. New York City's zoning ordinance, adopted in 1916, reflected both these movements and the efforts of Fifth Avenue merchants to protect their fashionable shopping district from encroachment by new garment manufacturers. That ordinance set the basic pattern for zoning ordinances to the present day.

Zoning ordinances were widely adopted by American municipalities in the 1920s. . . . This development reflected concerns with esthetics, health and safety, and protection of property investments. It was significantly stimulated by the Federal Government's publication of a Standard State Zoning Enabling Act, issued by the Department of Commerce's Advisory Committee on Zoning in 1924. Much state zoning law is still based on this model. By 1925, nineteen states had adopted statutes similar to this model; by 1930, some or all localities in every state were legally empowered to enact zoning ordinances.

Local subdivision regulations also came into widespread use in the 1920s in part stimulated by the Commerce Department's proposed Standard City Planning Enabling Act, issued in 1928. All fifty states now authorize local zoning and subdivision controls and more than 10,000 local governments have adopted them.

"The form of today's land use regulations, and often their substance as well, still commonly fall within the conventional patterns established in the 1920s," the Douglas Commission finds. Thus, the conventional zoning ordinance regulates land use, governs population density by setting minimum required lot sizes, and limits building bulk through height and setback requirements. Off-street parking requirements, minimum house size, landscaping, signs, and provision of various amenities may be covered. Subdivision regulations, under which individual lots are created out of larger tracts, regulate site design and relationships—size of lots, width of streets, length of blocks, etc. They often provide rules which in effect allocate costs of public facilities (streets, sidewalks, sewers, etc.) between the subdivider and local taxpayers.

Zoning Competition in Metropolitan Areas

Some 10,000 local governments have independent authority over land use decisions. With few exceptions, localities have almost complete autonomy in exercising these regulatory powers. . . . Some states authorize review of certain local land use decisions by a local agency of broader territorial jurisdiction, but normally such review is purely advisory. Metropolitan area planning agencies similarly have little power other than through persuasion.

Fragmentation of control is particularly serious in metropolitan areas. Within the 228 standard metropolitan statistical areas recognized by the United States Bureau of the Census, some 5,200 local jurisdictions have zoning ordinances and can make independent decisions on land use control.

The impact of such fragmented decision making becomes more obvious in considering actual situations. For example, independent zoning powers are exercised by: (1) 100 localities in the San Francisco metropolitan area; (2) 61 jurisdictions within Cuyahoga County (one of four counties in the Cleveland metropolitan area); (3) nearly 200 of the 238 cities, townships, and boroughs in metropolitan Philadelphia; (4) more than 112 of 129 localities in Cook County, Illinois (Chicago area); (5) more than 500 separate jurisdictions in the New York metropolitan area (as defined by the Regional Plan Association).

Certain key characteristics of regulations developed in the 1920s are important in considering land use regulation today. First, regulatory responsibility was delegated by the state to *local governments*—a significant factor in current problems of metropolitan area planning in regions in which numerous jurisdictions exercise independent zoning powers. Second, regulations were originally thought to be *self-enforcing*. Apparently early advocates of zoning controls felt it was sufficient simply to adopt the standards; they did not foresee the problems in administering the rules or the pressures for changes or special exemptions. Inspiration for regulation was largely *negative*—to keep out undesirable uses rather than to promote broader planning objectives. Finally, standards were *more lax* than most standards today and overzoning (allowing excessive acreage for business and industry) was common.

Today's regulations generally resemble those of the 1920s, but techniques have been considerably refined in hopes of achieving higher standards. For example, permitted uses are more specifically described . . . and higher performance standards demanded. Increasing reliance on some form of discretionary review by local authorities gives these authorities more control over the direction and pace of development. But it places heavy burdens on the zoning administration apparatus, and powerful pressures on those who must make important decisions often involving high financial stakes.

Finally, zoning ordinances of the 1960s have more restrictive requirements than those common in the 1920s. In particular, in recent years there has been a widespread reduction in permitted residential densities, especially in suburban areas.

Tighter zoning regulations may be inspired by commendable goals—the need to protect watersheds; to guard against premature or overly intensive development, with attendant congestion and pollution; or to prevent obnoxious or nonconforming uses of property. But it must be acknowledged that low-density development is often inspired by exclusionary objectives to prevent people of low- or moderate-income—

often minority group members—from being able to afford properties in the community.

While acknowledging varying local conditions and objectives, the Douglas Commission asserts that, from a "broad national perspective, however, it is reasonable to expect regulations to be directed toward achieving quality development, without needlessly increasing the *cost* of development, while at the same time assuring *fairness* to those affected by the system." Thus, "the most objectionable 'unfairness' of current regulations is the imposition of development costs which exclude people who could afford decent if less impressive homes.". . .

Exclusionary Zoning Policies

Exclusionary zoning may reflect prejudices against minority groups or against less affluent fellow citizens and the implicit desire of those who have "made it" to insulate themselves from the less fortunate. Often racial exclusion is achieved through economic exclusion, i.e., regardless of their stated intent, decisions which have the effect of raising the cost of housing inevitably limit access of the less affluent—who are often minority-group members.

Exclusionary zoning policies are also rooted in dollars-and-cents taxpayers' economics. Zoning is a local government responsibility, and the heavy reliance of local jurisdictions on the property tax as the major source of revenue encourages the tendency of localities to exercise "fiscal zoning," i.e., to seek to attract as residents those individuals or institutions who will pay as much or more in property taxes as they will demand in local services. The overwhelming reliance on property tax revenues to support local services (and the most costly local services are schools) leads many communities, particularly in suburban areas, to adopt policies to attract industry (preferably "clean" industry) and to limit residential developments which will attract families with large numbers of children which would burden local school resources. . . .

Zoning: Pluses and Minuses

In focusing on some of the shortcomings of current zoning controls and administrative practices, it is important to note that zoning controls have offered important public benefits to many communities. An overall assessment by the American Society of Planning Officials concludes that:

> Both zoning and land subdivision regulations have done much more good than harm. As difficult as the current problem of guiding urban development is, the situation is much better than it would have been without zoning and subdivision regulations. . . .
> The city of Houston is often cited as an example of the futility of zoning. It is the largest city—the only city with over 100,000 population—without a zoning ordinance. The claim is that Houston is no worse than any other city of its size in spite of its lack of zoning. . . . [Yet among] the defects in Houston that zoning has prevented in other cities are undersized lots; alley dwellings and overbuilding on residential lots; indiscriminate mixture of residence, commerce and industry; unbridled and irresponsible proliferation of signs and billboards; and a central business district that has sprawled and spread and left obsolescence and blight behind.
> Land use controls have been generally successful. If the prewar tempo of national growth had continued, there would have been little concern to improve these controls. But population pressures, technological change, economic advance, and social reform have demonstrated that what was once a satisfactory instrument to regulate urban growth is no longer adequate to the task.

Possibilities for the Future

The Douglas Commission concludes that achieving quality development requires promoting harmonious relationships within built-up blocks and neighborhoods without the enforced monotony of so many of our suburban subdivisions and guidance of timing, location and nature of development that has a positive impact on the living environment of community and region. The Commission proposes several approaches to achieve these aims:

1. *Increasing the scale of land development and redevelopment.* Many authorities agree that creation of large-scale projects such as "new towns" and large planned neighborhoods which "create their own environment" is the most

promising approach both for redeveloping ghetto areas and for creating suburban communities to house families of mixed income levels. The United States Advisory Commission on Intergovernmental Relations stresses this approach in its April 1968 report, *Urban and Rural America: Policies for Future Growth.*)

In city cores, redevelopment on a substantial scale is necessary because the effect of surrounding blight will soon negate an effort to redevelop a few scattered properties. Sound urban redevelopment investment seems to require an effort broad enough to change the character of the entire block or even the neighborhood. Dr. Jerome Rothenberg of Massachusetts Institute of Technology explains the reasons in testimony to the Douglas Commission: "The value of a particular piece of real property in an urban area depends not only on its own use but on the use to which neighboring property is put by its respective owners.". . .

2. *Guiding development through location and timing of public facilities.* Provision of highways, water and sewer lines is essential to development, and decisions on their location and timing are clearly critical to guiding development. Yet in many areas decisions on these facilities are made with scant reference to total community needs. Often the agencies which make the decision are in fact virtually independent of the local government. Many authorities feel that local officials ought to have greater control over location and timing of such public facilities.

3. *Pressure through location of government facilities and installations.* Decisions on location of government facilities (particularly Federal installations) also play an important part in local development. Under pressure from certain employee and civil rights groups, the Federal Government has recently moved to make availability of adequate housing for low- and middle-income Government employees a criterion in leasing space for Federal Government activities or in selecting and acquiring sites for new Federal installations. The regulation is currently in the form of an instruction

from the Commissioner of the General Services Administration's Public Buildings Service to GSA Regional Administrators. It declares that it shall be GSA policy "to avoid locations which will work a hardship on employees because (a) there is a lack of adequate housing for low- and middle-income employees within a reasonable proximity; and (b) the location is not readily accessible from other areas of the urban center."

These guidelines have no "teeth" however, and the employee-civil rights groups are pressing for issuance of a Federal Executive Order including enforcement sanctions. The Douglas Commission endorses this approach, proposing a finding of adequate existing housing for employees of all income groups before location of any major new Federal installation (employing more than fifty persons) in a metropolitan area. The impact of a Defense Department order issued in June 1967 which in effect compelled renters of off-base military housing to open facilities to minority groups suggests that such Federal Government pressure could be a potent tool in persuading local governments eager to attract Government facilities to make provision for development of low- and middle-income housing.

4. *Using Federal grants as a lever—the Workable Program requirement—and Federal funds for comprehensive planning.* "One of the roadblocks to providing standard, low-income housing in areas outside of central cities often has been the Workable Program . . . a set of requirements which must be adopted and at work in a city or a suburb as a condition for getting certain Federal grants for housing or community facilities from HUD [Department of Housing and Urban Development]. Some suburban communities that did not want low-income families simply did not meet Workable Program requirements," reports the Douglas Commission.

A community's failure to comply with such requirements has meant that neither private sponsors nor public agencies could afford to produce low-income housing in those communities because they could not get the benefits otherwise available for such projects. As a result, Congress has eliminated the Workable Program requirement on several new programs and a Senate-passed bill would cancel it for leased public housing.

To be effective in stimulating low- and middle-income housing construction, the Douglas Commission concludes that the Workable Program requirement "should be tied to things the cities want, such as sewer and water grants, with communities required to provide low-income housing before they can get the grants."

States and localities receiving Federal funds for planning assistance . . . are now required to include provision for housing for all income groups in their plans. The Commission recommends that such grants be conditioned on submission of comprehensive state studies of planning and land use controls and of possible need for state action to redistribute control powers to assure more orderly urban development. Further, the Douglas Commission recommends that "after a reasonable period of time" grants of . . . planning assistance funds be tied to the existence and enforcement by the states of local development guidance programs.

"Local governments should be required, as a condition for their continued exercise of control powers, to demonstrate that they are in fact making a significant effort to use such powers effectively," the Commission concludes. "At a minimum, the local development guidance program should require: (1) a locally approved compendium of development policies that land use controls are intended to achieve, covering such matters as transportation, housing, open space, air and water pollution; (2) a locally approved capital improvement program; and (3) evidence of the availability of trained professional employees, or consultants available on a continuing basis, to assist in formulating and administering local regulations."

5. *Need for government land purchase and compensative techniques.* The Douglas Commission urges that governments "must purchase land, or interests in land, where needed regulation will not be effective or will result in serious unfairness to individual owners or will be struck down by the courts as an unconstitutional 'taking.'" Many of these proposals have been aired by individual experts. The Douglas Commission is the first major national public body to give weight to such suggestions. . . .

6. *State government pressures to assure that local governments permit housing variety.* The Douglas Commission recommends that state governments amend planning and zoning enabling acts to include as one of the purposes of the zoning power the provision of adequate sites for housing persons of all income levels; to require that governments exercising zoning power prepare plans showing how such objectives will be carried out; and to require multicounty or regional planning agencies to prepare housing plans assuring available sites within each metropolitan area for development of new housing of all types and all price levels. . . .

7. *Possible court challenges to exclusionary zoning actions.* The Douglas Commission recommends that the Justice Department examine the constitutionality of various forms of exclusionary zoning and enter as *amicus curiae* [friend of the court; a party who suggests or states some matter of law for the assistance of the court] in court actions brought by aggrieved parties challenging such zoning where it appears to be unconstitutional. . . .

8. *Proposed changes in government structure.* It is clear that the vesting of zoning controls in numerous units of local government, each heavily dependent upon local property tax revenues to support essential services, poses serious obstacles to development and equitable distribution of low- and middle-income housing. To deal with these basic causes, rather than the surface symptoms, the Douglas Commission places heavy emphasis on the need to restructure local gov-

ernments in metropolitan areas to make them more respon-
sive to the needs of a broader cross section of the urban population and to make possible more effective coordination
within a metropolitan region. Such restructuring, combined
with lesser reliance on local property taxes and a greater assumption of expenses by the states, regional agencies and
the Federal Government, the Commission argues, offers the
soundest long-term approach to dealing with the root causes
of what it calls "metropolitan goal distortion."

To this end, the Commission recommends several steps
to enable competent local governments to guide urban development effectively, within limitations by state and Federal governments to assure responsiveness to broad segments
of the population and fair and effective treatment of interested parties. The Commission acknowledges that these recommendations cannot be achieved immediately, since they
require legislative and/or constitutional changes which
might be difficult to achieve. Among the Commission's
recommendations:

(a)   That the state governments enact legislation granting to counties (or to regional governments where such
exist) exclusive authority to exercise land use controls within small municipalities in metropolitan areas

(b)   That states require preparation of local development guidance programs and enact legislation denying land
use regulatory powers to localities that fail to develop such
programs after a reasonable period of time

(c)   That states enact legislation authorizing but not
requiring local governments to abolish local planning boards
as traditionally constituted—with the aim of eliminating
their administrative functions and retaining only their advisory role

(d)   That states enact legislation granting to large units
of local government the same regulatory power over actions
of state and other public agencies that they have over actions
of private developers—making clear at the same time "that

certain state and Federal policies, such as those relating to free choice for persons at all income levels, take precedence over local policies"

(e) That each state create a state agency for development planning and review, including research and technical aid to localities, and preparation of state and regional land use plans and policies

CEMETERIES AND LAND USE [7]

It is estimated that in the United States cemeteries occupy nearly two million acres of often choice land.

The report from which the above quotation comes goes on to say that "until recently, common burial customs have not affected the land use considerations of cities. . . . Cemeteries have seldom been any serious concern in planning the 'city scape'. . . ." But, now that urban areas are growing and the search for open space has become intense, the wastefulness of many urban graveyards, which are often large, poorly maintained, and underused, is being increasingly recognized.

In Pulaski, Tennessee, the once deteriorated and vandalized Old Pulaski Graveyard has recently been transformed into a public park as a result of a demonstration project conducted by the Pulaski city government. The demonstration was funded with the assistance of a grant of some $133,000 from the Department of Housing and Urban Development, under its programs for open space, urban beautification, and historic preservation. As a background to this local project, the demonstration also included a general analysis of the problems and potentials presented by cemeteries in urban settings. The findings of Pulaski officials have been recorded in an illustrated report, *Cemeteries as Open Space Reservations,* from which the above quotations come. The scope of the project included research into a variety of fields,

[7] From "Cemeteries Becoming Critical Factor in Land-Use Planning as Urban Areas Grow," by Martha Fisher, senior editorial associate. *Journal of Housing.* 27:527-9. N. 23, '70. Reprinted by permission.

ranging from legal and religious restrictions that govern the reworking of burial grounds to the land use problems that are being encountered as traditional interment practices persist in densely populated urban areas.

The Pulaski Rehabilitation Plan

The Pulaski cemetery, which had not been used for burial purposes since 1888, was described as abandoned and derelict before its rehabilitation was undertaken. Weeds and unmowed grass covered burial plots and many markers had been tilted out of position, while others were crumbled and broken. The cemetery had also been the victim of vandalism during its years of neglect and was considered a detriment to the neighborhood. Turning the rundown area into an attractive and useful open space and demonstrating how other localities could change similar problems to urban assets became the focus of the Pulaski project.

In the Pulaski demonstration, the actual reworking of the local cemetery involved research on local questions concerning religious beliefs, customs and superstitions, and legal regulations. It also required efforts at achieving widespread public acceptance of projected changes and some consensus from the heirs of those interred in the graveyard. In addition to contracting for standard construction and landscaping, it was necessary for the Pulaski designers to devise special techniques for documenting and storing the gravestones until they could be relocated for better display within the new park and for renovating the entire area without disturbing any burial plots.

When the project was completed, the deteriorated cemetery had been transformed into an attractively landscaped "passive" memorial park. Large flat monuments had been set in a rubble stone wall constructed along one side of the park and smaller gravestones were placed on the top surfaces of several low, curving walls, so that visitors can easily read the inscriptions. Free-standing monuments were placed throughout the park and a new memorial structure was constructed as the central focus of the quiet park. What had long been an eyesore in the community had been changed into a place of historic interest and had become an attribute to the surrounding neighborhood.

Ideas for the Future

According to Pulaski officials, the existence of old cemeteries or the need to plan for future burial grounds often present a diverse range of possible solutions. In almost all cases, the cemetery may be viewed as all, or as only part, of an open space that is the answer to the urban need for green relief. The characteristics of this green space may vary from quiet vestpocket parks to extremely large, functional "buffers" between two areas of incompatible land uses.

In presenting the findings of their general study, the Pulaski officials surveyed a variety of topics, ranging from the historical development of burial customs and cemetery designs to forecasts of future interment trends. In particular, the authors note the decline of small grid-patterned, church-controlled graveyards in favor of more spacious, privately operated memorial parks and the consequent changes, in many instances, away from hard-to-maintain monuments and site plans.

As for the fate of the older cemeteries, once maintained by descendants of the deceased, the Pulaski authors hold that surrounding neighborhoods have both influenced and been influenced by the condition of long-unused graveyards. While stating a general principle that cemetery conditions normally decline with a decrease in the interment rate, the Pulaski report points out that cemeteries in older, more well-to-do neighborhoods fare better than those surrounded by declining neighborhoods or around which industrial developments have grown up. Conversely, the report comments that poorly maintained cemeteries may have an adverse effect on adjacent properties. The primary factors determin-

ing the condition of older cemeteries, however, are stated
to be the existence of clearly defined control, continuing
care, and public interest.

Rehabilitation Guides

Outlining the procedures they consider advisable in undertaking the rehabilitation of an abandoned graveyard, the
Pulaski authors first emphasize the need to establish a clear
authority for the municipal government to assume control,
to rework the overall land parcel, and to use individual grave
spaces as plans dictate. The lack of such established authority, they say, is likely to engender unfavorable public senti-
ment.

A second preliminary requirement spelled out by the report is for a detailed study of the environment surrounding
the cemetery and of all proposed land use changes that might
affect the character of the immediate neighborhood. Only
by determining the future of the neighborhood is it possible
to insure that the planned open space will be related to the
needs of the immediate community.

Other factors that should be considered before actual reworking begins include the manner in which continuing
maintenance is to be provided in the completed park and
the possibilities for decreasing future maintenance costs. As
suggestions, the Pulaski authors propose the use of flush
grave markers or the planting of foot stones in mountings
flush against the ground; the elimination, wherever possible,
of curbings, fences, footstones, and superfluous plantings.
The possibility of relocating monuments for better display
within the cemetery is also recommended as a means of providing more attractive plans and more inexpensive maintenance. . . .

New Uses for Cemeteries

Renovation designs suggested by the Pulaski authors center around the concept of a passive memorial park as the

most appropriate use of cemetery land. The combining of passive-use areas with more active open spaces is seen, however, as a means of fulfilling more urban needs and of adding greater interest to the park area. Playgrounds are cited as "reserved use" areas that may easily be situated on large or small vacant spaces within the perimeter of a generally passive park. Or, assuming the availability of larger vacant tracts, the authors suggest the combination of several semi-active uses in one area. The proposals made in the report— arboreta or botanical gardens; nature, bridle, or bike trails; observatory facilities; and museums for local history—are suggestive of many other possibilities. In any event, a point to be borne in mind, the authors counsel, is the contribution to park maintenance that may be made through the inclusion of revenue-producing facilities.

Plans for the Future

As the Pulaski authors look at the growing land scarcity in urban areas, they predict for the future a greater acceptance of cremation and, possibly, a growing reliance on architectural structures such as crypts or mausoleums that will accommodate more than single burials. They also see, however, means through which traditional burial patterns could be adjusted to meet rather than conflict with urban needs. They propose the possibility of building terrace crypts into walls built to retain terraces artificially constructed of sanitary fill. Further, in areas normally considered unsuitable for most active land uses, as on tracts adjacent to airport runways or to freeway interchanges, cemeteries might be constructed as a means of making the best use of land that would otherwise remain vacant. In the design of new communities, the buffer characteristics of a cemetery may be advantageously employed to separate industrial and residential sections or to screen the planned community from possible undesirable development on properties adjacent to controlled boundaries. In all of these and many other feasible cemetery plans, the often neglected and wasteful, sometimes detrimental, burial ground is turned to the community's advantage.

Throughout the Pulaski report, society's demand that land be consumed for interment purposes and society's need for well-designed open spaces are considered side by side as problems that can be solved through combined land use planning. "It is apparent that the potential of cemeteries as multipurpose spaces is not being pursued because of social and economic resistance to innovative changes. But if this country is to accommodate the living as well as the dead then changes will have to be made."

III. OUR LAND AND ITS RESOURCES

EDITOR'S INTRODUCTION

Better use and care of our resources—river waters, coastal lands and waters, forest lands and mineral resources —relate directly to land policies, for both public and private holdings. These vast problems and the often uneconomic, careless way we have treated such resources to the detriment of the land and its continued productivity are explored in this section.

The section begins with an article on our polluted rivers. Then, a discussion by a *National Observer* reporter of the problems related to the Mississippi River illustrates the many complex governmental/economic aspects of water resources conservation.

Several articles follow dealing with our coastal areas, forest lands, and mining areas. The article on coastal areas by William S. Beller, physical scientist with the Environmental Protection Agency, is followed by two articles on our forests: one by Michael Frome, conservation editor of *Field & Stream*; the other, suggesting that we are in effect "mining" our national forests, by Dale A. Burk, environmental columnist for a Montana newspaper. Mining for minerals and coal (often by strip-mining) present obvious but often neglected aspects of land use. These are touched on in an article from the magazine *Environment* and an editorial from the New York *Times*. The problem of land use for power plants is considered in an article from *Science*.

Last, an article on the controversy concerning the transportation of Alaskan oil hints at the great land problems of Alaska, a state in which the Federal Government owns 95.3 per cent of the land.

CRISIS ON OUR RIVERS [1]

In central California, an hour's drive from San Francisco, lies the great, marshy, Huck Finn country of the Delta, where the Sacramento and San Joaquin rivers splay out into a thousand miles of wandering streams and bayous, shade-dappled by overarching oaks and cottonwoods, alive with catfish and bass. It's one of the country's biggest and most beautiful recreational areas close by a major metropolitan center. On a good summer day there will be tens of thousands of people lazing through the Delta in their houseboats and outboards, or driving down back roads for a shore dinner at one of the tumbledown hamlets by the water's edge.

And now the beauty of the area is being literally blotted out. In the name of flood control, the United States Army Corps of Engineers is strengthening the levees by stripping them of their vegetation and lining them with mile after mile of "rip-rap"—huge boulders that bury the shorelines under fortress-like revetments, destroying wildlife habitats and walling off any decent human contact between land and water.

Opponents say the $100 million project is an unnecessary desecration, a typical example of the damn-the-environment engineering mentality at work. Some deny it's needed at all, pointing out that the present vegetation has protected the banks for over forty years, since long before the present complex of upstream flood-control dams was built. If more protection actually *is* needed, say University of California soil specialists, there are alternative methods—like planting trees with stronger soil-holding roots—that the Corps has ignored in favor of its by-the-book rip-rapping. It is "pure vandalism," in the words of Representative Jerome Waldie

[1] From article by James Nathan Miller and Robert Simmons. *Reader's Digest*. 97:78-83. D. '70. Copyright 1970 by The Reader's Digest Assn. Inc. Reprinted by permission. Mr. Miller is a free lance writer and a Roving Editor for the *Reader's Digest*.

(Democrat, California), "the witless, heedless destruction of a great scenic resource."

Coast to Coast

Bad as it is, the Delta project is not unusual; the same thing is now happening all over the country. Indeed, it's high time Americans woke up to a crucial fact: The real crisis facing our rivers is not pollution; we will cure pollution when we're willing to spend the money. The real problem is the basic structural damage we're doing to our rivers that we'll *never* be able to repair. We're doing it at such a rate that within our lifetime we will render tens of thousands of miles of unspoiled streams unrecognizable.

Even conservationists don't realize how bad the situation is. They know of threats to a few national landmarks—Idaho's Hells Canyon, Florida's Everglades, New York's Storm King Mountain, etc.—plus perhaps a stream or two in their own areas. What they don't know is that the same thing is happening right now to river after river, in virtually every section of every state from coast to coast.

We can stop it, for most of the destruction is unnecessary. But first we must realize how widespread it is, and where the responsibility lies. Two typical river projects, one in Georgia and the other in the state of Washington, tell the story.

Planned Disaster

Observe the Alcovy River, a pure, free-flowing fishing and hunting stream that runs wild and beautiful through thousands of acres of hardwood swamps in central Georgia. Right now, the United States Soil Conservation Service (SCS) is planning to channelize the Alcovy.

Channelize? It works this way. First, SCS engineers knock down all woody vegetation within 30 to 100 feet of the stream. This allows farmers to install drainage pipes from the neighboring swamps into the river and also eliminates the habitat of waterfowl and songbirds. Then they scrape the stream's bottom free of muck and straighten its meanderings so that it can rush off floodwaters super-efficiently. This eliminates the pools that fish need for food and spawning areas. When they're all done, they have a perfectly engineered drainage ditch, an arrow-straight gash across the countryside that is almost totally devoid of life in its waters and along its banks.

Channelization's damage has left fish-and-game people aghast. A recent Alabama inventory of the channelization plans of the SCS, Corps of Engineers and Tennessee Valley Authority found 2,000 miles of stream projected for destruction *in this one state*. In Georgia, the 172 projects planned by the SCS will affect almost every one of the state's major fishing streams and lakes. Says Philip Aus, wildlife biologist of the United States Bureau of Sports Fisheries and Wildlife in Devils Lake, North Dakota: "The SCS is considering the possibility of watershed projects on nearly every stream in eastern North Dakota."

"The effects will be cataclysmic," says Professor Charles Wharton, Georgia State University ecologist. "Compared with these projects, strip-mining seems like a minor, local problem." Agrees Representative Ben Blackburn III (Republican, Georgia), "It's as far-reaching and disastrous a threat as any confronted in our natural history."

Crucial Facts

The obvious question is: Why *are* we channelizing these streams? The *official* reason is "flood control"; but to hydrologists, calling this kind of project flood control is like calling a forest fire a tree-clearing operation. For the swamps being wiped out are among nature's most effective flood-control devices—they slow down and blot up floodwaters and feed them into the ground-water supply—and their loss will simply dump all the water farther downstream.

The *real* reason was stated by Ralph H. Allen, Jr., chief of the Alabama State Game Management Section: Channelization's purpose is "to increase the wealth of a few landowners and to strengthen a Federal bureaucracy." On the Alcovy, for instance, the Government would pay $3,494,432 —a subsidy of $808 an acre—to dry up the farmer's land.

Behind this bureaucratic game lie three crucial facts that explain a large part of what we're doing to our rivers, and why:

1. To the engineering mentality, an undeveloped river is worthless. It may have high value to fishermen, birdwatchers and ecologists, but in terms of immediate economic gain it is like an untapped vein of gold—valuable only when you exploit it.

2. There are four main Government agencies whose job it is to do the exploiting: the SCS, the smallest, which is limited to upstream watersheds of 250,000 acres or less; the Corps of Engineers, the biggest, is in charge of flood-control and navigation projects on our main streams; the Bureau of Reclamation, whose assignment is irrigation and power dams; and the TVA, which handles all river development in its area. (One nondigging agency is also important: the Federal Power Commission, which licenses hydroelectric dams.)

3. The bureaucratic survival of these agencies demands that they keep digging; therefore, as they run out of rivers that really need developing, *they invent new needs.*

A perfect example of the latter is the way the SCS got into this business of channelization. When the agency got its small-watershed assignment in 1954, its job was to prevent floods and the erosion of farmland; its motto was, "Stop the raindrop where it falls." But then it began to run out of antierosion projects. So what did the SCS do? Because the words "flood prevention" were in its 1954 assignment, it began drying up farmers' swamps—in the process rushing raindrops downstream as fast as possible!

Self-Fulfilling Assumption

Which brings us to the second stream, the Snoqualmie River near Seattle. Here the Corps of Engineers is proposing a $50 million dam to "protect" the river's largely undeveloped flood plain—a valley that urban planners and environmentalists see as an ideal green belt around which to plan Seattle's future growth. What is the Corps' justification? Not that *present* development justifies the dam, but that *future* urban sprawl demands it. Thus the Corps has reversed *its* original flood-control assignment of protecting existing development, to the point where it is now building dams to protect houses that don't even exist.

In the process, the Corps is violating a basic principle of intelligent flood control. One of the hard lessons we've learned from past experience is this: Wherever you have a flood plain that isn't yet developed, *do everything possible to keep it undeveloped.* This is the cheapest and by far the most beneficial means of flood control. It's not simply that building on the flood plain is almost literally the same as building in the river, an open invitation to disaster; or that it destroys some of the finest land we have left for wildlife, recreation and agriculture. It's also that when we crowd houses and factories onto the plain we're making inevitable the building of costly dams, thus forcing the general taxpayer to subsidize the developers.

For all these reasons, Washington Governor Dan Evans has asked his department of ecology to investigate alternatives to the dam. "Once the dam is built," says Evans, "no matter how you zone the area or whatever else you try, the pressures will become overwhelming to allow 'higher use' for the land—which means the use that will bring the most cash return." Thus the Snoqualmie dam, like many others the Corps is planning, is a self-fulfilling assumption: building it will create the urban sprawl that will justify it.

How, then, did the Engineers get into this business of protecting *future* development? The same way the SCS got into channelization—through the back door:

In 1936, following a series of disastrous floods in the highly developed Mississippi Valley, Congress assigned the Corps to build dams to protect the millions of people then living on exposed flood plains. So diligently did the Corps do the job (it has since built more than 250 flood-control dams, costing over $5 billion), that after a while it began to run out of property to protect. Whereupon, very quietly, the Corps' aims began to change.

So quietly, in fact, that the changeover wasn't noticed until 1966, when a presidential task force investigated U.S. flood-control policy and came to this startled conclusion: "The major purpose of engineering projects is changing from the protection of established property to the underwriting of new development. . . . Thus the Federal Government inadvertently may encourage unwise flood-plain development. . . . Land developers may be enriched at public expense."

Quiet Alliance

That last sentence brings us to the crux of the whole thing, the secret of where the river bureaucracies get their power: the developers. Today, behind most big "flood-control" or "soil-conservation" or "navigation" schemes you'll find a quiet alliance between a bureaucracy and a special-interest group—the former providing the river and the subsidy, the latter the political clout that keeps the bureaucrats in business.

At the national level, for instance, a group of towboat operators, canal-construction companies, waterway shippers and local port authorities operates what is widely considered Washington's most powerful lobby: the National Rivers and Harbors Congress, whose every major aim—more canals, more rip-rapping, bigger locks—is faithfully echoed by the Engineers. Down at the grass-roots level, the regional salesmen for the big agencies are constantly addressing Rotary Clubs, farm organizations, chambers of commerce and others, and teaching them the bureaucratic ABCs of how to band together in a "watershed association" or a "conservation district" that can then apply to the river bureaucracy for a dam here or a channelization project there.

In the process, tens of thousands of acres of our finest land and hundreds of miles of riverbank are being blotted out *every year*. It's estimated that in ten years we will have blocked more than half of our rivers' natural flow, and twenty years later, 80 per cent. But even those rivers that remain undammed will have been largely rendered lifeless by rip-rapping and channelization.

The fact is that we are rapidly turning this magnificent natural resource into a piece of machinery.

This is not to say that *all* the big agencies' projects are worthless. In the future we will, of course, have to accept many legitimate sacrifices of natural areas in the name of economic efficiency. *Which is precisely the reason we must eliminate the illegitimate ones.*

Fundamental Truth

How do we do it? Here are four ways:

(1) *Forbid channelization,* unless it's absolutely necessary. Specifically, give state and Federal conservation agencies a veto over projects with damaging environmental effects. Representative Blackburn is now seeking such a change in the laws; it's one of the most important conservation actions before Congress.

(2) *Get help at the state level.* Any governor can veto a Federal project simply by saying he doesn't want it. Also, in the last couple of years sixteen states have passed wild-river or scenic-river laws, offering varying degrees of

protection to exceptionally beautiful streams. If such a stream is threatened in your area, pressure your legislature to defend it.

(3) *Stop flood-plain development.* About a dozen states now have flood-plain-management laws aimed at getting local communities to prevent population buildup where floods are inevitable. Under recently passed flood-plain zoning laws, Massachusetts has already protected 15,000 acres of salt-marsh flood plain, and is adding 1,000 acres a month to its protected list. A similar policy of buying flood-prone land has helped give Milwaukee one of the country's finest municipal park systems. But, so far, only a handful of communities have taken such action.

(4) *Prod Congress.* While new laws are essential, the fact is that Congress has the power *right now* to prevent the great bulk of the damage. Yet year after year it rubber-stamps the recommendations of its pork-barrel public works committees, which work hand-in-glove with the bureaucrats and developers. To see just how hand-in-glove, look at the letterhead of the dam-and-dredge National Rivers and Harbors Congress lobby; it lists, as the lobby's vice president and directors, *many of the key members of the House and Senate public works committees.*

A single set of figures shows the result. Last year Congress approved a $1.15 billion Corps of Engineers budget containing, as one small item, $23.8 million for planning new projects. At the same time, it reduced from $1.5 million to $1 million the *total* budget of the President's Council on Environmental Quality, which is supposed to assess the environmental impact of all Federal projects.

The fundamental truth is that we are doing to our rivers what Congress wants done, and the big bureaucracies are merely reflections of Congressional intent. So in the end it is up to us, the voters. The condition of America's rivers in 1980 will be a direct reflection of how much we cared about them in the 1970s.

A STORM ROILS THE MISSISSIPPI [2]

A great storm is quietly building up over the Mississippi that could become a raging environmental issue. At the very least, the fury of the simmering controversy—when it bursts —will affect some 35 million Americans whose lives are directly touched by the river.

The issue, on the surface, is ordinary and seemingly trivial. It is a proposal by the United States Army Corps of Engineers to deepen the channel of the Upper Mississippi from Cairo, Illinois, to Minneapolis-St. Paul. The Corps wants to deepen the channel from its present nine-foot depth to twelve feet along the 853-mile stretch.

At the moment, the fight over the proposal—and the possible effects on the environment—is largely out of public view. It is buried in the thousands of pages of pink-covered project studies made by the Corps of Engineers and in rather esoteric analyses by a handful of fretful conservationists and biologists. The validity of the conflicting arguments is being affected, too, by the almost imperceptible changes taking place in the river itself as it sweeps 2,348 miles from Lake Itasca in northern Minnesota down past New Orleans to the Gulf of Mexico.

The Engineers have talked about deepening the channel for decades. The Lower Mississippi already has a twelve-foot channel, and so does the Ohio River which empties into the Mississippi at Cairo. It is the Corps' view that the deeper channel is needed to permit the most economic use of the existing channels, and to enable cheaper barge freight to keep up with the population and industrial growth along the river from St. Louis to the Twin Cities.

[2] Article by David W. Hacker, staff writer. *National Observer.* p 1+. D. 28, '70. Reprinted by permission.

Big, Dirty Ditch

Few people paid much attention to the Engineers' proposal until a year or so ago when concern over environment became a major public issue. Now, the Corps finds itself, as George Lykowski, chief of the plan-formulative branch for the twelve-state north-central division puts it, "with the fish and wildlife interests on our back." Also lining up against the proposal are railroads and truck lines, which would get fresh competition from waterway users, and other critics who say the changes will turn the river into a "big, dirty ditch."

Making the channel, if the project gets a green light, is no cheap or easy task. Basically, it can be done in one of two ways, or through a combination of each way: Raise the water level or dig out the river's bottom.

Raising the water level would mean the flooding out of more land along the river, and the building of higher dikes and levees. In most places, topography alone would make it impractical to raise the river level by three feet.

Dredging the bottom requires a place to dump the mountains of "spoil"—mostly sand. It is not practical to move the stuff very far from the river, and critics insist the river banks can't stand much more filling in. If the spoil is dumped in the wetlands, important fish and fowl habitats would be destroyed.

Dredging is done with what is nothing more than a giant vacuum cleaner. A cutter head churns up the sand on the bed of the main channel. A pipe then sucks up this mixture of sand and water and discharges it on shore or at a river site away from the channel through a pontoon line. This is flexible and is floated into position.

There is no way to accurately forecast how much the deeper channel would cost until the Corps decides how to do the job. The engineers also are studying duplicate locks, to relieve the pressure of pleasure-boat operators who often are hung up at locks for hours at a time, while towboats are given priority for locking through. New locks also would be bigger, to accommodate the bigger tows that would ply the Upper Mississippi if the channel were deepened.

A Close-Up View

The dilemma—and the dissension that the plan is causing—can best be understood by taking a close-up view of a town that would be directly affected: Winona.

Winona is a town of 27,000 persons, in the southeastern corner of Minnesota, 110 miles south of the Twin Cities. At this point, the Mississippi runs east and west. The town is walled on the south by steep five-hundred-foot hills and on the north by the river. It is one of the Midwest's loveliest towns, with Lake Winona in the middle of it.

This lake, it's said, used to be the main channel of the river, but the sanding in of the river, which is an inexorable process, filled in the areas between the channels. The city of Winona is built on a sand bar.

The waters that brush Winona's levees make up Pool 5 and Pool 6, two of twenty-six pools created on the Upper Mississippi in the 1930s by the Corps by locks and dams for navigation purposes. These pools ensure there will be enough water for a nine-foot channel.

Recalls Harry Luedke, a dredger, "I remember before they put these locks in, the water would get real low in the summer. A man could wade across."

These locks and dams "made this a river," notes Mr. Luedke. The pools spread the river out over bottom lands, and turned hay meadows into marshes and feeding grounds for migrating ducks and spawning areas for fish. It made more water available for boaters too.

Winona's men are as avid hunters and fishermen as you'll find anywhere in the nation, but wildlife and sports are not Winona's only concern with the Mississippi. The river also spawns floods. Only frantic and heroic efforts at temporary diking kept the mighty river from washing out Winona in 1965, 1967, and 1969.

A Business View

Thus, for decades the city has tended to see the river as either a wildlife resource or a harbinger of disasters. But, recently, officials have decided that the river may be a source of industry too, and they set up a port authority, which is actively promoting the Frog Island industrial area and the River Bend Industrial Park.

Harold Doerer, a Winona businessman and member of the port authority, notes that Winona has a six- or eight-week longer navigation season than the Twin Cities, because the river here doesn't freeze up until later in the fall and opens up earlier in the spring. He sees Frog Island as a major center for warehousing, grain-storage tanks, oil terminals, and coal-storage areas.

"Victoria Elevator took over the one [grain] elevator we have here. Normally, they shipped out 20 to 25 barges a year. This year, they've shipped out over 100 barges."

Mr. Doerer is thinking big, and he is all for the barges with their heavier loads that would be made possible by a twelve-foot channel.

Less impressed by a deepening of the channel is Dr. Calvin R. Fremling, professor of biology at Winona State College. He points out that the hills overlooking Winona are not really hills, but the sides of a canyon. Winona is in a valley, cut by a glacial river. There is a relentless natural process for the river bed to fill in, and return to its original level, which is the hilltops. Thus, sanding in always has been the Mississippi River's greatest problem. The Corps has to dredge constantly to maintain even a nine-foot channel.

This sanding in was hastened, says Dr. Fremling, when the Corps built the locks and dams on the Upper Mississippi in the 1930s to create the twenty-six navigation pools. But, says Dr. Fremling, "the dams are creating catch basins for the silt and the sand."

Building the Bed

What this means is that the Corps is helping the river-bed to rise. Dr. Fremling calculates it has risen three feet in the past fifty years.

As the river-bed rises, of course, so does the level of the water. This, in turn, means floods with higher and higher crests, or more severe flooding.

This, obviously, was not the Corps' intention. But it is one of the subtle changes taking place, says Dr. Fremling, as a result of the Corps' rearranging of the river.

Dr. Fremling, and conservationists such as Raymond C. Hubley, Jr., United States Bureau of Sport Fisheries and Wildlife coordinator for the Upper Mississippi River Conservation Committee, and W. H. Dieffenbach, a biologist for the Missouri Department of Conservation, point out the tremendous dredging that must be done just to maintain the present channel. The spoil from this dredging lines the river. The sand does provide beaches and sand bars for recreational use by boaters, swimmers, and picnickers. But the spoil shrinks the river.

A twelve-foot channel would require far more dredging. Maintaining such a channel would require cleaning out those spots that now clog up, but at a depth of three feet greater, and cleaning out new spots where the river itself maintains a bare nine-foot channel.

Preliminary Study

In one pool, above Cap au Gris, Missouri, for example, a preliminary study showed that the Engineers had to dredge out 740,000 cubic yards of sand a year to maintain a nine-foot channel over a thirty-two-mile stretch of the Mississippi. That's equivalent to a load carried by fifty-seven one-hundred-car trains. For a twelve-foot channel, an additional 840,000 cubic yards would have to be dredged.

In this preliminary study, the Engineers figured they would have to scoop out 1.33 million cubic yards of sand every year. This is almost twice the amount needed to maintain the nine-foot channel, and it is only one tiny chunk of the river.

Corps officials say it may be three or four years before they finish studies on the upper river channel project and make a recommendation to Congress. At the moment, there's no doubt the Corps will recommend deepening the channel. Then Congress must authorize it, and then set aside money to pay for it.

It was Congress that decided in 1878 to give the voters access to cheaper goods through river freight, and charged the Corps of Engineers, which had been removing snags and wrecks from the rivers since 1824, with doing the job.

In 1878, the Corps began work on a 4.5-foot-deep navigation system, later raised to 6 feet, then 8 feet, then 9 feet, and now 12 feet. The Corps already has proposals for a 15-foot channel system. And, there are some persons who envision a 22-foot channel that would enable freighters to circumnavigate the eastern chunk of North America. They would come down the St. Lawrence Seaway, go across Lake Superior, down a canal to the Mississippi, and back to the Atlantic via the Gulf of Mexico.

That's the dream, but to some who see the twelve-foot channel proposal as an inexorable step toward "unkinking" the Mississippi, it's sheer nightmare.

COASTAL AREAS AND SEASHORES [3]

The United States clearly has a large stake in seeing that its coastal zone is developed in the best possible way. For this reason, all uses of the coastal zone must be con-

[3] From article by William S. Beller. a physical scientist with the Environmental Protection Agency. *Current History*. 59:100-4+. Ag. '70. Reprinted by permission of Current History, Inc. and the author.

sidered by those who might want to alter it. Furthermore, in most instances the long-term health of the coastal zone should dominate. These are recent conclusions, spawned by worried ecologists, supported by several high-level study groups and first introduced into Congress in a spate of bills in 1969.

The coastal zone is the area where the sea and the land meet and where the fingers of the sea or of the Great Lakes poke into the land. It is also where the effects of these meetings are strongly felt. Thus, the coastal zone includes the land, waters and the lands beneath the waters near the shoreline.

For legislative purposes, the definition of the coastal zone is made explicit and arbitrary, something nature neglected to do. In one such definition, the coastal zone is said to extend to the outer limit of the United States territorial sea. The territorial sea comprises state waters and reaches three nautical miles seaward for most coastal states. Historically, this was the distance a shore battery was able to propel a cannon ball.

There is no upper value limit that can be placed on the coastal zone, because it is integral to our lives. It provides an avenue for commerce, a nursery ground or habitat for most of our fish, a unique recreational area, a sink for our wastes, a storehouse of oil and other minerals, land for choice real estate developments and luxury hotels, sites for industrial development and a useful moat for national defense. More than 50 million people live in counties adjacent to the nation's coastal zone and use its resources.

Today there are about six times as many people in the United States as there were a century ago. They want services such as electricity, and places to relinquish their wastes. This means increased use of coastal waters. They make demands on the coastal zone in ways that may not be apparent: a pesticide that helps a farmer grow cherries of succulent size in a Michigan valley may result, under certain circumstances, in thousands of dead Coho salmon on the banks of Lake Michigan. By the same token, a factory that uses estuarine water to cool its equipment could pay taxes that upgrade the schools of the immediate area.

Who weighs the benefits against the costs? Even more important, how much benefit does a man receive from contemplating the wildlife in a salt marsh against the value to a community in filling the marsh with municipal wastes for a low-cost housing development?

A Piecemeal Approach

The nation has used its coastal zone in a haphazard way because during most of the life of the United States there seemed to be enough coastal area for almost every use. Then, as uses began infringing on one another, the Federal Government tried to preserve those it considered most precious: the protection of commerce, of course; the conservation of fish and wildlife; the striving for cleaner water; and, more recently, the nation's decision to try to conserve all aspects of its natural environment. . . .

The right of the Federal Government to regulate navigation is based on the commerce clause of the United States Constitution. The River and Harbor Act of 1899 exercised this right. It put the Army Corps of Engineers in charge of protecting the nation's navigable waters. (The courts have held that navigable waters include waterways that either in their natural or improved condition are used, or can be used, for floating light boats or logs, even though the waterway may be obstructed by falls, rapids, sand bars, currents, etc., and even though the waterway has not been used for navigation for many years.) The Corps keeps shipping lanes open and builds new ones; it has the sole authority to grant or deny permits to dredge or fill in the navigable waters of the United States. Through this work, the Corps has affected the shape and aquatic life of the nation's waters more than any other Government agency.

Since the turn of the century, the Corps has faithfully and expertly carried out its navigation mission, giving lesser attention to how its works might affect other values of the coastal zone. . . .

Yet the Corps could scarcely be criticized for the viewpoint it took through the years because trade was clearly important to the nation, and the voices of the conservationists were usually weak. Moreover, the public itself has only recently taken a profound interest in its natural environment. If the Federal Government is to be faulted, it should be in terms of not having had the foresight to anticipate the needs of the public, a task easily undertaken with the advantage of hindsight.

Certainly the nation's navigable waters have many more uses than simply to provide passage for ships. Such a view of United States waterways would destroy much of the value and beauty of the coastal zone. Recognizing this fact, Congress passed the Fish and Wildlife Coordination Act [of 1934, as amended in 1958]. This Act says that "wildlife conservation shall receive equal consideration and be coordinated with other features of water-resource development programs. . . ." In this way, Congress enlarged the scope of the River and Harbor Act of 1899. The Coordination Act requires that any Federal agency that intends to modify the course of a body of water, or anybody else who needs Federal permission to do so, must first consult with the Fish and Wildlife Service of the United States Department of the Interior and with the equivalent state body. The intent of Congress was to focus on the need to conserve wildlife as it had already focused on water-resource development. . . .

To make up for some of the deficiencies of the Fish and Wildlife Coordination Act, and to respond to increasing public interest in the problem of preserving the environment, the Secretary of the Interior and the Secretary of the Army signed a Memorandum of Understanding on July

13, 1967. Methods were set up under which the Corps would seek the advice of the Department of the Interior on questions relating to the natural resources and arising from dredging, filling or other work authorized by the Corps. If the Secretary of the Interior affirmed that impending work would have an adverse effect on fish and wildlife or other natural resources, recreation or water quality, then the Secretary of the Army would either deny a permit to do the work or impose conditions that he determined to be in the public interest.

The Corps used the Coordination Act and the Memorandum of Understanding when it rejected the application of land developers to fill in a large part of Boca Ciega Bay, near St. Petersburg, Florida. Although the Corps found that the proposed work would not interfere with navigation, the agency would not issue the permit because the fish and wildlife and other coastal resources of Boca Ciega Bay would be harmed.

The United States district court where the case was tried would not accede to the motion of the United States to dismiss the case. In this action, the court stated that the Fish and Wildlife Coordination Act does not give discretion to the Corps to deny permits on grounds other than navigation. The United States has appealed the case. Its outcome will test the essence of the Coordination Act, which relies in large part on the navigation authority of the Corps to help protect some of our coastal resources.

Use Through Water Quality

The common denominator for just about every use of the coastal zone is the cleanliness or quality of the water. It is easy to see the importance of clean water for drinking and for the protection of the health of fish and wildlife, swimmers in coastal waters, and even strollers along the beaches who have a passable sense of smell. The commercial and industrial users of the nation's waters are also interested in water quality: shippers whose craft could be harmed by hazard of oil in navigable waters or damaged by debris; power-station operators whose equipment is cooled by water diverted from streams (provided the water has not already been overheated by upstream operators) ; and industrialists whose products could be destroyed by contaminants in the water used in the manufacturing process.

Unlike navigation, which is a use of the nation's waters, water quality is a characteristic of the water. Its consideration in law was the nation's first major step toward achieving a healthful coastal environment.

In 1965, both houses of Congress unanimously passed the Water Quality Act of 1965, which states that it is in the public interest "to enhance the quality and value of our water resources and to establish a national policy for the prevention, control and abatement of water pollution." The act contains a requirement of historic significance— that water quality standards for interstate waters be set by the states, and be approved as Federal standards by the Secretary of the Interior. The standards identify uses of the waters, including agricultural, municipal, industrial, recreational, fishery and wildlife. They indicate the water quality necessary to support each use, and include plans to bring about and enforce this quality.

Control of water quality is necessary but in itself it does not guarantee the nation the best use of its coastal zone. Indeed, high water quality alone is not an assurance of a good coastal environment. If municipalities and industries turn to incinerating or burying more of their wastes in order to raise water quality, air and land pollution will increase. Hotels and condominiums might wall out beaches from public use. Thus, avoiding pollution is only one way of deriving the most benefit out of the coastal zone. While of the three factors pollution is the dominant one and, unlike the others, contains the seeds of assuring the nation of long-term dividends, still it suffers from the myopia of excluding other environmental and, to some extent, social and economic considerations.

Policy for the 1970s

By the end of 1969, the nation was ready for a strong policy on the coastal zone. The events of the year had laid the groundwork: the year had started out with the release of the highly influential report of the Marine Commission (Commission on Marine Science, Engineering and Resources), which among other things lamented our lack of knowledge of the mechanics of the coastal zone. Three weeks after the Commission report was released, a gas blow-out took place at an oil-drilling site about 5.5 miles from Santa Barbara, California, leading to a disastrous oil spill. In October, the Administration approved a strong program in marine science with emphasis on (a) devising a way to manage the nation's coastal zone in a beneficial manner; (b) getting the research needed by those who would manage the coastal zone; (c) finding a way to bring a body of water back to a healthy state; (d) contributing to a world-wide program aimed at understanding the oceans; and (e) increasing work in understanding the Arctic's natural environment. In the fall of the year, Congress appropriated $800 million for fiscal year 1970 to build waste treatment plants to stem water pollution, an amount several times greater than the Administration had requested. Throughout the year, it was clear that the public was beginning to realize the threat to the marine environment posed by a growing population despite the respites that might be expected from science and technology.

On New Year's Day, 1970, President Richard M. Nixon signed the National Environmental Policy Act of 1969. It created the Council on Environmental Quality, a body set up to be as close to the President and as influential as his Council of Economic Advisers.

The Act declares that it is national policy to encourage productive and enjoyable harmony between man and his environment; to help prevent damage to the environment; and to seek more understanding of the ecosystems that serve the nation. If this policy is successfully carried out, it signals a new era in this nation's use and enjoyment of its natural resources. The marine environment, and the coastal zone in particular, would benefit in large measure. . . .

The Marine Commission

In the early 1960s, the Federal establishment saw that the nation's relationship with its seas was bringing up critical problems, which would become unsolvable for future generations if something were not done soon. Futhermore, if the nation were concerned only with its present generation, with its present technology left unrestrained, the United States could utterly destroy its marine resources. Therefore, in 1966, Congress and the President created two marine bodies: the National Council on Marine Resources and Engineering Development to coordinate Federal activities in the marine field; and the Marine Commission. The job of the Commission was: first, to analyze all aspects of the marine environment including recreational, industrial, scientific and managerial; second, to recommend a marine program for the nation that would meet its present and future needs; and lastly, to estimate the cost of such a program.

To stress the importance of the Council and the Commission, Congress and the President made the Vice President the chairman of the Council; Cabinet officials were its members; some of the most eminent men in marine affairs and government organization in the country were appointed to the Commission. . . .

The Commission gave its formal report to Congress and the President on January 9, 1969. The importance of the report can be gauged by the reception the press gave to it on its release date five days later, when the Commission's findings appeared on the front page of just about every major metropolitan daily in the United States. Later in 1969 and in 1970, congressional committees held scores of hearings on a dozen or more bills derived in large part from the recommendations made in the Commission report.

The Commission gave much of its time to the problems of the coastal zone, and noted that the many claims on this area had outrun the present ability of local governments to deal effectively with these claims. The Commission recommended that each state set up it own agency with sufficient planning, coordinating and regulatory authority to ensure the healthy development of its coastal zone. The agency would have an overview of the state's needs with respect to the coastal zone and should be strong enough to surmount special pressures and local interests; to develop interstate arrangements where they are needed; and to amalgamate within the state the host of overlapping and often competing coastal-zone activities of the various Federal agencies. At the same time, Federal legislation would help the states by giving them guidelines for organizing their coastal-zone activities, and grants to help in the detail planning.

Unfortunately, often we do not know the extent to which our activities are endangering our marine resources nor, for that matter, the extent of the marine resources we have within our grasp. To help solve these problems, the Commission also recommended an extensive research program aimed at understanding the workings of our natural environment—the interactions among sea, air and land—in order to predict its course.

Tackling problems seemingly of more immediate and direct interest to the nation's citizens was a proposed network of "Coastal Zone Laboratories." These would examine the scientific and technical problems involving estuaries and the coastal zone. One great benefit from these laboratories would be their ability to advise their municipal and state governments about the technical factors that would affect the management of the coastal zone. Thus, the local bodies and the states would have the research data they would need to be able to manage their marine resources in an effective and rational manner.

The Problems Ahead

Congress has several bills in front of it in which plans for managing the nation's coastal zone are laid out. The bills differ in detail important in an administrative sense, but the aims are almost identical. In the Administration bill, grant money would be given to the coastal states to assist them in developing a comprehensive management program for the land and water resources of the coastal zone. The grants would not cover more than half the cost of developing the program, and the states individually would have to pay for the other half. If the Secretary of the Interior approves the coastal state's management program, the state is then eligible for operating grants, which would pay for half the costs of administering the management program, up to a prescribed dollar limit on the part of the Federal Government.

The keystone in the Administration bill is that before a state can get operating grants, it must show that it can require local zoning to conform with the state management plan. A number of local governments consider their zoning prerogatives as sacred, and almost forget that these powers were originally derived from the state governments. Regardless, it would be very difficult to try to manage a coastal zone in the bits and pieces local governments represent. States, and even multistate regions, would be the more logical units to use. Water and its resources are never conscious of political boundaries. Similarly, coastal-zone research should probably be done on a regional basis to be fully effective.

The United States, in recognizing its role in the coastal zone, is seeking to know this area as a complete system, not addressing isolated problems to the detriment of others. The nation is working to get the data needed to understand as fully as possible how the system operates so that the coastal zone can be enjoyed by all generations.

FOREST LANDS [4]

Forests even now cover an estimated one third of the land area of the United States. As sources of raw material, they play a significant part in the physical standards of American life. As conservers of soil and water, they are absolutely necessary if we are not willing to have our country become as denuded and flood swept as the Chinese hillsides and valleys. As environment for the highest type of recreational and esthetic enjoyment, including wilderness vestiges of the original America, they are essential to the happiness of millions of human beings.

In our modern age, forests serve as barriers to hot polluted air and restore the atmosphere with volumes of oxygenated air. In urban areas, they reduce harsh sounds and the effects of solar radiation, and limit the movement of wind, dust and snow. Economic, physical and social considerations demand that we maintain a bountiful forest resource. Yet the prolonged failure to protect and enhance these forests—based on the responsibility rather than right of land ownership—has contributed directly to the environmental crisis we face today.

Gifford Pinchot, the father of modern conservation and scientific forestry in the United States, made this plain. "The earth," he wrote, "belongs by right to all its people and not to a minority, insignificant in number but tremendous in wealth and power." Thus he saw forest manage-

[4] From "Forest Lands and Wilderness," by Michael Frome, conservation editor, Field & Stream. Current History. 58:343-8+. Je. '70. Reprinted by permission of Current History, Inc. and the author.

ment as a social issue. "The rightful use and purpose of our natural resources," he said, "is to make all the people strong and well, able and wise, well taught, well fed, well clothed and well housed, with equal opportunity and special privilege for none."

Pinchot strongly advocated Government regulation over privately owned forests, the need for which becomes increasingly apparent with the passage of years. When the first European settlers arrived, there was no such urgency. Forests covered 800 million acres of the continental United States, and the land was dense and dark with trees. The early pioneers might have known better than to indulge in waste and despoliation, considering that forests were no luxury in Europe and were already being managed with an eye toward perpetual yield. Or they could have learned from the Indians, many of whom practiced a form of conservation by taking no more than they needed.

Trees were useful, but barred the way of farms, homes, cities. The more felled, or burned, the better; there would always be more—such was the philosophy from colonial days to the latter part of the nineteenth century. True, there were a few early restraints. The British government, for example, reserved for the use of its navy a future supply of great white pines of Maine. But essentially, as long as forests and timber seemed limitless, concern and caution had no place in the scheme of things.

Maine was the first chief lumber source, supplying markets of the Atlantic Seaboard for more than two centuries; but by 1850 it showed the results of unrestrained exploitation. Then, for ten years, New York came to the forefront, followed by Pennsylvania, with its choice hardwoods and pines. Timber demands increased as the frontiers pushed westward. During the 1850s, prairie schooners and canalboats were made of wood, and railroads were laid on wooden ties. After the Civil War, there were new industries, new cities, new homes, all utilizing and clamoring for wood.

Thus logging came to the states bordering the Great Lakes, which in 1870 commenced a thirty-year leadership in lumber production.

The period was marked not simply by use, but by wasteful exploitation, followed by devastating fire. In 1871, the nation was shocked by the worst fire in United States history, at Peshtigo, Wisconsin, in which 1,500 persons lost their lives and nearly 1.3 million acres were burned. Disturbed by the wave of fire and destruction, the American Academy for the Advancement of Science two years later urged Congress and the states to recognize the need for "cultivation of timber and preservation of forests and to recommend proper legislation for securing these objectives." To pursue this program, the American Forestry Association was organized in 1875. Carl Schurz, the German-born Secretary of the Interior, called for a reversal of public opinion, "looking with indifference on this wanton, barbarous, disgraceful vandalism; a spendthrift people recklessly wasting its heritage; a Government careless of its future." As a result, in 1876 Congress enacted a bill providing for a study and report on the forest situation, and "the means best adapted to the preservation and renewal of forests."

During the same era, the Homestead Act of 1862 and subsequent laws were adopted by Congress presumably to encourage, assist and reward Americans who would open frontier lands and settle the West. But the land laws were bypassed and subverted and millions of acres passed into the hands of cattle syndicates, mining nabobs and speculators. The railroads were the real giants, receiving immense domains as "encouragement" to finance construction. Something like half the nation's forests were plucked into private ownership.

The National Forests

In the face of the dissolution of the nation's treasures, Yellowstone was set aside in 1872 as a public trust, "withdrawn" from any possible private claim and established as a national park. Thus the foundation was laid not only for additional national parks, but for the Forest Reserve Act of 1891, authorizing the President to withdraw portions of the public domain as "forest reserves." President Benjamin Harrison set aside reserves totaling 13 million acres, while his successor, Grover Cleveland, withdrew an additional 20 million acres. Theodore Roosevelt, however, made the greatest contribution, setting aside 132 million acres—very likely his greatest, most enduring contribution to the Republic—despite fervent, sometimes violent opposition. Today the national forests and national grasslands cover 187 million acres in forty-one states and Puerto Rico.

The 1897 Organic Act established the national forests on a firmer footing for the purposes of protecting watersheds and furnishing "a continuous supply of timber for the use and necessity of citizens of the United States." In fulfilling this mandate, Pinchot, the first Chief Forester, and other leaders of the Forest Service recognized that productive lands and an abundance of resources determine the quality of living of any nation. They were oriented to public welfare. Their underlying objective was that each generation should manage the land and its resources in such manner as to leave them to the next generation in a protected and productive condition. In due course, "continuous supply" became known as sustained yield, which means simply that if you are to have a continuous supply of timber, you must not cut it any faster than it grows. Or, the annual allowable cut must not exceed the increment of growth.

On this foundation, the National Forest System grew and developed. The Forest Service is the largest bureau in the Department of Agriculture. The Weeks Law of 1911 provided for purchase of forested lands in the East based on the need for watershed protection. Other laws were designed to advance forest research and to provide aid to state and private woodland management. In 1933, the National Plan for American Forestry, or the Copeland Report (named for its sponsor, Senator Royal S. Copeland [Democrat, New York, 1923-1938]), contained the most detailed statistics on American forest conditions ever compiled. It proposed a large extension of public ownership and more practical management of all timberlands. One significant premise was that the nation's 308 million acres of forest and brush land have a major influence on watershed protection. The report showed that, even when aided by public subsidy, private initiative had failed to preserve forest values: fire damage was eleven times greater on private lands than Federal lands, and only 0.85 per cent of private forests managed to assure continual growth of timber.

Subsequent studies substantiated the report. The *Timber Resources Review,* published in 1958, showed that annual saw-timber growth was 9 per cent higher than it had been a decade earlier, but that more desirable trees were losing ground to those of poor quality. It showed 60 per cent of commercial forest land divided among 4.5 million farmers and other private owners, mostly in small holdings—on which productivity and management were at their lowest levels. Yet the timber industry consistently greeted Forest Service warnings of potential timber shortages with derision and assurances that "growth exceeds drain," and sought at every turn to block proposals for regulation.

The Forest Service itself manages no more than 17 per cent of the nation's commercial forest land; other Federal agencies manage an additional 4 per cent. Private owners hold more than 73 per cent and state and local governments, almost 6 per cent. The state and private forestry program is intended to encourage better practices on 367 million acres of private land.

Industrial Forestry

Early in the century, industrial forestry was based on readily and endlessly available supplies of wood. The timber scouts went first, bringing the news of towering virgin forests. Then followed the sawmills and logging railroads. The flatlands of Mississippi and Louisiana, as an example, were easy to attack: by the 1920s, the land there was cut barren and the big mills had departed, leaving in their wake fierce fires fed by resinous slash scattered on the ground. In the depression years, vast acreages were left to county and state ownership for nonpayment of taxes. The industry suddenly found itself pressed against the last virgin timber frontier of the Pacific Northwest.

Drastic change was a necessity. Land-owning companies began to harvest timber in ways favorable to natural restocking. They became conscious of the need to cut selectively, leaving some trees to serve as a green protection against fire and to assure regeneration. Enlarged opportunities for foresters provided systematic management in place of hit-or-miss operations. In 1966, it was estimated that nearly 10,000 professional foresters were involved in industrial forest management, compared to fewer than 1,000 in 1941. "It is a tremendous base from which to carry forward more intensive management," said Bernard Orell, vice president of the Weyerhaueser Company, "even better forest fire prevention and control methods, and to refine through research utilization of the timber supply and the products which result."

Still, there remains the preponderance of small ownerships. The industry's answer to proposals for regulation has been its support of the voluntary American Tree Farm System. Each participating landowner is required to pledge support of basic land management principles, but unfortunately makes no pledge to match cut with growth, so that there is no assurance of scientific management with continuous production at an even rate.

Professor Albert C. Worrell, of the Yale School of Forestry, undertook in 1969 a cursory survey of small private properties, specifically for the purpose of determining timber supplies. He found that they contain more than their proportionate share of better growing sites, that they are physically capable of producing 4 billion cubic feet of soft-wood timber a year—equivalent to about 40 per cent of our present consumption—but that they are not producing any-thing near their potential. On nearly two thirds of the small forests covered in the survey, timber is harvested occasional-ly, but without any provision for a future crop.

The conclusions reached by Professor Worrell are most disturbing because they contain more questions than an-swers. "The forestry profession still cannot estimate how much timber our various forest types can produce under management," he wrote. "We are still resorting to rule of thumb averages."

Values of Multiple Use

But, of course, providing timber is only one use of the forests. Insofar as public lands are concerned, the national forests are managed under the Multiple Use-Sustained Yield Act of 1960. In a multiple use forest, the immediate values of the timber yield must be balanced with long-range protec-tion of soil, water, wildlife, wilderness and scenery, and with assurances that harvested areas will grow more trees for fu-ture timber needs. It is a must of multiple use to protect the flow and quality of water.

"The preservation of forests and game go hand in hand," wrote Theodore Roosevelt in 1893. "He who works for either, works for both." Today many foresters, technically oriented but ecologically ill-informed, insist that timber cut-ting opens the woodland, increasing the growth of herbs and shrubs for game, giving the impression that *deer* and *game* are synonymous and failing to mention that when one species moves in there is apt to be a mass exodus of many other species. The grizzly bear and wolf have been wiped out of the forests; the elk is confined almost entirely to the Western states. Even today, sportsmen report that clear-cutting [com-plete removal] of marginal timber on the steep slopes of the Rockies cuts off elk calving grounds, reduces the summer range, making the areas vehicle oriented rather than wild-

life oriented, destroying the scenic environment that lends
zest to sport—and this on public land. Little wonder, considering the timber sales budget of the Forest Service is *ten
times greater* than the budget for fish and wildlife habitat.

The obsession for clear-cutting represents one of the
major hang-ups in forest management on both public and
private land. Thanks to new types of machinery, it is now
possible to upend as many as 1,500 to 1,800 trees in the course
of a day, thus leveling a timber stand over hundreds of acres
in short order. Clear-cutting flattens various sized areas, destroying accumulated growth in one swoop.

Observers must focus close attention on the impact of
clear-cutting and rotation cycles on the life-community of
the forest. The mixed hardwood or hardwood-and-pine forest is a complex, diverse and stable association of plants, with
a tendency to maintain its ecological norm. There is plenty
of room for manipulation within the norm, along with growing timber on long rotations. Drastic changes outside the
norm—such as clear-cutting and the conversion of hardwoods
to pine—may be efficient in terms of technology and short-
range cellulose production, but are likely to prove disastrous
in the long run.

Yet vast areas of the Southland that once supported
mixed forests have been reduced to "even-aged" stands of
pine only, like apple orchards or orange groves, with few
plants desirable for game. True multiple use precludes using
forests as farm lots for such monoculture [single crop cul-
ture], which inevitably attracts rodents and insects, thus
creating the need for pesticides and insecticides (including
chlorinated hydrocarbons) and for fertilizers that ultimately take more out of the soil than they put into it. Hardwoods
take longer to grow and show a slower return in dollars and
cents, but they offer more value to the nation than the mass
production of low-quality wood at what must become a
steadily reduced rate.

The National Timber Supply Bill of 1969 represented
an intensive lobbying effort of the forest products industry

to establish logging as the primary role of public and private forests alike. The bill was advanced as a means of providing housing for the poor in American ghettos, yet its strongest boosters in the timber industry have been enjoying record financial returns from the uncontrolled and substantial export of logs to Japan. Simply stated, having cut most of their own holdings, they sought to continue the wave of liquidation in the publicly owned forests. The bill would have provided a timber improvement fund, to be created by the deposit of receipts from timber sales, but carried no safeguard for other values. Consideration of the bill was rejected in the House of Representatives by a vote of 229 to 150, though it may be brought up again in some other form. . . .

Industrial users of public lands, for such activities as timber, mining and grazing, have bitterly objected to what they call noneconomic set-asides of recent years, such as the Wilderness Law, the National Scenic and Wild Rivers Act, the National Scenic Trails Act, and the establishment of the Redwoods National Park and North Cascades National Park. Naturalists and citizen conservationists, however, consider these actions among the most vital efforts to protect the environment made by Congress in the twentieth century.

Wilderness Legislation

The Wilderness Law of 1964 was enacted by Congress in order "to secure for the American people of present and future generations the benefits of an enduring resource of wilderness." The law provides for use and enjoyment of wilderness, but in a judicious manner, designed to leave it unimpaired for future use and enjoyment. The law established a National Wilderness Preservation System, which at passage immediately embraced fifty-four units of the national forests, covering over 9 million acres, which had previously been classified administratively as wilderness. It also directed a review over a ten-year period of an additional thirty-four units, covering approximately 5 million acres, previously classed as primitive areas, for ultimate decision by Congress on their possible inclusion in the Wilderness System. Comparable roadless areas of the national parks and national wildlife refuges are being considered in like manner. Other areas could be added, areas presently called *de facto* wilderness—lands of the national forests which have not been reviewed but which qualify for study. In a highly important precedent-setting court decision handed down in the spring of 1970, the Forest Service was restrained from conducting a logging sale in the *de facto* wilderness of East Meadow Creek adjoining the Gore Range-Eagle Nest Primitive Area in White River National Forest, Colorado.

How much timber does wilderness deny? In the past decade, about one fifth of the nation's industrial wood has come from the national forests. About one half of the total area of the national forests is capable of yielding commercial timber crops. But only 5 per cent of the productive land is in the wilderness areas. Most of this 5 per cent is in the high elevations, where the cost of harvest is high and quality of timber is low. Actually, no more than 2 or 3 per cent of the long-range timber potential lies inside the wilderness.

On the other hand, wilderness is never single-use land. It provides watershed protection, hunting, fishing, hiking, and other forms of quality recreation in solitude away from congestion. It serves as a preserve for rare and endangered species of plants and animals. (Of 130 species of fish and game classified as rare, endangered or unique by their scarcity, more than 25 are known to live in the National Forest System.) Innumerable laws of nature can never be thoroughly understood without some access to conditions of the primeval.

This value applies not only to Federal areas but to others which may be unprotected as well. Thus, concerned citizens of Southern California have recently been making a heroic effort to raise funds in order to save a tract of the rare *Pinus torreyana,* which has absolutely no commercial value.

California has the unique distinction of having within its boundaries isolated plant communities found growing nowhere else in the world [comments William Penn Mott, Jr., director of California's state parks and beaches]. The Torrey pines found growing naturally only in San Diego County constitute an example of one of these unique plant communities. The preservation of the Torrey pines is of the utmost importance to scientists and ecologists throughout the world.

Such areas of value to the whole world are not generously supported. The nation is addicted to spending large sums in the pursuit of supersonics, space exploration and nuclear explosions, which may represent steps in the growth of human knowledge. But we already have life abundantly present around us, within touch of our fingers and sight of our eyes, and are barely beginning to understand it. A century hence others may look back and think how little we knew about soils, plants, animals, air and life itself. Perhaps one of the key roles of this generation is to insure the availability of resources such as the Torrey pines to the scientists and scholars of tomorrow.

What Future for Forests?

Securing an adequate resource of forest wilderness is one of the challenges facing the nation. There are others of great consequence, including the following:

First, forests need to be considered as an integral part of the city.

They lend charm and comfort to the crowded urban scene, provide daily reminders of man's relationship to nature, and enhance the supply of oxygen. However, growing conditions for city trees have steadily degenerated because of air pollution, drought, heat, erosion, disease, and concentrated use of the land; the loss of trees invariably speeds the destruction of other values. Even more serious, studies show that urbanization can raise the temperature by as much as ten degrees over surrounding woods and fields and cause a concentration of sulfur dioxide.

Urban conservation is a new art—seldom practiced, little understood. The primary target should be to provide more greenbelts, buffer strips, community parks and forests. A program should be conducted by means of Federal cooperation and cost-sharing with state and local governments, with a special goal of encouraging city and country forestry departments and private enterprise tree services.

Second, the relationship of forest trees to man and his survival is becoming evident.

Damage to trees and tree crops from various forms of air pollution has hit all sections of the country. The decline of citrus groves in Southern California is due in large measure to Los Angeles smog. Damage to thousands of acres of ponderosa pine in the Arrowhead-Crestline area of San Bernardino National Forest is attributed to the same source. In the Cumberland Plateau of Tennessee, Eastern white pines have been dying over thousands of acres. Investigation has finally traced responsibility to stack gas emissions from a large industrial complex, which includes a steam plant of the Tennessee Valley Authority and the Oak Ridge facility of the Atomic Energy Commission. This disease has been called white pine needle dieback or postemergency chronic tipburn (PECT).

Unless measures now being taken by various public and private agencies, and spearheaded by the United States Public Health Service, can successfully combat this problem in the near future, we can expect increasing damage to orchard, forest and shade trees [according to Dr. George R. Hepting, of the Forest Service]. We will also likely be recognizing certain kinds of damage to trees as caused by air pollution that we have not known the cause of before.

Trees are needed to combat pollution, both as monitors and as ameliorating agents. Moreover, the unlimited supply of pure air has always been taken for granted; but the only reason the earth's atmosphere contains oxygen for us to breathe is that oxygen is constantly given off by green plants. This means we cannot continue to allow forests to be replaced by jetports, freeways, shopping centers, barren suburbias and factories. It also means that management and the conservation of air must be implicit in the new science of environmental forestry.

Third, forest management needs to eliminate its own waste.

For generations, logging has been a destructive practice at best. About half the wood cut is left in the forest, then half the remainder is discarded in processing. Through research, scraps now go into fibreboard and particleboard, and promising work is being done on the utilization of limbwood and tops of trees which are now useless. But this is only the beginning.

As part of environmental forestry, the Forest Products Laboratory at Madison, Wisconsin, has been assigned the mission of helping lessen air and water pollution. This is based on recognition that woodpulp mills have been guilty of depositing wood residues and by-products in streams or the atmosphere; that air often is polluted by the burning of logging slash and sawmill residues, and that even the disposal of cast-off wood products at municipal dumps creates pollution. The common denominator is incomplete utilization. Thus scientists have set out to study the possibility of recovery of cellulose from mill effluents and to look for ways to use, rather than burn, logging slash, slabs and sawdust.

Fourth, although management has come a long way in the national forests and industrial holdings, it has hardly begun on the small woodlots which comprise three fifths of the nation's potential timber supply.

The National Association of State Foresters has urged Federal participation of 50 per cent of annual state expenditures in order to stimulate owner incentive for better management. There is a need to bring scientific management to more watershed lands; to increase wildlife concern in forest management plans; to expand the recreation business on private lands; to furnish technical and financial assistance to forest cooperatives, and to offer small woodland owners long-term loans at low interest rates in order to insure both softwood and hardwood for the future.

Above all, no landowner, large or small, should be able to control land use without regard for what his actions do to others. Ownership must be recognized as a trust to be exercised in the interests of other peope and the quality of the total human environment. For land is an integral part of all life and its resources remain part of the environment.

Perhaps the first rule to establish clearly for those who use and administer the land is that the economic parts of the forest life-community will not function without elements which lack commercial value but which are essential to its well-being. When this is clearly defined, we can proceed to sustain healthy forests for many years to come.

"MINING" THE NATIONAL FORESTS [5]

The embattled United States Forest Service, under indictment throughout the country with regard to its harsh methods of harvesting the national forest lands, has been severely criticized in an independent and extensive study conducted in western Montana at the request of Senator Lee Metcalf (Democrat, Montana).

Findings of the special study committee on the Bitterroot National Forest in western Montana were issued in mid-November. They immediately attracted nationwide attention; the Forest Service was attacked on the very grounds it most often uses to justify its practices, not only in Montana but throughout much of the lands under its charge: economics and multiple use. The study committee said the Service could not economically justify most of its management practices in the Bitterroot and that the principle of multiple use was not being applied in the forest.

[5] From article by Dale A. Burk, state editor and environmental columnist for *The Missoulian* in Missoula, Montana. *Nation.* 212:110-13. Ja. 25, '71. Reprinted by permission.

More important, the committee emphasized that the shortcomings are not limited to the Bitterroot alone, but are nationwide in scope. This came as no surprise to conservation organizations, notably the Sierra Club, that have long made this claim and that joined Montana citizens and conservationists in bringing about the investigation of the Bitterroot National Forest. They feel that the Bitterroot study will have far-reaching effects in bringing about better management of the public forest lands.

The study was conducted by a seven-man committee from the University of Montana's School of Forestry at Missoula. It was labeled a "select" committee, and was composed of three professional foresters, a professor of wildlife, a political scientist, a sociologist and an economist. . . . [The committee was chaired by] Dr. Arnold W. Bolle, dean of the Forestry School. . . . The unanimous report was issued with the admonition from Dean Bolle that the panel had undertaken the study "with the attitude that we would proceed only if we were convinced that our efforts would make a contribution to a better understanding of the problem and, hopefully, to eventual solutions."

Findings of the Bolle Committee

An earlier Forest Service study of the same area—labeled a task force appraisal—had focused attention on some problems in the Bitterroot, but had done little to help solve the hot controversy arising from the Service's insistence on clearcutting and terracing the steep hillsides of the Bitterroot, in the face of continued and growing opposition. Bolle's committee, while saying the Service's task force had done a commendable job of analyzing and publicizing the results of its investigation of the charges relative to timber management, pointed out that the task force suffered credibility since it was composed of agency personnel studying agency problems: "It is a psychological impossibility to evaluate one's own efforts objectively," Bolle's committee said.

Bolle's study group came up with findings of far greater consequence than "analyzing and publicizing." They were courageous in attacking some of the basic tenets of Forest Service doctrine, as well as the recently issued Public Land Law Review Commission report. [See "Public Land Law Review Commission Recommendations on Public Land Use," in Section V, below.—Ed.] Among their basic findings were:

1. Multiple-use management, in fact, has not been the governing principle on the Bitterroot National Forest.

2. Quality timber management and harvest practices are lacking. The committee added that consideration of the watershed, recreation, wildlife and grazing appear as afterthoughts.

3. The management sequence of clear-cutting-terracing-planting cannot be justified economically as an investment for producing timber from the Bitterroot Forest. The study team said it doubted the forest could continue to produce timber at the present harvest level—precisely the charge made by retired forest ranger G. M. "Brandy" Brandborg of Hamilton, Montana, who served as supervisor of the Bitterroot Forest for twenty years before retiring in 1955.

4. Clear-cutting and planting are expensive operations that should bear some relationship to the capability of the site to return the cost invested.

5. The practice of terracing—strips cut into a hillside on which to plant trees—should be stopped in the Bitterroot Forest. Existing terraced areas should be used for research.

6. A clear distinction is necessary between timber "management" and timber "mining." Bolle's committee said that timber management, the continuous production of timber crops, is rational only on highly productive sites where an appropriate rate of return on the capital invested can be expected. All other timber-cutting activities must be considered as timber mining.

7. Their findings in this field corroborated claims made in late 1969 by Brock Evans of Seattle, Northwest conservation representative of the Sierra Club. After an intensive

ground and aerial inspection of the Bitterroot, Evans claimed the timber harvest in the area was extractive, and called it mining rather than logging.

8. The Bolle committee did not oppose timber mining outright, but said that where it was to be practiced all other on-site values must be retained. They said that in the removal of residual old-growth timber from sites uneconomical to manage, hydrologic, habitat, and esthetic values must be preserved by single-tree selection cutting, there must be minimum disturbance of residual vegetation, and minimum, temporary roads.

9. The research basis for management of the Bitterroot Forest is too weak to support the practices used on the forest.

10. The Forest Service will have to recognize the need for total quality management, or the necessary financing will not be sought.

11. Manpower and budget limitations of public resource agencies do not at present permit essential staffing for multiple-use planning.

12. The qualitative need for specialists must first be resolved if the quantitative shortage of staff is to be resolved.

13. The Forest Service bureaucratic line structure as it operates is "archaic, undesirable and subject to change."

14. The Forest Service as an effective and efficient bureaucracy needs to be reconstructed so that substantial, responsible, local public participation in the processes of policy formulation and decision making can "naturally" take place. Bolle's committee commented in the report that public involvement must mean more than formal presentations of preconceived courses of action in which there has been no public participation.

15. The Bolle committee attacked the dominant-use philosophy of natural resources as promulgated by the Public Land Law Review Commission.

It appears inconceivable and incongruous to us at this time, with the great emphasis upon a broad multiple-use approach to our natural resources—especially those remaining in public ownership

—that any representative group or institution in our society would advocate a dominant-use philosophy with respect to our natural resources [the committee said]. Yet it is our judgment that this is precisely what is occurring through the Federal appropriation process, via executive order, and in the Public Land Law Review Commission's Report.

They suggested that any departure from a broad environmental approach was out of step with the interests and desires of the American people. The dispute over resource management arose from public dissatisfaction with the Bitterroot National Forest's concern for sawtimber production at the expense of other resource values. The committee said this shortchanging of values other than board feet is built into the Forest Service by legislative action and control, executive direction and budgetary restrictions.

"In a Federal agency which measures success primarily by the quantity of timber produced weekly, monthly and annually, the staff of the Bitterroot National Forest finds itself unable to change its course, to give anything but token recognition to related values, or to involve most of the local public in any way but as antagonists," Bolle's committee said. They added that as long as short-run emphasis on timber production overrides concern for related uses and local environmental quality, real change of management attitudes to other resource values is impossible.

"Mining" or Better Economics?

The problem may intensify if the Forest Service continues its extractive timber mining. The agency has caused considerable controversy with its unpopular management practices in the Bitterroot, and is costing the public money in the process. Bolle's committee, tackling the issue for the first time in economic terms—it had been viewed previously in terms of ecology, esthetics, wildlife, water yield, timber production and others—literally blew the Forest Service off the mountain in evaluating their practices on a dollars-and-cents basis. The Forest Service has persisted in spending the public's money in a losing proposition, and conservationists and senators have insisted this isn't limited to the Bitterroot.

Here, Bolle's committee simply couldn't find economic justification for the practices of clear-cutting, terracing and planting being done there. "The conclusions are clear and incontestable," the study team said. "Clear-cutting and terracing cannot be justified as an investment for producing timber on the Bitterroot National Forest. There are better and much more economic ways to provide for the nation's timber needs." Bolle's committee provided an illustration to support its contention.

Establishment (regeneration) costs after cutting were assumed at a conservative figure of $50 per acre, a rotation length of 120 years for ponderosa pine, an "optimistic" yield of 20,000 board feet per acre at rotation age, a stumpage value of $25 per 1,000 board feet, and an interest rate of 5 per cent, which the committee called conservative. They also made an "unrealistic but simplifying assumption" that there would be no additional costs during the 120-year growth period.

"If we invest the $50 in stand establishment and charge no other costs through the 120-year period, the stand at harvest would have to be worth $17,445 per acre in order to return 5 per cent on the initial public investment in regeneration," the committee said. They pointed out that if the actual yield were 20,000 board feet per acre, the stumpage value would have to be $872 per 1,000 board feet. Or if the stumpage value were actually $25 per 1,000 board feet (in 1970 dollars), the yield would have to be 697,000 board feet per acre.

"It would obviously be impossible to achieve yields of these magnitudes," Bolle's committee said. "It is enlightening to work the problem in reverse. In order to earn 5 per cent on the investment, with the yield and stumpage assumptions given, the stand would have to be established at a cost of $1.43 per acre." They added that if they set "more realistic

values" for costs, yields and interest rates, "the results become ludicrous."

Dominant Use or Multiple Use?

Why have the uneconomic practices been used? The
Bolle committee struck at the core of professional forestry
dogma—the sustained-yield timber management concept introduced into American forestry in the 1880s and 1890s by
early Forest Service chiefs Bernhard Fernow and Gifford Pinchot. The concept had been developed and rationalized in
the mercantile economies of Germany and France a century
before Fernow and Pinchot, and was developed in economies
characterized by stability, certainty, and, via the prohibition
of imports, a self-imposed scarcity.

With its implicit assumptions of scarcity, this dogma became the central dictum of professional forestry, and as dogma remains virtually unchallenged in American forestry
education.

The graduates of that education staff the Forest Service [Bolle's
study team said]. We found much evidence that a major element in
the Bitterroot controversy was just this professional dogma. "Productivity" we learned time and again meant maximum physical
production of sawlogs. Much timberland was being harvested os-
tensibly to "get it into production." The idea that a scraggly stand
of overmature timber could and does provide other values was alien
and largely absent from the thinking of most of the professional
foresters we encountered: this in spite of their lip service to "multiple-use."

The committee said that if productivity is held to mean
simply sawlogs at any cost, "then much of what we observed
was wholly rational." However, they seriously questioned
such a constrained definition and said that if productivity
includes recreation, watershed, wildlife and esthetic values,
much of what they saw in the Bitterroot could not be rationalized at all. "Certainly the idea . . . [of] clear-cutting a forest
to 'get it into production' is similar to the military rationale
of destroying a town to save it." The study team recommended that the Forest Service must be restructured to involve the

public in the formulating steps of its management policies—even if internal bureaucratic efficiency must be sacrificed as a result.

They also cited the need for research, saying that in the past "we didn't invest sufficiently in research and we didn't make optimum use of the limited research information that was available." They said that a vastly expanded research effort is the only solution to the question of how wild-land resources such as those in the Bitterroot can be used without having a deleterious effect on the natural environment. According to the study, such research would have application throughout the Rocky Mountain West.

The Bitterroot Valley is representative of a large part of the West. It is characterized by vast open space, low-population density, an economy based on wild-land resources, and a culture in transition from the "frontier" type with emphasis on exploitation to a more mature kind in which stability and environmental amenities are held in higher regard. Commodity resources such as timber, minerals and grass are increasing in value as the national economy continues to grow, but noncommodity resources such as wildlife, esthetics and recreation are increasing even more rapidly in value as the national stock of these items dwindles.

"We see the Bitterroot Valley faced with the same dilemma as so many other areas in the Rocky Mountain West," Bolle's committee said, "the need for more economic growth and development, but a strong desire to maintain or preserve a high quality natural environment."

The committee believes there is no reason to assume that economic development and environmental quality are mutually exclusive or irreconcilable. They say the problem, though badly handled in the Bitterroot and elsewhere, can be solved. "An objective appraisal of the situation leads to optimism, not pessimism," the committee said. "Trees can be cut without leaving an unsightly mess; roads can be built so they complement the natural beauty of the countryside;

disturbed areas can be rehabilitated; people can use the land for recreation without destroying it."

PROBLEMS UNDERFOOT [6]

Adverse environmental effects of underground mining and mineral processing run the gamut from air and water pollution to problems of solid waste disposal. There is, however, little public knowledge of the extent of these effects. A report written by United States Bureau of Mines personnel found that about 2 million acres of land have subsided (caved in) as a result of being undermined; that thousands of miles of streams and tens of thousands of acres of lakes have been polluted as a direct result of mining and mineral processing; that billions of tons of waste material from underground mining and processing are spread over millions of acres of land; and that hundreds of uncontrolled fires are burning in mining waste piles, or refuse banks, and abandoned mines. It is also noted in the report that

> Intense cooperative effort on the part of Federal, state, and local governments, the mining industry, educational institutions and an informed public are essential to the eliminaton or allevia-tion of past mistakes, and for the establishment of acceptable and feasible practices for future underground mining and mineral operations.

In view of this statement, it seems ironic that the report from which it comes has never been published. The report, "Environmental Effects of Underground Mining and of Mineral Processing," was compiled at the request of President Johnson and was supposed to have been finished by April 1, 1969. A draft of the report was completed by the deadline and contained more detailed information concerning subsidence, coal refuse bank fires, and underground mine fires than the Department of the Interior had ever released to the public.

[6] From article by Terri Aaronson, staff writer. *Environment.* 12:16-28. N. '70. Reprinted by permission of The Committee for Environmental Information, Inc. Copyright © 1970 by The Committee for Environmental Information.

However, the report is classified officially as a working draft—for use by the Department of the Interior staff. There is only one copy of the report available to the public—available to be read "on location" in the Department of the Interior. This is an unusual status for a presidentially requested report. Mr. Russell Train, when he was undersecretary of the Department of the Interior [Mr. Train is now chairman of the Council on Environmental Quality], claimed that the reason for not publishing the report was that Mr. Hollis Dole, assistant secretary for mineral resources, Department of the Interior, found the report to be "inadequate." Apparently, no attempt has been made to complete the report. Rather, when questioned by *Environment,* a spokesman for the Bureau of Mines insisted that no comprehensive study of the environmental effects of mining had ever been done. When questioned as to how he would explain the report, "Environmental Effects of Underground Mining and of Mineral Processing," the spokesman said that the report was merely a compilation of data from field office reports. Ralph Nader, on the other hand, has charged that the report was "suppressed" because it was embarrassing to the coal mining industry.

A copy of the draft report has been obtained by *Environment* and, while it without doubt does suffer from being a compilation and is in need of final editing, the report most certainly contains an extensive amount of information concerning underground mining and the environment.

Because of the unavailability of current data which apply to the environmental effects of mining discussed below, there has been no attempt to update the figures presented in the report.

Recommendations of the Report

The report, "Environmental Effects of Underground Mining and of Mineral Processing" (hereafter called "the Report"), states that "it is essential that the Federal Government take leadership by providing for a long-range program that will establish a compatible relationship between underground mining and processing activities and the preservation of an environment suitable for the welfare of present and future generations." The Report makes several recommendations to lessen the adverse environmental effects of underground mining.

Primarily, it is recommended that Congress declare adverse environmental effects of underground mining a national problem, but that the individual states assume the responsibility for correcting these adverse conditions. To assist the states in developing their own mine-related pollution abatement programs, it is recommended that the Federal Government assist the states both technically and financially, with such assistance going first to those states showing initiative in developing their own programs.

A series of grants for research into the understanding and control of the major adverse environmental effects of underground mining is recommended, with initial efforts to concentrate on eliminating water pollution associated with coal mining. Grants, the Report says, should also be given to determine the economic and social costs of underground-mine-related pollution.

Subsidence

The Report, making use primarily of 1966 figures, notes that of the 8 million acres of land undermined, approximately 2 million acres have subsided. Most of the subsided land, about 93 per cent, was in rural areas; however, the balance of subsidence, amounting to 158,000 acres, occurred in urban areas.

Subsidence occurs when the structures which support the overburden—the rock and earth above the mine—collapse or when the rock in the overburden falls into an underground gap between supporting structures. Subsidence can be triggered by sheering of rock, or a gradual bending and breaking of the overburden, or by a collapse of pillars left in underground mines as support. . . .

Subsidence, even in rural areas, is not without consequences. It causes damage to crops and natural water drainage patterns, and it results in decreased land values. Much more severe, though, is damage from subsidence in urban areas. There, damage ranges from cracks in and dislocations of subsurface pipelines and other facilities, to cracks in sidewalks and roadways, to caving of pavement and buildings. . . .

The Report estimates that, unless adequate preventive measures are taken, 2.5 million acres of undermined land will subside between now and the year 2000. Preventive measures consist primarily of improving overburden support techniques and of backfilling mines. Backfilling a mine is a technique whereby the mining wastes, consisting of rock and low-grade ore, are placed back into the mine after its initial removal for processing. Unfortunately, this fairly expensive process is practiced more often in metal mines, where subsidence is minimal, than in coal mines.

Although it is estimated that millions of dollars of damage to property has occurred from subsidence, there are no exact figures. Nor are there figures on how often and to what extent mine operators pay surface landowners for subsidence damage. Very often subsidence is caused by mines long abandoned by companies which are now defunct. Conversely, a landowner may not wish to report subsidence damage because it lowers the property value of his land. In any case, Pennsylvania is the only state with legislation making the mine operator responsible for subsidence resulting from his operations. In addition, Pennsylvania has created the Anthracite and Bituminous Coal Mine Subsidence Fund which permits noncommercial property owners to buy insurance to compensate for damages from subsidence. However, very few property owners have chosen to make use of this insurance. . . .

Water Quality

It is estimated that approximately 9,000 miles of streams and 22,000 acres of lakes and other impoundments have been adversely affected by underground mining and mineral processing. There are two types of water pollutants stemming from mining, one physical and one chemical. Physical pollutants consist of fine silt or coarse, chemically inert grains of ore or of associated rock. Most physical pollutants do not come from the underground mine, but rather from the processing plant, which is ordinarily located in the vicinity of the mine. There minerals are processed to upgrade or concentrate the ore. Vast quantities of waste are often rejected by processing and are usually heaped in extensive piles, or refuse banks. These banks are subject to erosion and spillage if not constantly maintained. The Report notes that almost 2,000 waste piles at abandoned or inactive mine sites are presently contributing to water pollution. "The majority of these piles resulted from the processing of bituminous coal."

Another way that coal processing, particularly, is a source of water pollution stems from the fact that 93 per cent of the coal processed in the United States is "wet-cleaned" to remove dust from the finished product. The liquid used to clean the coal picks up fine coal particles and is known as black-water. More than half of the coal processing plants examined in preparing the Report were releasing large quantities of black-water into adjacent streams. . . .

The major chemical water pollutant from mining is "acid mine drainage," which is most often a result of the mining and processing of coal, but also of copper and other metal sulfides (compounds of sulfur). Certain sulfide minerals are naturally associated with coal and some metals. Sulfides exposed to air and water when the ore is mined and processed may react chemically with air and water to produce sulfuric acid. Further reactions between the acid, which becomes dissolved in water passing through the mine or in rain washing through refuse banks, and minerals in the surrounding rocks result in the addition of other ions, such as aluminum and manganese, to the water. The final acid water very often drains into streams and other waterways.

The amount of damage done to aquatic life in a stream affected by acid drainage depends on the amount of acid and the natural buffering or neutralizing capability of the water. According to the Report, "Small amounts of acid mine drainage severely limit biological productivity, and result in the elimination of the less resistant plant and animal species. . . ."

Additional pollution of waterways from mining is a result of various chemicals used in cleaning and processing the ore. Often these chemicals are lost during processing and enter waterways through accidental spills, direct effluent, or the overflow or leaching of settling ponds. . . . Another type of water pollution due to mining involves radioactive ores. Waste piles from uranium mining and processing are often subject to erosion and spillage. . . .

Water pollution due to mining affects more than local water quality. The Report states, "The total environmental impact of water pollution from underground mining and mineral processing has not been assessed." Water pollution from mining can adversely affect intakes and outlets for industrial and public water supplies, pumps, lock and dam facilities, highway structures, and barges and boats. Annual damage to such structures runs into many millions of dollars. In 1961 the Public Health Service stated that annual damage from acid mine water in the Monongahela River in Pennsylvania alone exceeded $2.2 million; that estimate included only some of the affected instream facilities. The Federal Water Pollution Control Administration (now the Federal Water Quality Administration) estimated that, because of water pollution from mining, the economy of Appalachia loses a minimum of $7.5 million annually in water-oriented recreation income.

Water pollution from mining is not an impossible problem, but it is a very expensive one with which to deal. . . . Waste piles contributing to water pollution can be regraded or stabilized to minimize their addition of physical pollutants, at least to water systems. Techniques for reducing the pollution potential of processing plants are sophisticated, but also usually expensive. . . .

In the near future all states will have to have established water quality standards, as directed by the Water Quality Act of 1965. The mining industry will be regulated by these standards. Already, water quality laws have affected mining operations. Some mine operators have claimed that the cost of meeting even current standards are prohibitive and have closed their mines.

However, despite current legislation, water pollution from mining is growing, not receding. The Report claims that if known methods of control which are only 70 per cent effective are universally applied to mining operations during the ten-year period 1965 to 1975,

the problem will still continue to grow to greater proportions. Only the development of . . . technology which approaches 95 per cent effectiveness and its total application between 1970 and 2000 will reverse the present pollution trend and ultimately minimize the problem.

Solid Waste

Solid wastes from underground mining are generated both in the mining and finishing processes. The wastes generated are usually stored in refuse banks which grow to be man-made mountains, up to seven hundred feet high and over one mile long. Prior to 1966, approximately 18.5 billion tons of waste were generated by the mining industry, including wastes from surface-mined coal processing, but not including displaced overburden. This accumulation was spread over 1.8 million acres of land surface. Surface mining generates enormous quantities of solid waste; underground mining generates smaller, but still sizable amounts. Copper mining is responsible for the greatest amount of solid waste from underground mining. However, underground mining of coal, responsible for 12 per cent of the industry's solid waste, presents a greater problem because its wastes are deposited on highly valuable land, primarily in five heavily populated eastern states. The copper industry, located in the West, dumps its wastes on sparsely inhabited low-value land.

Vast accumulations of solid waste from underground mining present the most hazardous local effect in mountainous areas, such as Appalachia, because of the danger of an unstable bank collapsing, starting a landslide of mining wastes.

One such disaster in Aberfan, Wales, in 1966 killed more than 150 residents, most of them children, when an 800-foot-high refuse bank slid into the town. Often refuse banks are made unstable by persons who use portions of the refuse for roadfill, railroad ballast, and other construction purposes.

Air pollution is also a hazard of the vast heaps of waste. Fine particulate matter in refuse banks is easily borne aloft by wind. The airborne dust is particularly bothersome to nearby communities. The Report makes no mention of possible pathologic consequences of the dust except to note that radionuclides in dust from uranium mine waste piles may be harmful: "Very little is known about the effect of long-term exposure to low concentrations of radioactive isotopes such as radium-226, thorium-230, and other radionuclides." In Colorado, there are three communities immediately adjacent to uranium waste piles and several communities within two miles of such a pile. Some of these wastes have been used in local construction projects as landfill. As many as 4,000 houses and other buildings in Grand Junction, Colorado, a uranium mining center, have been built on uranium wastes. Radon gas, a product of the radium in the mine waste, has been implicated in the induction of lung cancer in uranium miners. Several Colorado public schools, built on the mine wastes, are contaminated with unsafe levels of radon gas. Recently there has been some success in stabilizing uranium mine refuse banks, and their use in construction has been halted.

Water pollution from solid waste banks is due to water filtering through the banks, picking up acid which then may enter adjacent streams. Environmental problems of solid waste from underground mining can largely be controlled through careful construction of the refuse banks or by leveling, compacting, and seeding with grass. Perhaps best of all would be to use the wastes to backfill the mines, simultaneously reducing the hazard of subsidence. There is currently a great deal of research into practical uses for the wastes generated each year by underground mining. This is a pressing need, as conservative estimates of waste accumulations from underground mining alone exceed 2 billion tons annually by the year 2000.

Burning Coal Refuse Banks

The coal industry has a particular solid waste problem in that its wastes are highly combustible. Often these wastes are dumped onto huge banks which can ignite and burn for extended periods of time, often years. The banks may ignite by spontaneous combustion, by lightning striking them, or as a result of a forest fire. Or, coal refuse banks may be ignited by campers not completely extinguishing fires on the banks or by persons dumping rubbish on or near a bank and burning it. Whatever the cause, once they are ignited coal refuse bank fires are particularly difficult to extinguish.

A United States Bureau of Mines survey in 1963 showed that 495 coal refuse banks were burning at the time. The northern portion of the Appalachian Region contained 90 per cent of the fires. In 1963 half of the fires were reported to be in the late stages of burning; however, no indications were made as to how long it would be before the fires were burned out. Judging by their history, some are probably still burning. The 1963 survey noted that 290 of the burning banks were at abandoned mine sites. Such fires are often allowed to burn themselves out. . . .

There is no way yet known of effectively extinguishing all coal refuse bank fires. Rather, current emphasis is placed on avoiding ignition, either by proper construction of the refuse bank to allow a minimum flow of air through the bank, by keeping out as many combustible materials as possible, by sealing exposed faces with clay, or by choosing a site which will minimize exposure of the bank to wind and rain. It is also wise to establish a vegetative cover on the refuse bank and to post notices to keep trespassers, who may ignite the bank, away. It would be advantageous to develop uses for the coal wastes and thereby reduce the size of the problem. . . .

Underground Mine Fires

One of the most hazardous aspects of coal refuse bank fires is the possibility that they might ignite an underground coal seam. Underground coal mine fires are a threat to any nearby community. They emit smoke and noxious fumes over large areas, often cause subsidence by destroying supporting pillars, and contribute to water pollution by contaminating groundwater with sulfuric acid. In addition, "Fires in abandoned mines and virgin coal deposits have a destructive and demoralizing effect upon a community," according to the Report.

Underground mine fires may be started by refuse bank fires if a coal seam beneath the refuse bank is covered by only a thin layer of overburden. Abandoned strip mines often serve as a place to dump rubbish which may then be burned, and if a coal seam adjoins the abandoned pit, an underground fire may be started. The United States Bureau of Mines estimates that at least 65 per cent of abandoned mine fires in the eastern coal area begin in this way. Fires in outcrops—places where coal seams are on the surface—may be started by a trash fire, a camp fire, lightning, or spontaneous combustion. A fire in an abandoned mine may begin during active mining, as a result of a gas explosion, defective wiring, or some other incident. The fire may have been sealed off from an area of active mining, or the mine could have been abandoned because of the fire. Once a fire has begun, it may continue for decades. One fire near Laurel Run, Pennsylvania, has been burning for more than fifty years. Another, at New Straitsville, Ohio, was ignited in 1884 and still burns, although during the 1930s the Works Progress Administration invested over $1 million in efforts to extinguish it.

The Report identifies 237 underground mine fires. Presently, the United States Bureau of Mines claims to have identified a total of 292 fires. As of June 1, 1968, Bureau of

Mines projects to control mine fires in Pennsylvania alone involved estimated expenditures of $16 million by the Federal Government and $5 million by the State of Pennsylvania. It is estimated that this investment will protect property valued at approximately $2 billion, coal reserves of about 110 million tons, and a population of approximately one million. The damage from underground mine fires may be seen in the cost of the fire at Laurel Run: subsidence due to the fire burning out mine supports, and to poisonous gases, largely carbon monoxide emitted to the surface, caused the abandonment of 170 homes, a church, and several businesses.

Fires in the Western Coal Field, an area extending south from Montana to Arizona and New Mexico, do not have the potential for the same sort of damage as those in the East because western coal reserves are in sparsely populated areas. However, these fires do endanger grazing land by emitting lethal gases and they also may ignite grass fires and forest fires. Additionally, 66 per cent of the nation's coal reserves are located in the Western Coal Field. Western coal will be increasingly needed in the future. The Report claims that underground mine fires "pose an immediate threat to millions of tons of coal reserves and conceivably could destroy a much greater tonnage if comprehensive fire control measures are not undertaken." . . .

The Report claims that a concerned public is a prerequisite in controlling mine fires. Present indifference is demonstrated by the fact that two uncontrolled outcrop fires are advertised as tourist attractions. Rather, public interest might insure proper mining procedures and adequate fire prevention precautions.

Status of the Report

The Federal Government is supposedly taking a firm stand on pollution abatement. But it has quietly filed away a report which could inform the public of a kind of pollution of which most people are unaware.

The Report was not left unpublished because the problems with which it dealt were diminishing or were being taken care of. Legislation has not affected to any extent adverse environmental conditions associated with underground mining. The Report found that:

state requirements are not uniform; many are complex and difficult to interpret; and in some cases, do not apply to existing conditions. Enforcement of applicable laws may range from strict adherence to the letter of the law to a degree of permissiveness bordering on the absurd. Limited efforts are being undertaken to clarify existing legislation and make it more effective.

Until those "limited efforts" are drastically expanded, this country will continue to have its land, air, and water unnecessarily defiled by the effects of underground mining and mineral processing. The first step in passing effective laws concerning the environment is to inform the public of the extent of the problem. Surely, it would be in the public interest to make the report, "Environmental Effects of Underground Mining and of Mineral Processing," available.

LAND USE AND POWER PLANTS [7]

During the 1960s problems of environmental pollution emerged as a major national issue, and it now seems evident that in the 1970s this issue will be broadened to include the politically sensitive question of land use planning and controls. The fact that the United States lacks a coherent land use policy is highlighted by the persistent controversy over the selection of sites for new facilities for the generation and transmission of electricity. Efforts to overcome the threat of energy shortages are running head on into opposition from people afraid that the new power plants and transmission lines being proposed will put a blight on the environment.

[7] From "Land Use: Congress Taking Up Conflict Over Power Plants," by Luther J. Carter, staff writer. *Science.* 170:718-19. N. 13, '70. Copyright 1970 by the American Association for the Advancement of Science. Reprinted by permission.

Several current legislative initiatives that represent steps toward a national land use policy are being taken either wholly or partly in response to this "crunch" over the siting of power facilities. . . .

The Nixon Administration will propose legislation on the location and certification of power plants. In Congress, Senator Edmund S. Muskie (Democrat, Maine) is also developing powerplant siting legislation, and Senator Henry M. Jackson (Democrat, Washington) , another key legislator on environmental matters, already has won approval of the Senate Interior Committee for the initial draft of a bill to require the states to make a major commitment to land use planning and regulation generally.

Industry Opposition

The private utility industry, taken as a whole, has indicated plainly that it will oppose any proposals to give the Federal Government a major say in the siting and certification of power facilities. In fact, some observers, aware of the frustrations of those congressmen who have long and unsuccessfully promoted efforts to tighten the regulatory hold of the state and Federal governments over the utilities, doubt that any meaningful legislation will be enacted.

Nevertheless, given the present concern in Congress about potential shortages of power and about environmental quality, the prospects for legislative action may be brighter than heretofore. Even some legislators who usually have taken a laissez-faire attitude toward the utilities appear to feel that Congress must do something to help resolve the conflict between the siting of power plants and protection of the environment.

According to the Federal Power Commission, twenty years from now the United States will be producing three times the amount of power that it is producing today. Some three hundred additional sites for nuclear and fossil-fuel thermal plants of five hundred megawatts or larger will be needed, the majority of the plants to be huge facilities in the 1,000- to 4,000-megawatt range. A 3,000-megawatt thermal plant requires a site of from 400 to 1,200 acres, the size depending upon whether the plant is a nuclear plant or a fossil-fuel facility requiring extensive coal and ash storage areas.

Moreover, while overhead electric transmission-line rights-of-way already cover nearly 4 million acres and extend for several hundreds of thousands of miles, twenty years hence—barring a breakthrough in underground transmission technology—the nation's countryside will be laced with great new swaths of overhead transmission rights-of-way. For instance, whereas today there are 67,000 miles of extra-high-voltage lines, by 1990 there will be some 165,000 miles of such lines, to say nothing of the many thousands of additional miles of lower voltage lines that will have been built.

Many of the new thermal plants will be built along sea-coasts, estuaries, and large lakes and rivers and will draw on these bodies of water for purposes of condenser cooling. In other cases rivers will be dammed to form large reservoirs to provide cooling water and thousands of acres of bottomland will be inundated. For part of their peaking power, utilities will look to pumped storage hydropower units and these too will have a major esthetic and ecological impact. Such facilities have an upper reservoir—which may be built on top of a scenic mountain or palisade, such as Storm King on the Hudson—which releases water to generate power during hours of peak demand and which is then refilled during off-peak hours by pumping water up from the river or reservoir below.

And, even if the best available pollution-abatement technology is used in the new thermal plants, damage from air and thermal pollution can result if plant sites are not chosen with full knowledge of meteorological patterns and the assimilative capacity of the body of water into which cooling water is discharged. In sum, the big push on the part of the electric utility industry to meet projected power needs will alter, if not degrade, a significant part of the American landscape.

"Piecemeal" Regulation

As noted in the recent report *Electric Power and the Environment* sponsored by the White House Office of Science and Technology (OST), "preconstruction reviews of the expansion plans of [utilities] are generally piecemeal, uncoordinated, and incomplete," although a few states such as New York, California, and Maryland are now trying to improve on their past procedures. The situation is no better at the Federal level, and, while a Federal license is required for nuclear and hydropower plants, none is required for fossil-fuel plants, which produce most of the power.

The legislation that President Nixon will send to Congress will be based on these major recommendations of the OST report: (1) utility expansions should be planned at least ten years ahead of construction and the plans should be made public at least five years before construction; (2) a state or regional agency should be designated to review and approve plans for large new power facilities—with the Federal Government to step in and perform this role if a state fails to act; (3) an expanded program of research and development, to be financed largely from utility rates, should be undertaken to achieve such objectives as better pollution controls, economical long-distance underground transmission, and perfection of such advanced concepts as the siting of power plants on offshore islands or in large "energy centers" or parks.

The utility industry accepts the view that it should put more money into research. And, through its recently established regional "reliability councils," the industry is now making a better effort at long-term planning of new generating and transmission facilities. But shortly before the OST report appeared, the Edison Electric Institute (EEI), which is the most important of the industry trade associations, stated that no need for Federal legislation with respect to siting procedures was evident. Further, the EEI held that each utility should be free to decide whether to follow any new certification procedure provided.

Moreover, in commenting on the OST report, an industry spokesman later told *Science* that many power companies would strongly object to a requirement for public disclosure of plans five years ahead of construction. The effect of such disclosure, he said, would be to encourage land speculation and jack up the cost of sites not yet purchased and also the cost of transmission rights-of-way. Authors of the OST report had felt that if higher land costs resulted from advance disclosure this would by no means offset the advantage of allowing plenty of time for the public and the environmental protection agencies to evaluate the utility's plans.

Con Ed Needs Help

Not all utilities oppose congressional action with respect to the siting of facilities. For instance, in a hearing last August, Charles F. Luce, former Under Secretary of the Interior and now chairman of the board of Consolidated Edison of New York, told Senator Muskie's Subcommittee on Intergovernmenal Relations that "if this committee can show the way and find solutions, we will all be thankful."

Con Ed's plans to increase its generating capacity have encountered increasing public opposition. Luce said that what is needed is a certification procedure in which a utility would have to go to only one agency. That agency would give the utility a conclusive yes or no answer as to whether its plans meet all zoning and environmental protection standards. At present, utilities must obtain approvals from a multiplicity of agencies and local governments.

Senator Muskie's bill on the siting of power facilities . . . would have licenses for new bulk power facilities issued by a Federal agency, not by a state or regional agency as contemplated in the OST report. Federal certification would be a final step in a procedure carried out largely by regional boards appointed by the state governors and made up of persons in no way connected with electric utilities. These boards, which would establish advisory councils to encourage participation by interested citizens in the analysis of plant-siting questions, would decide whether plans for proposed facilities meet appropriate siting criteria. But utilities have great political clout, and, in Muskie's view, final action on siting plans should come at the Washington level and not be left to state or regional agencies that might be too weak to reject plans posing environmental hazards.

Air and water quality standards are, of course, based on such criteria as the maximum water temperatures compatible with fish life and the threshold levels at which air pollutants such as sulfur dioxide become a health threat. The standards concept is central to the antipollution legislation enacted under Muskie's leadership since 1964. If exacting air and water quality standards are to be met, the sites for large new industrial facilities such as power plants *must* be chosen with a view to the assimilative capacity of the airshed or watercourse into which cooling water or treated wastes are to be discharged. Pollution-control technology alone may never be good enough to protect the environment.

The bill by Senator Jackson, which recently received the Senate Interior Committee's unanimous approval, would establish a national land use policy under which the siting of power facilities would be considered along with other activities of significant environmental impact. Terms of the bill are still tentative, but, in general, this measure would require that the states establish an agency for the planning and control of land use and submit a state land use plan to a new cabinet-level Land and Water Resources Planning Council.

Projects having a major environmental impact, such as those involving the construction of highways, dams, and airports, would be denied Federal funds if the new state agency were not set up and the land use plan submitted to Washington within five years. The state plans would be prepared in consultation with Federal agencies, but, as the bill is now drafted, Federal approval of the plans would not be a prerequisite for funding of construction projects. Even so, given the traditional abhorrence with which many politicians have viewed large-scale public planning, the Interior Committee's adoption of the Jackson bill is remarkable. Senator Jackson, the chairman, is a liberal on most domestic issues, but the Republicans on the committee include some senators who are highly conservative.

Testifying on the Jackson bill, Harry G. Woodbury, a senior vice president of Con Ed of New York and a former chief of civil works for the Army Corps of Engineers, indicated general approval of the measure. But while Con Ed clearly is an exception within the industry in this regard, it is not the only utility now willing to have the public better represented in the consideration of plant-siting questions. Another is Northeast Utilities, a holding company for several utilities in southern New England.

Northeast has given $180,000 to the Fund for the Preservation of Wildlife and Natural Areas, a group said to be Boston Brahmin in tone, to support a citizens' evaluation of two possible pumped storage projects in the Berkshires. Quite understandably, Lelan F. Sillin, Jr., president of Northeast, has expressed indignation at the fact that some conservationists have questioned the good faith of this company initiative.

Dummy Corporation

However, by having generally failed to take the public into its confidence in the past, the utility industry is itself to blame for the skepticism with which it is now viewed. In some cases utilities have practiced outright duplicity. A prime example of this came to light recently in hearings conducted by Representative Henry S. Reuss (Democrat, Wisconsin). Reuss discovered that, in 1963, Potomac Electric

Power Company (PEPCO) used a dummy corporation—dubbed Idamont, Inc.—to purchase a site bordering a part of the Potomac estuary now considered important as a fish and wildlife habitat and as having prime recreational value. Not until this past spring and summer did PEPCO reveal its ownership of the property and announce that it was considering building a 2,535-megawatt complex of generating facilities on the site. The likely result of such sleight of hand is to bring nearer the day of comprehensive land use planning and controls by public agencies.

THE EVILS OF STRIP-MINING [8]

The old and evil practice of strip-mining, according to a recent report in . . . [the New York *Times*], is spreading and booming. More than 35 per cent of the nation's annual production of coal now comes from this kind of "mining" in which huge electric shovels gouge out the topsoil to get at readily accessible seams of coal.

State laws nominally require that the mine operators reclaim the land by grading it and restoring topsoil. In practice, the strip miners usually leave a wasteland, barren, treeless, virtually unusable.

This ravaging of farmland, pasture, and woods in single-minded pursuit of cheap coal is a desecration. It pollutes the land as decisively as the dumping of mercury pollutes a river and the congestion of automobiles pollutes the air, and it is just as intolerable. When millions of tons of coal lie below ground available to conventional mining methods, there is no good excuse for this kind of pollution. If necessary the nation's electric power users can well afford to pay slightly higher prices for conventional coal rather than "save" by buying strip-mined coal.

The United States Government is in a good position to stop this iniquitous practice since the Tennessee Valley Au-

[8] Editorial, "The Great Soil Swindle." New York *Times*. p 32. D. 22, '70.
© 1970 by The New York Times Company. Reprinted by permission.

thority is the largest single purchaser of this coal. But the power of example is not enough. Federal legislation is needed to outlaw strip-mining.

In the 1930s, the Federal Government undertook numerous and costly soil conservation programs when wind storms turned the prairies into a dust bowl. Yet the Government today stands by, silently, impotently, as coal operators lay waste the land and scatter topsoil as recklessly as the dust storms ever did. Why the contrast? The answer can only be that nobody made money out of the dust storms but the Consolidation Coal Company, the TVA and other private and public entrepreneurs are profiting from this rape of the land.

Greed and convenience are no longer justifiable reasons for taking a green and pleasant land and turning it into a waste of rubble. It is time to curb the strip miners to protect the face of America.

DEVELOPING ALASKAN LANDS [9]

The Interior Department reported today that an oil pipeline across Alaska would create unavoidable environmental damage, but it recommended that the line be constructed because the oil was so crucial to the country.

A staff report, which officials said represented the current position of the department listed dozens of different ways that the eight-hundred-mile, $1 billion project would disturb the ecology of the vast Alaskan wilderness.

But the report said that the oil in the rich new field on the Arctic North Slope was "essential to the strength, growth and security of the United States," and that stiff regulations on the pipeline's construction and monitoring of its operations would "reduce foreseeable environmental costs to acceptable levels."

[9] From "Alaska Pipeline Is Upheld by Interior Agency Study," by David E. Rosenbaum, Washington bureau staff member. New York *Times*. p 1+. Ja. 14, '71. © 1971 by The New York Times Company. Reprinted by permission.

A study group of Interior Department technical, geological and environmental specialists spent two years preparing the 195-page report and detailed regulations that the builders must follow.

The report was described by the department as "tentative" and subject to change following public hearings. . . . But Interior officials said that it was highly unlikely that the substance of the conclusions would be altered.

The report was required by the Environmental Policy Act, under which Government agencies must submit a statement to the Council on Environmental Quality about the impact on the environment of their proposed actions.

A consortium of seven major oil companies wants to build the pipeline from Prudhoe Bay on the Arctic North Slope to Valdez, an ice-free, deep-water port on Prince William Sound [see map]. The oil would then be transported by freighter to the continental United States.

Because the line must cross Federal lands, it cannot be built without a permit from the Interior Department. . . .

[In] April [1970], a Federal court . . . [in Washington, D.C.] issued an injunction preventing issuance of the permit until the report on the environment had been submitted. Following the hearings and the final report, the department will have to go to court to get the injunction dissolved. . . .

The injunction was obtained by three environmental groups: The Wilderness Society, Friends of the Earth and the Environmental Defense Fund, Inc. . . . There has been an intense struggle between developers and conservationists since an oil pool of more than 10 billion barrels was discovered on the North Slope in 1968.

The fabulous strike has been conservatively valued at $60 billion, which could be delivered by pipeline to Valdez for about $1 a barrel. Competitive leases and royalty payments to the State of Alaska also would run into billions of dollars.

© 1971 by The New York Times Company. Reprinted by permission.

Broken line traces route of the proposed pipeline.

Conservationists' View

But conservationists have argued that construction of the project and moving the hot oil across the state would destroy the country's largest natural wilderness.

Referring to the debate between the developers and the conservationists, the Interior Department report stated:

> For those to whom unbroken wilderness is most important, the entire project is adverse because the original character of this corridor in northern Alaska would be lost forever.
> To others, the opening of this remote country is a proper development that can be defended on both economical and recreational grounds.

The department, however, said that the primary argument for the pipeline was not based on economics but on national security. The oil on the North Slope is vital to the country if it is not to become overly dependent on oil from the politically unstable Middle East, the report said.

If construction of the pipeline is begun promptly, the report said, 500,000 barrels a day will be available by 1975, rising to 2 million a day by 1980.

The department's report and specifications will require substantial changes in the oil companies' original plans for the pipeline. The companies had proposed laying 90 to 95 per cent of the line underground, in the permafrost, the frozen layer of gravel, sand and ice that covers much of Alaska.

The oil, flowing at about 180 degrees Fahrenheit, would be certain to melt this permafrost, resulting in serious erosion. Not only would the erosion itself cause ecological damage, but also, if the erosion left the pipe unsupported, it might break with the weight and cause severe spills.

The department's specifications stated that only 52 per cent of the line could definitely be laid underground safely, although some other areas might be found safe after drilling. The department would require that the rest of the line be built above ground.

Other Regulations Listed

Other specifications require crossings for big game animals, protection for fish spawning grounds and controls on water and air pollution.

Safeguards would be taken against oil spills, but the report acknowledged that "there is a probability that some oil spills will occur even under the most stringent enforcement." However, the possibility of a major spill was said to be "remote."

The oil companies would be required to bear the cost of repairing the damage from any spill.

The department called its regulations "the most stringent environmental and technical stipulations ever imposed upon industry for a project of this nature." But it acknowledged that there would be a "residue of unavoidable effects."

Among these, it listed the destruction of wilderness area and wildlife habitat. "It is clearly recognized that no stipulation can alter the fundamental change that development would bring to this area," the report stated. But given the urgency for the oil, the report said, the pipeline "would create the fewest number of environmental problems of all alternate means considered."

In addition to the pipeline, the oil companies plan to build a road, about 375 miles long, to move equipment and materials during the pipeline construction. The road must be built in such a way as to avoid erosion.

The total effort was believed by Interior Department officials to be the largest single private construction project and private capital investment in history.

[In February 1971 Secretary of the Interior Rogers C. B. Morton indicated that a decision was still to be reached on the question of constructing the pipeline from Prudhoe Bay to Valdez.—Ed.]

IV. OUR LAND AND RECREATION

EDITOR'S INTRODUCTION

When we think of public lands we most often think of our national parks; and for most citizens this is the section of our public lands about which most is known. Today we are also becoming publicly aware of the great population pressure upon these parks. In this section the first article deals briefly with the United States National Park Service and its director, and the remaining articles reflect new concerns about possible national park areas.

Thus, the second article, by a professor of forest land use at Yale University, considers our wilderness areas. It is followed by an article on efforts to establish a Prairie National Park in the Midwest, where the vast original prairie lands have been nearly lost. Finally, two selections from the *Wall Street Journal* discuss the wetlands and other scenic areas not yet part of the National Park System.

THE NATIONAL PARK SERVICE [1]

As director of the United States National Park Service, George B. Hartzog, Jr., is a leading caretaker of America's natural environment, and the national park system that he manages serves as a model to scores of other nations. The United States opened the world's first national park at Yellowstone in 1872. Thirty-four years later the National Park Service was set up as a bureau within the Department of the Interior, and it currently employs nearly 6,000 persons who administer some 265 areas, including national monuments, historic sites, recreational lakeshores, seashores, and park-

[1] From biographical sketch of George Benjamin Hartzog, Jr., National Park Service director. *Current Biography*. 31:18-20. Jl. '70. Reprinted by permission from the 1970 issue of *Current Biography* © 1970, The H. W. Wilson Company. Also available in *Current Biography Yearbook 1970*. p 173-5.

ways, and thirty-two operational national parks. Parts of that huge complex are endangered by the same overcrowding and man-made pollutants that plague the rest of the earth's environment.

Recognizing the urgency of the problem, Director Hartzog has aimed his program not only at developing new ways to accommodate visitors without damaging park ecology, but at educating the public to achieve a greater harmony with their environment. Before his appointment as director of the National Park Service in 1964, Hartzog had served the bureau for almost twenty years, becoming its associate director in 1963. . . .

Less than a year later, on January 6, 1964, Hartzog was sworn in as director of the National Park Service, succeeding Conrad L. Wirth, who retired after twelve years as head of the bureau. Hartzog inherited the supervision of his predecessor's Mission '66, a ten-year program to expand visitor facilities, roads, trails, and staff and to establish new historical sites and recreational areas. By the time the program ended in 1966, the National Park Service had added forty-nine new areas, including the Virgin Islands National Park, the Cape Cod National Seashore, and the Independence National Historical Park in Philadelphia.

Parkscape U.S.A.

In 1966 Hartzog launched Parkscape U.S.A., a new far-reaching plan for the national park system "to make the beauty and the history of the land a richer and more meaningful part of the daily life of every citizen." Its expressed goals were to expand the beauty and recreational features of urban parks managed by the National Park Service and to acquire new urban parklands; to cooperate with other Federal and state agencies in improving park and recreational facilities not directly under the Park Service's control; to expand assistance to the ninety other nations with national park systems; to communicate the value of parks in an effort to help people to live in harmony with their environment;

and to complete the national park system by 1972. (According to Robert Cahn, who in 1968 wrote a Pulitzer Prize-winning series of articles for *The Christian Science Monitor* entitled "Will Success Spoil the National Parks?," the last goal is unlikely to be achieved "even in a decade," because of "lack of funds, plus opposition from various sources to any new park.")

To implement his new projects, Hartzog reorganized the National Park Service on a functional rather than a professional basis. A new headquarters was planned for Harpers Ferry, Virginia, in which all interpretive and publicity services would be consolidated, and a new office of urban affairs was established in December 1967 within the Washington headquarters. To acquaint the public with ecology and man's place in his environment the National Park Service started the National Environment Education Development program (NEED) in 1967. Pilot programs have been run with fifth-grade students, and it is planned eventually to provide training for students throughout the elementary and secondary years. A corollary program of Environmental Study Areas using parklands as outdoor classrooms for people of all age groups has also been established. In 1968 the first annual Summer in the Parks program was launched in Washington, D.C., providing city children with daily trips to outlying parks and recreation centers and sponsoring various entertainments in the city's parks.

History of the Service

Historically, the National Park Service has had two main goals: to preserve the natural and historic heritage of the nation and to provide enjoyment for visitors to its land. With its road building, expansion of visitor facilities, and publicity featuring visitor statistics, Mission '66 seemed to many critics to put an alarming emphasis on just one of those goals, and in 1966 a 60,000-word report for the Conservation Foundation asserted that overuse of the parks had already resulted in "ecological deterioration." The number of visitors to the national park system has continued to increase each year since then—there were 152 million in 1968—but Director Hartzog has taken steps to help ensure that the visitor can enjoy his stay without inflicting damage. He has, for example, declared a limited war on the automobile. Early in his administration he announced a new road policy, asserting that the national parks "stand today at the same crossroads as do the American cities—some of which seem on the verge of choking on their automobiles. Just as noise, congestion, and pollution threaten the quality of urban life, they have begun to erode the quality of the park experience."

The new policy declared that park roads should not be links in the Federal highway network; that the National Park Service must not be obliged to accommodate new types of camping vehicles; that every park road should provide a scenic or educational interest in itself; and that research should be conducted on the feasibility of such mass transportation systems as tramways, monorails, and hydrofoils. The park director has not always been allowed to carry out that policy, but at Mesa Verde National Park in Colorado he was able to cancel a contract for a high-quality road leading to newly excavated cliff dwellings. Instead, a winding, narrow fire road was to be used after slight improvements.

Hartzog views privately owned lands within the nation's parks as one of the National Park Service's biggest headaches. Although those pockets of land, or "inholdings," take up only about 300,000 of the 27 million acres in the park system, they are all too often clustered around major scenic attractions and disfigured by ramshackle buildings. Such small settlements as Wawona Village in Yosemite create administrative problems for already overtaxed park rangers and unscrupulous real estate speculators have occasionally acquired land that they scar with unsightly roads and tiny plots of camping ground. The National Park Service's chronic shortage of funds and rising land values have hindered it from acquiring the inholdings. Testifying before a House Appropriations subcommittee in April 1968, Hartzog estimated that it would cost the Government $119 million to buy the same land that would have cost $59 million in 1961. The Park Service director would like to see an annual Congressional appropriation for a special fund that would allow his bureau to purchase those properties as they become available on the market.

As director of the National Park Service, Hartzog must contend with a vast array of special interest groups both in and out of the Government. On the one hand, conservation groups like the Sierra Club and the Wilderness Society exert pressure on him to retain the pristine purity of the parks, while on the other, lumber, mining, grazing, and hydroelectric power industries resist the establishment of new parks and restrictions in present ones. Within the Government the National Park Service often has its disagreements with the Bureau of Public Roads, the Forest Service, the Bureau of Reclamation, and the Army Corps of Engineers. Hartzog spends much of his time dealing with Congress, testifying at hearings, meeting with individual members, and studying the large body of legislation that affects the national park system. He is an accomplished public speaker and an adroit political strategist. On Capitol Hill he is reportedly highly respected, although some leading conservationists are said to consider him too much of a "wheeler-dealer."

The preservation of historic sites has been one of Hartzog's special concerns. In 1965 he represented the Department of the Interior on a special committee on historic preservation. The committee's report helped to bring about the National Historic Preservation Act of 1966, which established a program of assistance to states in preserving historic sites that would be administered by the National Park Service. The bill also authorized matching grants for the acquisition and administration of nationally significant buildings by the National Trust for Historic Preservation, of which Hartzog is a trustee. Under another provision a seventeen-member National Advisory Council on Historic Preservation was set up. (Hartzog serves as its executive director.) . . .

Although he recognizes the gravity of the environmental crisis, Hartzog is optimistic. He feels that public awareness and concern can reverse the trend. At a recent environment seminar he told his colleagues, "I sincerely believe that the idea of an environmental ethic—embracing the concept of human ecology—the interdependence and the interplay of everything on this planet as it relates to the human condition—is an idea whose time is fast approaching."

CARING FOR OUR WILDERNESS AREAS [2]

To begin with, one must recognize that the idea of a wilderness is a matter of social and human attitudes, and is not a consistently definable concept. One cannot say, "this is a wilderness," and find general agreement. The definition of a wilderness varies with the cultural background, education and desires of the individual.

The origin of the word *wilderness* is shrouded in antiquity. *Wildren* is Middle English for savage, from the Old English *wildēoren,* of or like wild animals. Etymologically, the word means the place of wild beasts (or just animals). Consequently, it means a place where nature is largely uncontrolled by man and where natural (another hard word to define) processes prevail.

The Bible contains many references to "wilderness," although the particular meaning is often uncertain because of translation problems. In general, the biblical reference meant a place apart, arid and uncultivated—a wasteland. This meaning is consonant with much of the area on which biblical experience is based. A wilderness area today can be large or small, and highly variable as to what grows or lives on it. In the United States, wilderness is usually, but not necessarily, associated with forested lands, with which this country is plentifully endowed.

[2] From "Wilderness and Forests Tomorrow," by Kenneth P. Davis, professor of forest land use, School of Forestry, Yale University. *Current History.* 59:91-4+. Ag. '70. Reprinted by permission of Current History, Inc. and the author.

The concept of a forest conjures up many things: a feeling of time and of things enduring; of great trees, some of which have survived the vicissitudes of centuries and are the oldest living organisms on this planet. To some, the forest is dark and forbidding, a place of mystery and hiding. Our folklore is full of such images: of great beasts lurking, of danger, of wild spirits, or a refuge for hunted man. To those who know the forest, it is friendly, a place of life. It is endlessly interesting and changing as one comes to understand the myriad life relationships between plants and animals. One should never be lonely there; the cities are a place for loneliness. An answer to the question "What is a wilderness?" then can be given only by individuals in terms of their outlook and interests. The definition is a social and a human matter that transcends definition of particular pieces of land as a wilderness area.

Wilderness Concepts and Attitudes

To the first settlers from Europe on the eastern shores of this country, the "wilderness" stretched for illimitable distances westward; much farther, in fact, than they imagined. Because they did not intend to live like the Indians already there, this wilderness was something to be conquered, cleared, settled and made fruitful on their terms.

As settlement proceeded westward, forests were cleared for farms, towns and cities. It is well to bear in mind that practically all of the United States east of the Great Plains was originally heavily forested. The same was true of most of the Pacific West.

This sketch of history gives one major concept of wilderness: the situation when the first European settlers came. They regarded the frontier, the wilderness, as an obstacle, something to be conquered and controlled. The facts of settlement in the New World and the frontier spirit have historically and naturally colored much of our outlook and attitude regarding natural resources and wilderness.

In sharp contrast is a second concept of a wilderness as a vignette of natural ecological and groundcover condition that should be kept in its original state. This idea has scientific meaning, but is not very practical as a general approach. It is somewhat museumlike.

Nature does not stand still. The trees and other plants grow and die whether or not they are affected by man. Natural forces of change—fire, storm, insects—operate crudely, often more so than man. To withdraw all protection such as forest-fire or insect-epidemic control from an area may lead to the destruction, not the preservation, of the forest. Protection *from* man is also equally important; individuals and groups of people can be very disturbing to natural conditions.

For these reasons, this preservation concept of wilderness has been applied to the designation of specific and usually rather small areas that represent certain specific forest or other ecosystem types of scientific interest. These are termed Natural Areas and a substantial number of them have been established in the United States. They constitute wilderness in a limited sense, are protected, and are available to people for study only.

A third general wilderness concept is rather subjective and personal. In memory, a forest we once roamed as a child was a wilderness. It may have been much man-influenced but that did not matter. Many of us have nostalgic memories of such areas and of their passing with increasing urbanization.

This general concept has much practical application. East of the Great Plains there is practically no virgin forest or other wildland that has not been affected by man. But in many areas the kindly and durable forest has become reestablished as farm fields and pastures have gone out of agricultural use, and as natural regrowth has followed cutting in forested areas. Many of these areas are very attractive; they constitute a wilderness in the remaking. With reasonable protection they are or will become areas that provide wilderness experience.

The Wilderness Preservation Movement

The frontier, as the pioneers knew and felt it, passed with the nineteenth century in this country. Soon after the middle of the century, railroads spanned the continent and by the end of the century a basic transportation network was complete. True, there were many and large areas of little or no settlement or other development but they were explored, mapped and known.

An appreciation of wilderness, of nature, of natural areas and the out-of-doors developed with the passing of the frontier. Rather naturally, it developed in the cities, with urban people who were the farthest removed from nature and were often those who least understood the realities of living in wildland areas. A movement with philosophical, religious, romantic, ethical, political, ecological and primitive components was applied to a social need for wild areas and for direct contact with nature in general. It grew to be a naturalist cult in some respects.

The name of Henry David Thoreau (1817-1862) is associated with the beginnings of this movement. He was the founder of a literary genre of nature writing. Other prominent names associated in one way or another with this general movement and continuing into the twentieth century include John James Audubon, John Muir, George Perkins Marsh, Francis Parkman, Jr., Gifford Pinchot, Theodore Roosevelt, Samuel H. Hammond, Frederick Law Olmstead, Charles Sprague Sargent and Aldo Leopold. The movement was led by a few dedicated people in a generally unconcerned country.

The development of the nature-wilderness-forest preservation movement in the late 1800s and early 1900s is a fascinating story but only some high points of action can be traced here.

The world's first instance of large-scale wilderness preservation in the public interest occurred on March 1, 1872, when President Ulysses S. Grant signed an Act designating over two million acres of northwestern Wyoming as Yellowstone Park. (Roderick Nash in *Wilderness and the American Mind*)

The park was created by a generally uninterested and apathetic Congress and public, and for a long time there was uncertainty over what to do with the area and how to administer it. But it was a beginning, and from it came the present National Park System.

The next major action was the withdrawal, primarily in the West, of millions of acres from the Public Domain lands as Forest Reserves. This began in the 1890s and continued into the next decade. Again, this act was urged by a few farsighted and dedicated people and was more or less slipped through the Congress without general public support. Gifford Pinchot was a major architect. The reserves were transferred from the Department of the Interior to the Department of Agriculture in 1905 and renamed National Forests, and the United States Forest Service was then born with Gifford Pinchot as its first chief. Primarily through purchase of privately owned lands, mostly during the 1920s and the 1930s, National Forests were established in the eastern United States and the present National Forest System of some 183 million acres of federally owned and managed lands developed.

In later years, other and large federally owned areas were designated or acquired for public purposes. The Bureau of Land Management in the Department of the Interior is charged with the continuing management of all lands remaining in the public domain—about 300 million acres—reversing a former general and rather vague policy that all of these lands were subject to "ultimate disposal" from Federal ownership. There are also large areas managed for fish and wildlife by the Bureau of Sport Fisheries and Wildlife and some other public agencies. Extensive state parks and other state landownerships have developed. All of these areas have something to do with wilderness and wilderness experience. So do many large forested areas in private ownership. The frontier is gone, but large wildland areas remain.

There was a mixture of motives and purposes behind these earlier large-scale public land reservations. They included concern for nature, for wilderness and for preservation of some of the frontier, and a desire for the use of all forest and related resources in the public interest. Conflicts of interest were inevitable and they still continue. The early Forest Reserves were resented in the West as withdrawing lands from private entry and development and not in keeping with a frontier spirit. There was and is sharp disagreement between those who desire to restrict public lands for particular uses such as wilderness and National Parks, and those with a broader concept of applying, under management, some combination or blending of wildland resources uses for outdoor recreation, for timber production, for grazing of domestic livestock, for fish and game, as well as for wilderness. There is a continuing search for balance and harmony in land use in a political democracy.

National Interest in Wilderness Lands

The Government's interest in wilderness has continued strongly over the years. Beginning in the 1920s, the United States Forest Service initiated the designation by the Secretary of Agriculture of a large number of wildland areas, mostly in the mountainous West, for wilderness-primitive recreational use, with other uses sharply restricted or eliminated. Nearly ninety such areas, aggregating about 14.5 million acres, have been so designated over the years. Areas of wilderness character are also held in the federally owned National Parks and National Wildlife Refuges but prior to the 1960s they were not considered specifically for wilderness designation.

A continuing tide of concern about wilderness preservation culminated, in 1964, in the passage by Congress of

the Wilderness Act (Public Law 88—557. 88th Congress)
following long debate. The act establishes a National
Wilderness Preservation System of federally owned lands
". . . to secure for the American people of present and
future generations the benefits of an enduring resource
of wilderness." Wilderness is defined as "an area where the
earth and its community of life are untrammeled by man,
where man himself is a visitor and does not remain."
Prohibited are roads, any commercial enterprise, use of
motor vehicles or aircraft, and any structure or installation
(with some exceptions for emergency human health and
safety protection). A major feature of the act is that wilderness areas are recommended by the President and approved
by act of Congress and consequently can be changed only
in the same manner.

At the time of passage of the act, fifty-three wild or
primitive areas aggregating some 9.1 million acres previously
designated in the national forests that met wilderness
criteria established in the act were taken into the system.
In addition, a total of 115 areas aggregating nearly 50
million acres of Federal lands of some wilderness potential
in the National Forests, National Park System, and national
wildlife refuges and rangeland areas are to be reviewed over
a ten-year period for possible inclusion in the system. As
this is written, the review is in progress and definite statistics cannot be given.

Permanent Wilderness

A formal and permanent Federal wilderness system
consequently now exists and will be enlarged in the future.
It cannot be over-emphasized, however, that it is a great
mistake to think that all opportunities for wilderness experience can or should be encompassed in this Federal
system. There are millions of other acres, public and private,
large and small, whether formally designated or not, that

can and do provide opportunities to see nature and enjoy outdoor recreation and wilderness experience.

A much larger objective is to use all lands, wild or otherwise, not only to conserve them to meet man's physical needs but to satisfy his deeper needs for beauty and refreshment of spirit. A well-managed forest *can* be a place of usefulness and pleasure forever. There has to be some blending of use with preservation.

The Future of Wilderness Areas

Establishment of a wilderness area is a first step, but keeping it so is a continuing need. Speaking as a professional forester who has spent years in the forest, sometimes with backpack, sometimes with saddle and packhorse, and sometimes on canoe trips into wilderness areas, I know stubborn realities must be faced if a wilderness is to serve its human purposes. Wilderness is a human point of view; to the wild animal there is no such thing as a wilderness—it is just home. As the act defines it, a wilderness is an area in which man is a visitor.

Let me explain a little. The Hiawatha concept of parting the branches to let us travel through and cutting boughs for our bed at night is appealing but inapplicable when a great many people do the same. By the facts of terrain and trails, only a very small portion of a wilderness area is traveled to any extent. There are only so many natural routes and logical places to camp, especially on horseback. Actual travel and use consequently must be concentrated in a relatively small area.

By their basic nature, wilderness areas cannot withstand heavy human use without controls. Neither the noble red man, the frontiersman, nor the present-day citizen is noted for natural conservation impulses; these have to be acquired. On main routes of travel, trails or portages, I have seen human-bestowed litter of all kinds and stripped trees that look like plucked chickens. Visitors also start forest fires on occasion; they bypass inadequately constructed or maintained trails and unsightly shortcuts develop.

There is real need to inculcate and apply a wilderness ethic of human behavior, and at the same time to face the necessity for commonsense provision of facilities of certain kinds and in certain places. These facilities are needed to preserve the very thing a wilderness area was established for—to preserve nature untrammeled by evidences of man. Too often and increasingly, such evidences are painfully apparent, but they are sometimes swept under the carpet by romantic but unthinking enthusiasm about the truly wonderful and healing nature of a wilderness experience.

A larger question in the future of wilderness areas is the interests of the many versus the few. Only a relatively few are equipped and financially able to enjoy a wilderness experience in a large area. What about the many who cannot go beyond a day's walk or an overnight trip? Their interests count, too, and have led to the consideration of the concept of travel corridors in some large wilderness areas from which a more dispersed pattern of use, accessible to more people, is possible.

The problem of use, essentially the problem of protecting wilderness *from* people and at the same time making such areas available to them, will confront wilderness area management in the future. There are no easy or simplistic answers. Wilderness areas are for people to see and to appreciate, to enjoy but not to destroy, to use but not to abuse, to have now and in the future as part of our American heritage.

FOR A PRAIRIE NATIONAL PARK [3]

There are people who love the prairie as others love the sea. They love the feel of its black, spongy soil, the splen-

[3] From "Prairie Partisans Move to Save Grasslands," by John Noble Wilford, science news reporter. New York *Times.* p 1. O. 17, '71. © 1971 by The New York Times Company. Reprinted by permission.

dor of its many wild flowers and the sweep of its tall grass blowing in the wind. They feel, with Willa Cather, that "the grass was the country," and that its roots ran deep and shaped the heartland of a nation.

But those who love the prairie have to look hard now-adays to find any real prairie left to love. It has been plowed under, grazed over and covered by concrete and people.

Partisans on Offensive

Now, before it is too late, a small but fervent group of prairie partisans—scientists, conservationists, seed growers and businessmen—is making some progress in its efforts to hold on to whatever virgin prairie is left and to restore some lands to their former wild grandeur.

Prairie—the word is from the French for meadow—is a generally flat and fertile terrain covered with tall perennial grasses and an abundance of native flowering plants.

Partisans are buying up wild prairie ahead of the real-estate developers, fencing off relic prairies, restoring prairie-like fields for state parks and even attempting to establish a prairie national park.

"Man has probably misused the earth's grasslands more than he has misused any other plant environment vital to man," Dr. Roger C. Anderson, director of the University of Wisconsin Arboretum, told a recent conference of prairie experts in Madison, Wisconsin.

The original prairie stretched from Indiana west to the Rockies, from Texas north through the Dakotas and into Canada. To the east the grass was tall; to the west, short. Only an occasional stand of cottonwood or grove of burr oak, usually by a stream, broke the sea of grass.

About all of the prairie left now are patches of grass and flowers on some rocky hillsides and sand ridges, along a few railroad rights-of-way and in old and forgotten cemeteries like the one in the cornfields out from . . . [the] small farming community [of Plainfield, Illinois].

This rare relic of virgin prairie vegetation . . . was discovered not long ago by Dr. Robert F. Betz, a botanist and
ecologist at Northeastern Illinois University in Chicago.
He has found about eighteen other prairie cemeteries in
the Chicago area, all of which he hopes to fence off and
preserve.

Reclamation Projects

In similar moves, several Midwestern universities are
reclaiming patches of prairie for scientific, historical and
esthetic reasons. The Nature Conservancy, a land conservation group, is buying prairie remnants in Illinois, Wisconsin,
Minnesota, Nebraska and Kansas.

A group of Wisconsin citizens recently rescued eighty
acres of prairie near Kenosha from the reach of real-estate
developers. Illinois has acquired 2,000 acres of unplowed
land sixty miles southwest of Chicago for the development
of the Goose Lake Prairie state park, a restored prairie
planned for research and recreation.

Jim Wilson, a mail-order seed grower in Polk, Nebraska,
estimates he has supplied native grass and wildflower seed
for some 3,000 acres of what he calls "soul plantings"—
the miniprairies established by school groups, landscape
gardeners and homeowners. . . .

And on a grander scale, state leaders and scientists
in Kansas are pressing the Federal Government to establish a prairie national park in the Flint Hills, a relatively
unspoiled region south of Manhattan and near the eastern stretch of the Santa Fé Trail. In arguing their case,
the Kansans point out that there are parks for the mountains, forests and seashore—but not for the prairie.

Attitude Changing

To Dr. Betz, the Northeastern Illinois professor, the
new interest in saving the prairie reflects a gradual change
in public attitudes toward nature.

"A few years ago we had a real crisis from our point of view," Dr. Betz said. "Almost none of the prairie had been saved. What was left was endangered, and the few of us who worried about it had almost no support from the public. We were just 'dicky-birds'—you know, nature lovers."

Now, Dr. Betz said he is in constant demand to speak to civic and school groups about the prairie. Through the Prairie Restoration Society, a branch of the Sierra Club organized by Chicagoans who are concerned with prairie preservation, he has raised money to try to save such remnants as the old cemeteries. . . .

The Indians managed the prairie very well, Dr. Betz explained. They were hunters and so never turned over the sod, exposing the soil to the erosion of wind and rain. They put up no fences and so the buffalo never overgrazed any one area. And, either by accident or to herd buffalo, they often set fire to the prairie grasses in the fall or spring, thereby killing off encroaching weeds and forest seedlings, but not the deep-rooted perennials of the prairie. . . .

Surviving Cemetery

The cemetery prairie survived because its land was never plowed like the surrounding cornfields and because it was burned off nearly every fall by a farmer down the road who wanted to discourage hunters. The burning kept the weeds out.

The edge of the cemetery showed the value of prairie vegetation as defense against erosion. At the edge there was a one-foot drop into the cornfield. In more than a century of plowing, water and wind have stripped a foot of soil off the cornfield—rich soil that was a product of millions of years of evolution through prairie growth and decay.

Having this "standard of comparison" between the unspoiled and the cultivated land, Dr. Betz said, is one of the reasons scientists are interested in saving relic prairies.

But since there are few relics like the old cemeteries, most scientists and conservationists attending the Second Midwest Prairie Conference, which was held . . . [in September 1970] at the University of Wisconsin, said that they were concentrating their efforts on prairie restorations—taking land that has never been plowed and only lightly grazed and planting it with native grasses and flowers.

A model restoration is the sixty-five-acre Curtis Prairie, developed on the outskirts of Madison by the University of Wisconsin. It was started in the 1930s by the old Civilian Conservation Corps. University students and professors combed hillsides, rural cemeteries and railroad rights-of-way to find the dozens of wild prairie plant species.

Only now, more than thirty years later, can the field be considered a reasonably authentic example of wild prairie, for the process of restoration is that slow and difficult.

Dr. Grant Cottam, chairman of the university's botany department, explained the process during a walk through the restored prairie. The field had been a pasture. If it had been cultivated for any length of time, Dr. Cottam said, it might have taken a century or more to restore it.

When the prairie seeds were sown, the first growth was mostly downward. For the first few years, prairie flowers and grasses concentrate on extending deep roots.

The Curtis Prairie is burned over nearly every fall. Besides killing off nonnative competition, Dr. Cottam said, the burning also somehow seems to increase the length of the growing season and "give us five times as many flower-ing plants the next spring."

Effects of the Railroads

Weeds—the annuals whose roots are shallow but whose seeds are ubiquitous—are "by all odds, the toughest problem facing the prairie restorationist," said Jim Wilson, the Nebraska seed-grower.

Weeds compete with the native plants for moisture, nutrients and growing space. Despite the burnings, Dr. Cottam still found clumps of bluegrass in the Wisconsin restoration, vestiges of the field's days as a pasture.

Another problem is the dwindling sources of native seeds. Railroad rights-of-way used to be the best source. They were unplowed and were burned frequently to keep down the wild plants. But Southern Illinois University botanists reported at the prairie conference that railroads are increasingly using chemical herbicides to clear the rights-of-way. The spraying destroys the natural vegetation and encourages the growth of weeds.

Relic Prairies

Most relic and restored prairies are too small to provide food and shelter for many of the original prairie wildlife, except for hawks, doves, sparrows, gophers and mice. The larger animals, especially buffalo and elk, have long ago vanished from the area.

At a fifteen-thousand-acre test site in northeast Colorado, scientists participating in the International Biological Program are attempting the first comprehensive study of grassland ecology. They are charting the living and eating habits of 60 species of mammals, 138 kinds of birds and more than 3,000 types of insects that depend on prairie grass.

In Illinois, a private citizens' group organized the Prairie Chicken Foundation to "preserve and perpetuate the prairie chicken." Though once an endangered species, the prairie chicken is now making a slow comeback, primarily because nesting sanctuaries were provided in areas of remnant prairie.

Leaders of the Kansas drive to establish a national prairie consider thirty thousand acres "a minimum if the native fauna as well as the native flora is to be preserved."

The first proposed site for the park lay west of the Blue River, just north of Manhattan, Kansas. But cattlemen objected, the Corps of Engineers went ahead with a dam and people started building cottages and marinas where the prairie park would have been.

On a visit to Kansas . . . [early in 1970], Walter J. Hickel, Secretary of the Interior, had some encouraging words: "I still think there is a need for . . . a Prairie National Park and I think Kansas would be an ideal location for it."

Driving south of Manhattan, where the sky is big and the fields have never been plowed and bluestem grows by the side of the road, Dr. Lloyd Hulbert, a Kansas State University botanist, considered what a prairie has to offer. "People go to see glaciers and mountains," Dr. Hulbert said. "Perhaps they would like to see what the prairie was like. It's part of our heritage, and it's a chance to get away from civilization. That's becoming a more important consideration all the time."

NATURE'S NURSERIES [4]

Wetlands, as ecologists define them, are areas in which there is no clear-cut border between land and water—areas such as swamps, marshes, bogs or tidal flats. The Department of the Interior's Fish and Wildlife Service estimates there were about 125 million acres of wetlands in what's now the United States when Columbus came to this hemisphere. By 1955 "reclamation" activities in the form of dredging, draining and filling had left only 74.4 million acres. Today it's estimated there are 60 million acres, and they are going fast.

Conservationists are particularly worried about marshes— both salt and freshwater—because they are at the same time the biologically most productive and perhaps the least appreciated natural areas on earth. Most people particularly those in urban areas, tend to regard marshes as "mosquito-infested swamps" that are best filled in.

But ecologists point out that such areas teem with plant

    [4] From "Threats to Wetlands Where Sea Life Breeds Upset Conservationists," by William E. Burrows, staff reporter. *Wall Street Journal.* p 1+. O. 30, '70. Reprinted by permission.

and animal life. And, together with adjacent tidal flats, creeks, streams and bays, any given marsh helps form a single biological system that's vital to the life cycles of many creatures that range far afield both on land and in water.

Salt marshes, for example, are called the "nurseries of the sea" because they provide spawning and nesting grounds for birds, fish and mollusks that may live out most of their lives far away. It is calculated that two thirds of the ocean's sport and commercial fish either begin their own lives in wetland areas or feed on other creatures spawned in wetlands.

Short-Range Interests

"And the beauty of it all is that you don't have to do anything to it but leave it alone," says Roland Clement, a biologist with the National Audubon Society.

A particular source of frustration to many conservationists, including Mr. Clement, is the frequent failure of those who control wetlands to look beyond their short-range economic interests. Mr. Clement sighs impatiently as he picks up a recent issue of *Area Development,* an industrial planning magazine, and points to an article titled: "Why Not Choose Marshlands for Your New Plant?" The author, an engineer, advocates "marginal land reclamation," which is "fast turning the wastelands of bog and swamp . . . into desirable industrial sites."

"For these people," comments Mr. Clement, "salt marshes are cheap, and therefore that's the place to put their plant." But, he argues, such an attitude sacrifices the long-range good of many for the short-range fiscal convenience of a few.

"Everybody insists that his little bit of destruction can and should be accommodated because it will not, by itself, destroy the ecosystem," says Mr. Clement. "But bit by bit we're giving the whole damned thing away."

Though the process of the filling and draining of U.S. wetlands has been going on for centuries, it has accelerated rapidly in recent years. "Everyone wants a view of the water, and all of the good land is gone," observes James Haskell, a consultant to Maine's Environmental Improvement Council, a newly formed state agency. "Only so-called marginal land is left, so developers are turning to swamps."

Increasingly, though, the developers are running into opposition. Conservationists are trying to block several development schemes in various areas of the country, and they have already succeeded in some places. Community action last spring stalled a West German chemical firm's attempt to build a $100 million plant near a resort area in Beaufort County, South Carolina, and conservationists currently are battling a plan to extend runways at New York's Kennedy International Airport into a wildlife preserve area of Jamaica Bay on the south shore of Long Island.

Conservationists have persuaded some state governments to enact legislation to protect wetlands. The New Jersey state legislature just this fall [1970] passed such a bill aimed at protecting the state's remaining wetlands. (The Open Space Institute, a conservation group that has compiled reports on wetlands use, says that in New Jersey, "which may once have possessed the finest estuarine resources on the entire East Coast," nearly thirty-five thousand acres of tidal marsh have been drained, filled and developed since 1953.) Massachusetts, Connecticut and some other states already have enacted strong wetlands laws.

Law Prohibited Damage

But conservationists have found that such laws by no means provide ironclad protection of wetlands. In some instances loopholes are left that allow development despite the objections of ecologists, and in others enforcement has proved a problem. Conservationists in Maine were shocked last May when a newly passed state wetlands law was declared unconstitutional by the state supreme court.

The Maine law prohibited the changing of coastal swamps, marshes, bogs, beaches or other lowlands by removing, filling, dredging or draining sanitary sewage into them without approval of municipal authorities and the newly created state Wetlands Control Board.

The law was challenged by a Wells couple who owned land near the Webhannet River at Wells Beach. They had started to fill the land ... but were enjoined to stop under the new law.

They appealed, and the supreme court overturned the law on the ground that the benefits from preserving wetlands are statewide and that the cost of preservation should be publicly born. "To leave (the Wells couple) with commercially value-less land in upholding the restriction presently imposed is to charge them with more than their just share of the cost of this statewide conservation program," the court said in a unanimous decision.

Prefers Local Action

That decision has "left Maine without a wetlands law," says John N. Cole, editor of the Maine *Times,* a weekly newspaper noted for its concern with conservation issues. But he adds: "I'm not a big believer in the legislative route anyway, because when the legislature does something, most people think the problem is solved."

Mr. Cole says he prefers community action in the form of local laws, and he suggests that conservationists trying to get such laws enacted concentrate on more than just the preservation of wetlands. "What you have to do is find economic alternatives," he says.

A case in point, he says, is a widely publicized controversy over a proposed oil refinery at Machiasport, Maine. Machiasport, situated near the northeast tip of Maine, has the only port on the U.S. East Coast deep enough to accommodate oil supertankers. When an oil company wanted to build a refinery there, conservationists blocked the move on the ground that an oil spill would severely damage the estuary.

The people of Machiasport, like many others in Maine, suffer from chronic unemployment. For the most part, they favored the refinery plan.

"The people of Machiasport didn't vote for oil," Mr. Cole says. "They voted for work. The conservation groups really failed there. They were out there throwing rocks at the oil man, but they didn't provide economic alternatives."

The Price Goes Up

The immediate commercial impact of draining and filling wetlands is evident here in Wells. William Abbott, the Wells harbor master, estimates that two small lots on the harbor, recently advertised for a total of $45,000, would have sold together for around $2,000 before the harbor was built.

But even in economic terms Wells is paying heavily for whatever benefits it's getting from its harbor project. For one thing, unforeseen problems in construction have caused the cost to balloon. "Before that project started, they said it would cost $1 million," says Robert L. Dow, research director for Maine's Department of Sea and Shore Fisheries. "Now it's past $2 million."

Moreover, another expensive problem has arisen. An estimated fifty thousand cubic yards of sand have swept off beaches adjacent to the Wells harbor and settled on its bottom since 1967, when the marina was completed. The results are twofold: The area's beaches are shrinking and the sand will probably have to be redredged out of the harbor every three years.

Noting that the town currently gets combined income of only about $6,000 yearly from the restaurant and the marina, Mr. Dow questions the economic wisdom of the whole project. "Dredging will cost $30,000 to $40,000 every three years," he says. "In addition, they've lost $30,000 a year in clams. Finally, Abbott told me the marina would be operational only 40 per cent of the year. I don't understand the economics."

Building Plenty of People

Harbor master Abbott, on the other hand, contends that the demands of a growing population will eventually make the harbor complex pay off. "They aren't building any more land," he says, "but they're building plenty of people."

Mr. Abbott says he has trouble understanding the reasoning of those who complain that wetlands reclamation disrupts wildlife.

"We're all interested in wildlife, but is wildlife going to take over man or is man going to take over wildlife?" he asks. "There was an oil spill in the Gulf of Mexico that killed millions of birds. That's a good thing. Those birds were polluting the Gulf of Mexico. . . . I'll tell you something about polluting water," he continues. "The excrement of twenty-five ducks has the potency of a family of six people. The Federal Government is raising ducks and geese to pollute man."

The man-versus-wildlife argument upsets many ecologists. "People think we're looking at birds and flowers," says a spokesman for the National Audubon Society. "But we're for people. Marshes are a functional necessity. They hold the water line and anchor the coast. Inland marshes even out the water flow and can hold up to sixteen times their own weight in water, which helps control flooding."

Buying Up Wetlands

For conservationists trying to preserve wetlands, one of the most effective—though expensive—methods has been simply to buy them up. Wetlands in many areas have been purchased by private groups, notably the Washington-based Nature Conservancy and the Audubon Society, or by state and Federal agencies.

The Nature Conservancy is the most active private agency in this field, often buying up threatened land and then reselling it to government agencies, which frequently require much more time to raise the money.

Occasionally, however, even ready cash can't forestall developers. The Nature Conservancy was thwarted . . . when the owner of a twelve-thousand-acre island lying at the mouth of the Cape Fear River in North Carolina sold it for $5.5 million to developers who plan to turn it into a resort complex.

The island includes nine thousand acres of salt marsh in its natural state and is a bird and fish habitat.

The Nature Conservancy had offered to meet the selling price of the island and then resell it to the state, but its offer was rejected.

There's still a chance that development can be halted, however; Governor Robert W. Scott of North Carolina has expressed disappointment over the sale and hinted that state approval may be withheld for dredging required to build a bridge connecting the island with the mainland.

SAVING THE SCENERY [5]

Thorn Creek Forest just south of densely populated Cook County, Illinois, is a rare reminder of how many parts of mid-America looked when Abe Lincoln was a boy. Century-old oaks and hickories shade the steep hillsides above the creek. Deer, raccoon and the great horned owl are among some 150 wildlife species found in its eight hundred acres.

The forest also happens to be a choice piece of real estate located directly in the path of Chicago suburbia fast advancing from the north. Most of its area, in fact, is now in the hands of Park Forest South Developers Inc., a Chicago company that proposes to make the woodland the centerpiece of a self-contained "new town" to be developed with Federal help.

Preservationists have organized to keep the forest intact. But the Department of Housing and Urban Development [HUD] has given its tentative approval to housing construction in and around 260 of the woodland acres.

Thus, another struggle to save a scenic tract from the bulldozers is under way. But with one important difference. This time the conservation forces have two new weapons that could alter the outcome: The National Environmental

[5] From "New Federal Programs May Strengthen Effort to Guard Environment," by Burt Schore, staff reporter. *Wall Street Journal.* p 1+. O. 27, '70. Reprinted by permission.

Policy Act [NEPA], in effect since January 1 [1970], and the President's three-member Council on Environmental Quality [CEQ], which the act created.

Trying to Sway HUD

NEPA, as the law is called for short, requires Federal agencies to make detailed reports on any of their activities "significantly affecting the quality of the human environment." To the Council it assigns sweeping oversight authority as well as the primary role in developing new policies to protect the environment.

A prime hope of the Thorn Creek defenders is that HUD administrators will come around to their viewpoint by the time their final report on the proposal to aid the new town is filed. Currently, department officials maintain they have already struck a compromise by rejecting an initial development plan that threatened to chew up considerably more woodland acres than the present proposal. But at the urging of the proforest forces, the environmental council, headed by Russell Train, who is President Nixon's top environment adviser, is questioning HUD's apparent willingness to sacrifice choice parts of the forest.

Largely due to the conservationists' efforts, a committee representing all parties with a stake in Thorn Creek Forest has been formed by the Northeastern Illinois Planning Commission to reexamine plans for the woodland. Still to be heard from in Washington are such nature-minded agencies as the National Park Service and the Forest Service. One possible result: A further compromise requiring that the new town developer switch housing sites to tracts within the forest containing fewer choice trees.

"We're trying to use the council as an ombudsman," says Rutherford Platt, a Chicago attorney representing the Open Lands Project, one of the forest preservation groups. "HUD would like to smooth over our objections. But the Council has a unique position under the law to bring them out into the open."

Concerned Bureaucrats

Mr. Platt's appreciation of the Council's role is shared by other environment activists, many of them within the Federal bureaucracy itself. "No one can tell us now that we are acting without some basis in law," says one Transportation Department man whose job is to curtail neighborhood and scenic damage by highways and airports.

NEPA enthusiasts already can point to several instances where Government policy on highway aid, river damming and other activities subsidized or licensed by the Federal Government apparently is shifting "to create and maintain conditions under which man and nature can exist in productive harmony," as the act prescribes.

Thus the Army Corps of Engineers, after prodding by the environmental council, has begun to study alternative ways to finish the controversial Cross Florida Barge Canal. The objective: To leave more miles of the unspoiled Oklawaha River free of dams and other construction. Even though the project is about a third completed, there's still time to scrap one of the two major reservoirs planned, corps officials say. . . .

Cases Pending

So far NEPA's clearest and most unanticipated impact has come through its use in suits brought by private environment groups. In most of these cases, ironically, Government agencies and their Nixon-appointed chieftains have been the principal targets.

One action, seeking to block construction of an interstate highway that would knife through the Boston suburb of Somerville, Massachusetts, even names Chairman Train as a defendant. But such legal moves are privately welcomed as support for the Council's own efforts by Mr. Train and his colleagues, Pulitzer prize-winning newspaperman Robert Cahn, who is on leave from *The Christian Science Monitor,* and geophysicist Gordon MacDonald, former vice chancellor of the University of California at Santa Barbara.

As of August 1 [1970], NEPA had been cited in 18 Federal court cases, 16 of them against the Government, a Council staff study shows. Most of these cases are still pending, but one lawsuit resulted in an injunction last spring barring [former] Interior Secretary Walter Hickel from granting a Federal right-of-way for an Alaska road from the Yukon River to the North Slope. [See "Developing Alaskan Lands," in Section III, above.—Ed.] The Wilderness Society and other plaintiffs argued in part that the Interior Department had failed to make the required environmental impact statement for the trans-Alaska oil pipeline, whose construction depends on completion of the road. . . .

There is evidence, however, that NEPA guidelines pushed by the Council are beginning to affect decisions within agencies that have long been accused of insensitivity to environmental concerns.

The Atomic Energy Commission now requires applicants to supply an environmental impact statement prior to public hearing on licenses for nuclear power reactors. One of the first such reports, from Connecticut Light & Power Company and other New England utilities seeking approval for a second nuclear unit at their Millstone Point plant near Waterford, Connecticut, went to twenty-five state and Federal departments for comment this summer.

The procedure gave HUD officials the chance to express concern about the effect of the unit's high-voltage transmission lines on scenic areas or urban planning. Similarly, Interior Department men wanted to know if the lines might conflict with a Connecticut Valley parkland corridor it now has under study. The utility responded that it was considering both matters in its planning. The license probably wouldn't be held up on power-line questions, "but the procedure certainly puts a public spotlight on the applicant to live up to what he said he was going to do," comments an AEC staff man.

By citing NEPA, Transportation Department environment men seem to have stalled—and perhaps blocked permanently—a bridge-expressway project that threatened to flood disruptive traffic into the quiet narrow streets of old Charleston, South Carolina, a historic community with some 425 restored residences.

The project, designed to provide a second direct link between Charleston and suburban James Island across the Ashley River, has had powerful backing from the Charleston Chamber of Commerce, city and county officials and the state highway department. Yet J. D. Braman, who has just retired as assistant transportation secretary for environment, delayed Federal clearance because of the potential threat to historic sites.

Mr. Braman feared he might not be able to hold this position indefinitely. With NEPA guidelines in effect, though, Mr. Braman was able to suggest in a letter to Charleston Mayor J. Palmer Gaillard . . . that the widening of streets in old Charleston for the bridge approach might have an adverse environmental impact and thus violate the new law.

Gebney Howe, Jr., an attorney representing old Charleston opponents of the bridge, sounded a similar theme when he met with local bridge boosters. . . . "For the first time, the other side was on the defensive," Mr. Howe recalls.

One man swayed by Mr. Howe's arguments was Charleston County Council Chairman Richard Seabrook. He is now convinced that NEPA requirements could delay the bridge for three to five years and that it would be wiser to push instead for construction of a freeway that would span the Ashley well north of old Charleston. Mr. Howe believes state highway officials, too, ultimately will adopt that view.

V. TOWARD A NEW PUBLIC LANDS POLICY

EDITOR'S INTRODUCTION

Nearly one third of the United States is owned by the Federal Government, over 700 million acres. Over 300 million public land acres exist in Alaska alone; 187 million acres are in national forest lands; 25 million acres are in national parks; the remaining acres are in coastal areas and the like.

It is these lands, their management, use, and possible disposal which are now up for review since a congressional commission reported on policies for these lands in June 1970. As a result it is expected that within the next several years the President and Congress will consider new legislation governing such lands.

The congressional commission referred to was the Public Land Law Review Commission and its voluminous report was entitled *One Third of the Nation's Land*. The report and comments on it are dealt with in this section.

The first selection is a report on the commission and its most salient recommendations; the next excerpts the basic concepts and major recommendations of the report.

There follow three articles appraising the report: one from *Life* magazine; the next from *Not Man Apart*, a magazine of the Friends of Earth organization; then a critique by Michael Frome, the conservation editor of *Field & Stream*. Another article by Mr. Frome suggests alternative goals which should be sought in devising a new public lands policy.

The section closes with excerpts from President Nixon's second environmental message to Congress.

REVISING U.S. LANDS POLICY [1]

A congressional commission, after a massive five-year study recommended ... [on June 23, 1970] that the one third of the nation's land that is federally owned be largely retained by the Government, but that major changes be made in its management and use.

Foremost among the recommended changes were the following:

1. That Congress reassert its constitutional primacy in supervising the public lands and curb the President's power to shift public land from one use to another

2. That public land laws be revised to help such commercial activities as mining, the timber industry and agriculture

3. That land be made available to states for urban expansion

4. That the United States Forest Service be shifted from the Department of Agriculture to the Department of the Interior

A 342-page report containing these and 350 other recommendations was presented to President Nixon and congressional leaders . . . by members of the Public Land Law Review Commission.

First in Two Centuries

The study was the first comprehensive assessment of public land use in the two centuries of the nation's history, during which Congress and other agencies have passed thousands of laws and other enactments dealing piecemeal with the problem.

President Nixon . . . said it "will have without question a very great effect on the policy of this country."

[1] From "Revised Policy for U.S. Lands Asked in Study," by Gladwin Hill, national environmental correspondent. New York *Times*. p 1+. Je. 24, '70 © 1970 by The New York Times Company. Reprinted by permission.

"It is essential to plan now for the use of that land," he continued, "not do it simply on a case-by-case basis, but to have an overall policy."

First reports from conservationists were unfavorable. Portions of the report appear to follow closely policies that have been advocated by the grazing, mining and timber industries and that have been criticized by conservation groups.

The nineteen-member commission was created by Congress in 1964 to chart a future for the 755 million acres of land—out of the nation's total of 2 billion acres—in the hands of Federal agencies.

Half of the Federal land is in Alaska, and nearly all of the rest is in the eleven contiguous Western states, although there are tracts in all the states.

The largest portion—some 450 million acres—is under the Interior Department's Bureau of Land Management, with 187 million more acres under the Forest Service and lesser amounts under Interior's National Park Service and Fish and Wildlife Service.

The commission's recommendations generally call for an array of new legislation to remedy what one official called "the chaotic jungle" of land laws going back to 1792.

The commission's chairman, Representative Wayne N. Aspinall, Colorado Democrat, said he hoped the 1971 Congress would start taking up the proposals and that the implementation process would be completed in "six or eight years."

This prospect was regarded by experienced Washington observers as uncertain. The recommendations of three previous Federal land study commissions in the last century were largely blocked by conflicting interest-groups. And many of the new proposals plainly contain the seeds of high controversy.

Judicious "Multiple Use"

The report, while repeatedly stressing judicious "multiple use" of public lands with solicitude for environmental values, hewed closely to policies advocated by the timber, mining and grazing industries, which conservationists have denounced as overly exploitative.

The initial reaction of one conservation leader—Hamilton Pyles of the Natural Resources Council of America—to the report was that it was an "emasculation" of public land controls. Others suggested that the proposals were so disputable that they would provide a new rallying point for environmentalist opposition.

The report, commission leaders acknowledged, deliberately by-passed the question of long-term conservation of such exhaustible resources as metals, coal and oil—leaving such considerations, a spokesman explained, "to the normal operations of the market place."

"The commission saw no reason for superimposing the views of Government executives on the decisions of business executives," the commission's director, Milton A. Pearl, a specialist in real estate law, told a news conference.

Representative Aspinall, chairman of the House Interior Committee, said the commission's constant concern had been to balance commercial uses of public land with recreational and environmental objectives, and that this accommodation was constructive because "nature is one of the worst offenders, in regard to maintaining environment."

The commission comprised, in addition to Representative Aspinall, six senators, six members of the House of Representatives and six nongovernmental appointees of President Johnson, among them Laurance S. Rockefeller, a leading conservationist.

President Nixon told Mr. Aspinall at the White House that he knew the report contained "a great deal of very helpful information and recommendations, many of which of course will be accepted and, we trust implemented." . . .

Other major recommendations of the commission were the following:

1. Termination of grants of Federal land to states and institution of a system of "in lieu" payments to states that have large amounts of nontaxable Federal land

2. Consolidation of scattered responsibility for land into one Senate committee and one House committee, and on the executive side into one Cabinet department

3. "Phasing out" of the 20,000 existing vacation homes on public lands, and adoption of a policy of "occupancy uses" (settlement) "only where suitable private land is not abundantly available"

4. Revision, but not outright repeal, of the basic 1871 mining law, which some officials and conservationists have called a scandalous device for illegitimate acquisition of public lands

Communities Supported

Another feature of the report was explicit support for communities depending on commercial activities on public lands, such as logging and grazing.

Although public lands provide only 3 per cent of cattle forage nationally, Mr. Pearl said there was no thought of phasing out this seemingly marginal activity because in some localities entire communities depended on it.

"Through its timber management and sales policies," the commission said, "the Federal Government over the years has in effect made a commitment to communities and firms that it will make timber available to assure their continued existence."

The commission's study was essentially a continuation of business that Congress left hanging in 1934, when it passed the Taylor Grazing Act prescribing management policies for public lands "pending their final disposition."

This has been construed as presupposing ultimate Federal relinquishment of public lands, and has generated perennial demands for transfer of land to states and private parties.

A Contrary Conclusion

The commission's conclusion, Mr. Pearl said, was that "the bulk" of public lands should be kept in Federal ownership—although that term did not appear in the report and the recommendations contained myriad ways in which tracts of public land could end up in other hands.

The report contained eighteen broad policy "concepts," 137 numbered recommendations, and some 250 less formally stated ones.

It was described as representing the "consensus" of the nineteen commission members, whose signatures were on it, although not corresponding with their views in every detail.

In one of the footnoted dissents to sections of the report, two members from Nevada, Senator Alan Bible [Democrat] and Representative Walter S. Baring [Democrat], opposed the termination of Federal land grants to states. Federal land makes up 86.4 per cent of Nevada, the highest proportion after Alaska's 95.3 per cent.

The Federal Government "owes" nearly one million acres of land to 15 of the "lower 48" states under historic grant provisions still unconsummated. The commission recommended that these obligations be settled within ten years.

For Alaska, the commission recommended "immediate establishment" of a joint Federal-state natural resources and regional planning commission to expedite the transfer to the state of the 104 million acres granted to it with statehood but delayed until Congress acts on the land claims of Alaskan natives—Eskimos, Indians and Aleuts.

The commission said "Congress has largely delegated to the executive branch its plenary constitutional authority over the rental, management and disposition of public lands" and urged that Congress reassert this authority, "immediately review" existing executive decisions regarding land disposal, and delineate explicit ground-rules for presidential latitude.

Recommendations on Resources

"Mineral exploration and development should have a preference over some or all other uses in much of our public lands," the commission said. "We recognize that [it] will in most cases have an impact on the environment or be incompatible with some other uses."

The panel recommended that successful prospectors on public lands be given title only to specified subsurface minerals rather than surface land (now obtainable for no more than $5 an acre), but should be able to buy surface acreage at "the market value."

The report advocated private development of oil shale lands in the West, a major reserve that has been frozen because of Federal uncertainty about viable policies.

Similarly, the commission proposed exploitation of the vast outer continental shelf oil reserves under "flexible methods of pricing" in place of the present bonus bid-fixed royalty system.

In regard to timber, much of which comes from national forests, the report was characterized by some observers as reflecting the philosophy if not the details of the proposed industry-sponsored National Timber Supply Act, which conservationists have denounced as sanctioning a "raid" on forest resources.

On up to one fourth of national forest land, the commission said, commercial timber production should be formally classified as "the dominant use," while "those lands having a unique potential for other uses should not be included in timber production units."

The commission favored replacement of the century-old and virtually inoperative Homestead Act and related laws with "statutory authority for the sale of public lands . . . for agricultural purposes . . . at market value in response to normal market demand" with "no artificial and obsolete restraints such as acreage limitations on individual holdings, residency requirements and the exclusion of corporations as applicants."

Regarding the problem of expanding population, the commission recommended making some public land available for a prototype "new city" to explore policy.

The commission held 37 sessions, 10 of them regional public meetings, between July 1965, and . . . April [1970], and heard nine hundred witnesses. Its forty special studies, made by staff members and contractors, make a stack of volumes a foot high and six-feet long. The commission spent $7.104 million—$286,000 less than its budget.

PUBLIC LAND LAW REVIEW COMMISSION RECOMMENDATIONS ON PUBLIC LAND USE [2]

Feeling the pressures of an enlarging population, burgeoning growth, and expanding demand for land and natural resources, the American people today have an almost desperate need to determine the best purposes to which their public lands and the wealth and opportunities of those lands should be dedicated. . . .

For reasons that we will detail, we urge reversal of the policy that the United States should dispose of the so-called unappropriated public domain lands. But we also reject the idea that merely because these lands are owned by the Federal Government, they should all remain forever in Federal ownership. . . .

Future disposal should be of only those lands that will achieve maximum benefit for the general public in non-Federal ownership, while retaining in Federal ownership those whose values must be preserved so that they may be used and enjoyed by all Americans.

While there may be some modest disposals, we conclude that at this time most public lands would not serve the maximum public interest in private ownership. We support the

    [2] From a report to the President and the Congress. United States. Public Land Law Review Commission. *One Third of the Nation's Land*. Supt. of Docs. Washington, D.C. 20402. '70. p 1-16.

concepts embodied in the establishment and maintenance of the national forests, the National Park System, the National Wildlife Refuge System, and the parallel or subsidiary programs involving the Wilderness Preservation System, the National Riverways and Scenic Rivers System, national trails, and national recreation areas. . . .

Our studies have also led us to the [conclusion] that the Congress has largely delegated to the executive branch its plenary constitutional authority over the retention, management, and disposition of public land. . . .

We, therefore, recommend that: Congress should establish national policy in all public land laws by prescribing the controlling standards, guidelines, and criteria for the exercise of authority delegated to executive agencies. . . .

We [also] recommend that: Congress assert its constitutional authority by enacting legislation reserving unto itself exclusive authority to withdraw or otherwise set aside public lands for specified limited-purpose uses and delineating specific delegation of authority to the executive as to the types of withdrawals and set asides that may be effected without legislative action. . . .

Public land management agencies should be required by statute to promulgate comprehensive rules and regulations after full consideration of all points of view, including protests, with provisions for a simplified administrative appeals procedure in a manner that will restore public confidence in the impartiality and fairness of administrative decisions. Judicial review should generally be available. . . .

For "Dominant Use"

Statutory goals and objectives should be established as guidelines for land use planning under the general principle that within a specific unit, consideration should be given to all possible uses and the maximum number of compatible uses permitted. This should be subject to the qualification that where a unit, within an area managed for many uses, can contribute maximum benefit through one particular use, that use should be recognized as the dominant use, and the land should be managed to avoid interference with fulfillment of such dominant use. . . .

Federal statutory guidelines should be established to assure that Federal public lands are managed in a manner that not only will not endanger the quality of the environment, but will, where feasible, enhance the quality of the environment, both on and off public lands, and that Federal control of the lands should never be used as a shield to permit lower standards than those required by the laws of the state in which the lands are located. The Federal licensing power should be used, under statutory guidelines, to assure these results. . . .

Statutory guideliness [should] be established providing generally that the United States receive full value for the use of the public lands and their resources retained in Federal ownership, except that monetary payment need not represent full value, or so-called market value, in instances where there is no consumptive use of the land or its resources. . . .

Statutory provisions [should] be made to assure that when public lands or their resources are made available for use, firm tenure and security of investment be provided so that if the use must be interrupted because of a Federal Government need before the end of the lease, permit, or other contractual arrangement, the user will be equitably compensated for the resulting losses. . . .

The United States [should] make payments in lieu of taxes for the burdens imposed upon state and local governments by reason of the Federal ownership of public lands without regard to the revenues generated therefrom. Such payments should not represent full tax equivalency and the state and local tax effort should be a factor in determining the exact amount to be paid. . . .

Statutory authority [should] be provided for the sale at full value of public domain lands required for certain mining activities or where suitable only for dryland farming, grazing of domestic livestock, or residential, commercial, or industrial uses, where such sale is in the public interest and important public values will not thereby be lost. . . .

Legislation [should] be enacted to provide a framework within which large units of land may be made available for the expansion of existing communities or the development of new cities. . . .

Statutory authority [should] be granted for the limited disposition of lands administered by the Forest Service where such lands are needed to meet a non-Federal but public purpose, or where disposition would result in the lands being placed in a higher use than if continued in Federal ownership.

The administration of some programs, such as recreation, can be accomplished just as well, if not better, by state and local government units; in other instances, Federal public lands are required for construction of schools and other buildings that provide state or local government services.

We find that it is in the best interest of all concerned to encourage state and local governments to assume complete responsibility for the maximum number of programs that those levels of government can and will administer and to acquire title to the required land in order to permit the proper level of investment to be made.

We, therefore, recommend that: legislation be enacted to provide flexible mechanisms, including transfer of title at less than full value, to make any federally owned lands available to state and local governments when not required for a Federal purpose if the lands will be utilized for a public purpose. . . .

We find that the division of responsibility for the development of policy and the administration of public lands among congressional committees and several Federal departments and agencies has led to differences, contradictions, and duplications in policies and programs. Not only have these factors been administratively burdensome, but they have also been the source of confusion to citizens dealing with the Government.

We, therefore, recommend that: responsibility for public land policy and programs within the Federal Government in both the legislative and executive branches should be consolidated to the maximum practicable extent in order to eliminate, or at least reduce, differences in policies concerning the administration of similar public land programs. . . .

In making public land decisions, the Federal Government should take into consideration the interests of the national public, the regional public, the Federal Government as the sovereign, the Federal proprietor, the users of public lands and resources, and the state and local governmental entities within which the lands are located in order to assure, to the extent possible, that the maximum benefit for the general public is achieved. . . .

Major Recommendations

The Environment: Environmental quality should be recognized by law as an important objective of public land management, and public land policy should be designed to enhance and maintain a high quality environment both on and off the public lands. . . .

Federal land administering agencies should be authorized to protect the public land environment by (1) imposing protective covenants in disposals of public lands; and (2) acquiring easements on non-Federal lands adjacent to public lands.

Those who use the public lands and resources should, in each instance be required by statute to conduct their activities in a manner that avoids or minimizes adverse environmental impacts, and should be responsible for restoring areas to an acceptable standard where their use has an adverse impact on the environment.

Public land areas in need of environmental rehabilitation should be inventoried and the Federal Government should undertake such rehabilitation. Funds should be appropriated as soon as practical for environmental management and rehabilitation research.

Congress should provide for the creation and preservation of a natural area system for scientific and educational purposes.

Timber Resources: There should be a statutory requirement that those public lands that are highly productive for timber be classified for commercial timber production as the dominant use, consistent with the Commission's concept of how multiple use should be applied in practice.

Federal programs on timber production units should be financed by appropriations from a revolving fund made up of receipts from timber sales on these units. . . .

Timber production should not be used as a justification for acquisition or disposition of Federal public lands.

Controls to assure that timber harvesting is conducted so as to minimize adverse impacts on the environment on and off the public lands must be imposed.

Range Resources: Public land forage policies should be flexible, designed to attain maximum economic efficiency in the production and use of forage from the public land, and to support regional economic growth. . . .

Public lands, including those in national forests and land utilization projects, should be reviewed and those chiefly valuable for the grazing of domestic livestock identified. Some such public lands should, when important public values will not be lost, be offered for sale at market value with grazing permittees given a preference to buy them. Domestic livestock grazing should be declared as the dominant use on retained lands where appropriate. . . .

Mineral Resources: Congress should continue to exclude some classes of public lands from future mineral development.

Existing Federal systems for exploration, development, and production of mineral resources on the public lands should be modified. . . .

Competitive sale of exploration permits or leases should be held whenever competitive interest can reasonably be expected. . . .

Legislation should be enacted which would authorize legal actions by the Government to acquire outstanding claims or interests in public land oil shale subject to judicial determination of value.

Some oil shale public lands should be made available now for experimental commercial development by private industry with the cooperation of the Federal Government in some aspects of the development. . . .

In future disposals of public lands for nonmineral purposes, all mineral interests known to be of value should be reserved with exploration and development discretionary in the Federal Government and a uniform policy adopted relative to all reserved mineral interests.

Water Resources: Congress should require the public land management agencies to submit a comprehensive report describing: (1) the objectives of current watershed protection and management programs; (2) the actual practices carried on under these programs; and (3) the demonstrated effect of such practices on the program objectives. Based on such information, Congress should establish specific goals for watershed protection and management. . . .

Congress should require federally authorized water development projects on public lands to be planned and managed to give due regard to other values of the public lands.

Fish and Wildlife Resources: Federal officials should be given clear statutory authority for final land use decisions that affect fish and wildlife habitat or populations on the public lands. But they should not take action inconsistent with state harvesting regulations, except upon a finding of overriding national need after adequate notice to, and full consultation with, the states. . . .

Public lands should be reviewed and key fish and wildlife habitat zones identified and formally designated for such dominant use.

A Federal land use fee should be charged for hunting and fishing on all public lands open for such purposes.

The states and the Federal Government should share on an equitable basis in financing fish and wildlife programs on public lands.

State policies which unduly discriminate against nonresident hunters and fishermen in the use of public lands through license fee differentials and various forms of nonfee regulations should be discouraged.

Intensive Agriculture: The homestead laws and the Desert Land Act should be repealed and replaced with statutory authority for the sale of public lands for intensive agriculture when that is the highest and best use of the land.

Public lands should be sold for agricultural purposes at market value in response to normal market demand. Unreserved public domain lands and lands in land utilization projects should be considered for disposal for intensive agriculture purposes.

The states should be given a greater role in the determination of which public lands should be sold for intensive agricultural purposes....

The allocation of public lands to agricultural use should not be burdened by artificial and obsolete restraints such as acreage limitations on individual holdings, farm residency requirements, and the exclusions of corporations as eligible applicants.

The Outer Continental Shelf: Complete authority over all activities on the Outer Continental Shelf should continue to be vested by statute in the Federal Government. ...

Protection of the environment from adverse effects of activities on the Federal Outer Continental Shelf is a matter of national concern and is a responsibility of the Federal Government. The Commission's recommendations concerning improved protection and enhancement of the environment generally require separate recognition in connection with activities on the shelf, and agencies having resource management responsibility on the shelf should be required by statute to review practices periodically and consider recommendations from all interested sources, including the Council on Environmental Quality....

Outdoor Recreation: An immediate effort should be undertaken to identify and protect those unique areas of national significance that exist on the public lands.

Recreation policies and programs on those public lands of less than national significance should be designed to meet needs identified by statewide recreation plans. . . .

The Federal role in assuming responsibility for public accommodations in areas of national significance should be expanded. The Federal Government should, in some instances, finance and construct adequate facilities with operation and maintenance left to concessioners. . . .

Private enterprise should be encouraged to play a greater role in the development and management of intensive recreation use areas on those public lands not designated by statute for concessioner development....

The direct Federal acquisition of land for recreation purposes should be restricted primarily to support the Federal role in acquiring and preserving areas of unique national significance; acquisitions of additions to Federal multiple use lands for recreation purposes should be limited to inholdings only.

The Land and Water Conservation Fund Act should be amended to improve financing of public land outdoor recreation programs....

Occupancy Uses: Congress should consolidate and clarify in a single statute the policies relating to the occupancy purposes for which public lands may be made available.

Where practicable, planning and advanced classification of public lands for specific occupancy uses should be required.

Public land should be allocated to occupancy uses only where equally suitable private land is not abundantly available....

Public lands should not hereafter be made available under lease or permit for private residential and vacation purposes, and such existing uses should be phased out....

A new statutory framework should be enacted to make public lands available for the expansion of existing communities and for the development of new cities and towns....

Tax Immunity: If the national interest dictates that lands should be retained in Federal ownership, it is the obligation of the United States to make certain that the burden of that policy is spread among all the people of the United States and is not borne only by those states and governments in whose area the lands are located.

Therefore, the Federal Government should make payments to compensate state and local governments for the tax immunity of Federal lands.

Payments in lieu of taxes should be made to state governments, but such payments should not attempt to provide full equivalency with payments that would be received if the property was in private ownership. A public benefits discount of at least 10 per cent but not more than 40 per cent should be applied to payments made by the Government in order to give recognition to the intangible benefits that some public lands provide, while, at the same time, recognizing the continuing burdens imposed on state and local governments through the increased use of public lands....

Land Grants to States: No additional grants should be made to any of the fifty states.

Within a relatively brief period, perhaps from three to five years, the Secretary of the Interior, in consultation with the involved states, should be required to classify land as suitable for state indemnity selection, in reasonably compact units, and such classifications should aggregate at least 3 or 4 times the acreage due to each state. In the event the affected states do not agree, within two years thereafter, to satisfy their grants from the lands so classified, the Secretary should be required to report the differences to the Congress. If no resolution, legislative or otherwise, is reached at the end of three years after such report, making a total of ten years of classification, selection, and negotiation, all such grants should be terminated. . . .

The satisfaction of Federal land grants to Alaska should be expedited with the aim of completing selection by 1984 in accordance with the Statehood Act, and selections of land under the Alaska Statehood Act should have priority over any land classification program of the Bureau of Land Management. . . .

Administration: The Forest Service should be merged with the Department of the Interior into a new department of natural resources.

Greater emphasis should be placed on regional administration of public land programs.

The recommended consolidation of public land programs should be accompanied by a consolidation of congressional committee jurisdiction over public land programs into a single committee in each House of Congress.

The President's budget should include a consolidated budget for public land programs that shows the relationship between costs and benefits of each program. . . .

Statutory authority should be provided for public land citizen advisory boards and guidelines for their operation should be established by statute.

THE CONFLICT OVER PUBLIC LANDS [3]

The public lands have always been the arena where Americans fought for their dreams. The dream of wealth, the dream of home, the dreams of peace and escape chase each other across the history of these lands like streaks of light across the western sky. They are now, as they have always

[3] From "This Land Is Our Land," by Donald Jackson, staff writer. *Life*. 70:34-42. Ja. 8, '71. © 1971 by Time Inc. Reprinted by permission.

been, inseparable from our national destiny. What we do with them tells a great deal about what we are, what we care about and what will become of us.

Public lands . . . are the share of the American bounty that has come down to us, and even now that bounty seems extravagantly rich. After a century and a half of carelessness and conflict, the land still retains its capacity to inspire and to console. It is a kind of drawing account for the spirit, and there are many who cannot believe that such an account can be overdrawn. It is the last and hardest lesson; the *idea* of the land is infinite, but the land itself is finite. We may be the first generation of Americans to recognize its limits.

"We abuse the land," the great naturalist Aldo Leopold wrote in 1948, "because we regard it as a commodity belonging to us. When we see land as a community to which we belong, we may begin to use it with love and respect. There is no other way for land to survive the impact of mechanized man."

The problem was serious then, when we had no overall land policy and few alarums. It is even more serious today, paradoxically, because we *do* have a policy. Its outlines were charted by the Public Land Law Review Commission [PLLRC] in a report released . . . [on June 23, 1970]. The commission's report was drawn up by men who believe in the "commodity" approach that Leopold rejects, and consequently it gallops headlong in the wrong direction.

The implications are enormous. Public land includes national forests (187 million acres), national parks (23 million) and what is called the public domain—Federal land not classified for forest, parks or other special purpose. Its 470 million acres are made up of the great roadless bulk of Alaska (350 million) and the high, sage-covered plains of the intermountain West. The public domain represents a theoretical windfall of 2.3 acres for every man, woman and child in America. But much of it is inaccessible, difficult if not impossible to turn to profit, or—increasingly—already occupied. Don't rush out to find your acreage. There is liable to be a cowboy there grazing his cattle, or a mining company in search of Eldorado, or a trailer-borne family looking for a smog-free weekend, or a hunter, a cyclist, a camper. They are busy with their own dreams.

The land may be used for private profit by lumbermen and ranchers, both of whom pay fees for the privilege, and by miners, who don't. Through the years it has been pressed and stretched, folded and trampled. Clear-cutting (cutting down all the trees in a given area) in national forests has left stump-littered moonscapes. Open-pit and strip-mining have gouged craters from mountainsides. Overgrazing of arid land has caused erosion, siltation and floods. Cyclists have dug mountain trails into ditches, mobile campers have overrun national parks, hunters and hikers have sullied the canyons. Most of the remaining open land is either protected by special legislation (such as wilderness) or flawed. The demand for it escalates with the population and with urban discomfort.

The need to protect it, to husband the remaining land and referee the increasingly bitter contests for it is self-evident. The conflicts are both historical and novel: How much woodland should be cut for timber, how much preserved for watershed and wildlife, hunters and campers? Should mining be permitted in a *de facto* wilderness? And how should we compare the relative values, the one economic and the other spiritual? Can hunters, jeep drivers, snowmobile jockeys and cyclists coexist on the public range with cattle and sheep? Should roads penetrate the back country for the mobile majority, or should it remain inviolate for the purist minority? Hard questions, boiling to a head now because of the pressure of numbers on the dwindling land, and raised repeatedly by conservationists feeling their developing political muscle.

The Public Land Law Review Commission was chartered by Congress in 1964. The commission might have laid down guiding principles for the uncertain future, furnished a vision, confronted the waste of our past and established binding priorities, but the report it issued does none of these things. Instead it emphasizes the commodity value of land, it

limits its vision to the year 2000, it avoids guidelines by buck-
ing that responsibility to Congress, and, worst of all, it es-
chews the idea of land as an ecological community. Instead it
sees land as a continuing killing-ground of competing
demands.

But there are too many of us now, with too many and
varying claims on our land, the claims colliding with one
another and with the land itself. The men who represent us
must resolve conflicts involving logging, hunting, camping,
always mindful of the condition of the ground. It is there that
the dilemma comes into focus.

"There were 10,000 elk hunters in here last weekend,"
forest ranger Jim Dolan was saying. "Ran everybody else off.
They tear up the roads and trails, and what's the sport? The
elk are artificially fed and stocked, it's put-and-take just like
the trout in the streams. It's more outright killing than
hunting."

Dolan administers a 220,000-acre district of the Snoqualmie National Forest in the Cascade Mountains of Washington. Douglas fir trees pack the western slopes of the range,
ponderosa pines dominate the crest and the eastern side, in-
terspersed with larch pines, turning yellow-brown . . . in
November, lodge-pole pines and patches of willows. The
forest walls the mountain roads, and behind it clouds bounce
off and drift down the snowy mountain draws like formless
pillows. "We have everything in this district," Dolan said.
"Glaciers on one end and cactus on the other.

"I'm trained as a forester," he said, "and I was always
timber-oriented, I guess. But I'm getting more critical of the
logging. The timber people talk ecology, but I never see them
do much about it. Clear-cutting is the easy way. It's forestry
without imagination. We're moving much more to selective
cutting." . . .

About half the trees in Dolan's district are classed as
commercial timber—suitable for sale. On the fringes of the
district, blocks of privately owned timber land alternate with
public land. "On the private land they sometimes leave their

slash [unusable branches] burning and they log the creek beds. That takes away the animals' escape area.

"We have to have some of these products, I know. People have to live in wood houses. But we also need a buffer."

On the roadside a covey of hunters loaded a dead elk into a pickup. It was snowing lightly, the flakes powdering the branches of the Christmas-tree-sized firs. "I don't think you can legislate the best use of this land," Dolan said. "We have to decide that here, on the ground, knowing about the ground."

A Critique of the Report

The Public Land Law Review Commission was weighted with western congressmen and senators (as are the Interior Committees of both House and Senate) whose constituents have been extracting income from public land for generations. The chairman was Representative Wayne Aspinall [Democrat] of Colorado. "It was Wayne's show," one member said. "He ran it. He got what he wanted."

In some ways their report has a biblical quality—"on one page it says Love Thy Neighbor," a critic commented, "and on the next it's an eye for an eye." There are some love-thy-neighbor recommendations: a general policy of retaining the lands in Federal control rather than selling them off in the easy-come, easy-go style of the nineteenth century; an insistence on public participation in decisions affecting public lands; the suggestion that "environmental quality should be recognized by law as an important objective of public land management" (though not *the* important objective). Still, the report emits the unmistakable smell of commerce from almost every page. "Their philosophy was simple," says conservationist John Dewitt. "It was, 'What's posterity ever done for us?' " Nowhere in the report is there a *sense* of the land, a feeling for its extra-economic values, for the truth of it rather than the facts of it.

The mining law of 1872, which permits mining companies to claim public land and get title to it, even in national forests, is allowed to stand. Mining is, in fact, deemed to have a "preference over some or all other uses on much of our public lands." Forest land "highly productive for timber" is to be "classified for commercial timber production as the dominant use" (this would affect 30 per cent or more of the national forests) and "managed primarily . . . so as to maximize net returns to the Federal treasury." Rather than the careful limits on livestock grazing now enforced by the Bureau of Land Management (which manages the public domain), "no limits would be placed on the number of animals to be grazed." The language of the report gives it away. The word "use" appears thirty-one times in the first three pages; Leopold's "respect" is absent. It is "management" and not stewardship, "resource" and not amenity, "feasible" and not desirable, quantity and not quality.

The report's recommendations are merely that, and not law. Yet the report weighs authoritatively on our future, lugging with it an investment of $7 million and five years. And the seventy-four-year-old Representative Aspinall, as chairman of the House Interior Committee, controls the flow of legislation affecting public lands.

The report suggests that much of the decision-making power currently held by executive agencies be shifted to Congress. This comes at a time when the agencies, particularly the Forest Service and Bureau of Land Management, are developing more environmental responsibility and when "multiple use" (as opposed to dominant use) has taken hold as an operating principle. Forest Service Director Edward Cliff, whose agency still operates too often on the premise that the purpose of trees is to make boards, mirrored the change recently when he confessed his programs were "out of balance to meet public needs for the environmental 1970s. . . . Our direction must be and is being changed." The change is visible in the field. . . .

Finding the "Best Use" of Public Land

In plotting the direction of public land policy, Representative Paul McCloskey of California said recently, "the his-

tory of the United States gives us pause." Public land history
is a saga of blitzkrieg peppered with fraud. Land speculators
abused the homestead laws, gold miners shredded the Sierras,
fast-buck lumbermen chewed up the pine forests of the North
Woods. "Let us develop the resources of our land," were the
words of Daniel Webster, who made a few dollars himself on
public land—and generations of exploitation followed.

Down to today. Five years ago an Arizona housing developer planted gold on a piece of land he coveted, filed a claim
under the mining law, dug up the gold, acquired title and set
about building houses. Once he had title, it was his property
to do with as he liked. Another ingenious entrepreneur filed
a mining claim on a national forest in the West and opened a
house of lively repute. The local sheriff declined to prosecute,
so the U.S. Attorney charged the operator with violating the
mining law and had the establishment closed.

The PLLRC report stressed "maximum economic efficiency." "And that," says Hamilton Pyles of the Natural Resources Council, "is what got us into the mess we're in. It's
more efficient—cheaper—to strip-mine, to dump waste into a
river, to clear-cut."

"We need a conservation version of this report," says
Boyd Norton of the Wilderness Society, "the master plan this
commission didn't produce. All we can do is fight a defensive
action." Curiously, both the conservationists and the report's
authors are on the political defensive, the conservationists because of the weight and momentum of the report, the commission because of the growing political clout of the ecological forces.

Finding the "best use" of public land is a many-layered
dilemma without simple answers. Retaining the land in Federal control does not guarantee wise decisions. Circumscrib-
ing private use confronts cherished tenets of the American
creed—individual liberty, private property. The demand for
the land's yield—for minerals, lumber and beef as well as
recreation space—will continue to increase. Protecting the

environment requires hard political, economic and even cultural decisions.

Norton and other conservationists, recognizing the critical relation of land to the overall problem, believe that something akin to an "environmental NASA" is necessary. They envision a ten-year program which would marshal scientific and technological expertise, backed by the kind of political and financial support that insured the success of the American space effort. The superagency running the program would have the muscle in its field that NASA does now—and that the President's Council on Environmental Quality, in its advisory capacity, does not. Its goal would be to channel American skill and confidence toward conserving the environment without sacrificing social or economic gain. "We should make an enormous commitment of resources and study and money," he says, "to come up with answers: to develop new recycling techniques, to find alternate means of energy, perhaps solar power, to relate cities to ecology and make them more livable." "What we're talking about," says his colleague Harry Crandell, "is just this: What makes a good day for a human being?" And how many do we have left?

A BLUEPRINT FOR CORPORATE TAKEOVER [4]

Now we have the PLLRC [Public Land Law Review Commission] report after five years of work and the expenditure of $7 million. I have this report titled *One Third of the Nation's Land*. It should be titled "A Blueprint for Corporate Takeover of 724.4 Million Acres of Land Which Now Belongs to All the People of the United States." The plan is to turn over public lands to lumber, mining, and oil interests, to the big stockmen and the big land barons. What they don't want will be turned over to states, counties, and cities, which

[4] From "The Public Land Law Review Commission Report," by Angus McDonald, former research director of the National Farmers Union. *Not Man Apart.* 1:18-19. Ja. '71. Reprinted from *Not Man Apart,* Vol. 1, No. 2, Jan. 1971. Copyright © by Friends of the Earth.

are largely controlled by real estate interests. And whatever these interests don't want will be turned over to land speculators, who will build new cities and towns and extend urban sprawl. If anything is left after this division of the spoils, it may be reserved for conservationists, fishermen, and wildlifers.

Land Grab

This is the idea I get, at least, after reading the 342-page PLLRC report. Because I have known Wayne Aspinall for a good many years, I didn't expect much. But I never expected this. This is the biggest land-grab proposal in history.

The PLLRC report calls for "a policy of large-scale disposal of public lands towards the end that future disposals may be restricted and lands held in Federal ownership where values must be preserved so they may be used and enjoyed by all Americans." What the report writers mean by this contradictory sentence is that all Americans can enjoy whatever is left after the special interests get through.

This is quite apparent as you get to the heart of the report. After discussing in detail how timber, minerals, and rangeland should be handled, the authors lamely add that we must be sure to give *some* consideration to the environment. They are aware that devastation will surely result, but they plan for you and me to pay for the damage. Costs of restoring the environment are to be charged to the taxpayers. If any of the stockmen or lumber and mining companies make an effort to undo the damage, they are to be paid for it or have it subtracted from the fees they pay. Stockmen now pay only a few cents a head for grazing; mining companies pay $2.50 to $5.00 an acre, and lumber companies, so far as I know, pay only the nominal value of the timber they cut. The authors suggest that in some cases, it may be impossible to restore the landscape. This is one of the honest statements in the report.

The commission's report is particularly bad in regard to timber cutting. It suggests a crash program to get rid of old trees. It indicates that all commercially valuable timber is to be sacrificed. The authors deprecate past practices of the

Forest Service (which, in many instances, has been negligent in protecting forests from the ravages of lumbermen). Their complaint is that the USFS hasn't been negligent enough.

The report is also particularly bad in regard to grazing. Big cattlemen, as the authors of the report must have known, think they own the grass on public lands. A Bureau of Land Management study proved that 5 per cent of the grazing permittees controlled more than 52 per cent of the land grazed; 74 per cent of all BLM forage was allotted to only 11.4 per cent of the permittees.

Commission Report on Grazing Lands

Under present practices, those holding original permits are given preference in the renewal of permits. Regardless of the deterioration of the range, the commission report recommends that:

> Private grazing on public land should be pursuant to a permit that is issued for a fixed statutory term and spells out in detail the conditions and obligations of both the Federal Government and the permittee, including provisions for compensation for termination prior to the end of the term. . . . Most disturbing to permittees . . . is the fact that permits may be canceled at any time if the land covered passes from the administrative control of the particular agency issuing the permit, as by withdrawal or exchange. . . .

> We recommend, too, that the kind of public purposes for which a grazing permit may be canceled should be identified in the permit. . . . We recommend that permittees should be compensated when permits are canceled to satisfy other public uses. . . .

> Public lands including those in national forests and land utilization projects should be reviewed and those chiefly valuable for the grazing of domestic livestock identified. Some such public lands should, when important values will not be lost, be offered for sale at market value with grazing permittees given a preference to buy them. Domestic livestock grazing should be declared as the dominant use on retained lands where appropriate. . . . Modern land management methods, developed to prevent the recurrence of conditions which existed between 1900 and the thirties, preclude the necessity for the Government to continue to control lands that are primarily valuable for grazing. . . .

Disposal of those lands which are principally valuable for grazing would reduce Federal administrative costs. More importantly it would place the management and use of the forage resource in the hands of those who normally manage productive resources in a free enterprise economy, and thus provide an incentive for the investment needed to make those lands fully productive. In private ownership, economic efficiency would tend to cause the lands to move into the hands of more efficient operators, and thus lower the cost of livestock and improve the health of the industry.

I have quoted at length what the PLLRC said about grazing on the public lands to give the full flavor of its philosophy.

We should be mindful of the fact that grazing on public lands is a privilege, not a right. Livestock owners have for years received a tremendous subsidy—which was mainly restricted to a few large operators. When the Secretaries of Agriculture and Interior decided, after a thorough study, that Federal grazing fees should be raised, there was a great outcry. There was such an outcry, in fact, that [former] Secretary Hickel postponed putting the increase into effect. But many small stockmen were actually in favor of the increase; they were having to pay six or eight times as much to graze their livestock on private or state lands.

Dominant Use

One of the fanciest phrases in the report is *dominant use*. Dominant use means that cattlemen will get the grass, timber companies will get the lumber, mining companies will get the minerals, and the general public will get next to nothing. There is a good deal of long-winded language in the report about pollution, the environment, recreation, and so on. But if you analyze all the semantic tricks, you will come to the conclusion that interest in the environment is an afterthought. The PLLRC seems to be mainly interested in one thing: exploitation. It turns out that the commission is unhappy that the land was ever withdrawn in the first place. It chides Theodore Roosevelt and other Presidents for having the wisdom to withdraw 700 million acres of public domain to save it from the ravages of commercial exploitation.

I appeared before a House committee in 1953 to oppose the Wesley D'Ewart proposal to turn over public grazing land to stockmen. If you don't remember D'Ewart, you may remember another man who favored the proposal; his name is Richard Nixon. I was surprised to learn recently that he, by executive order, put into effect a proposal to accelerate timber cutting on public lands—a proposal that Congress had decisively voted down on February 26th ... [1970].

The PLLRC got around to most every problem that has worried the exploiters for many years. It dusted off the old myth that public lands belong to the states. The United States Constitution and state constitutions provided that these lands belong to the Federal Government and the United States Supreme Court has reaffirmed this several times. It did so in the Ivanhoe decision, the Pelton Dam decision, and the California-Arizona decision. Yet the PLLRC complains that the states should have these lands and waters.

The commission devotes quite a few pages to the Implied Reservation Doctrine. In layman's language, this means that the U.S. Government has a right to use the water on its public lands. This right supersedes any pretended rights under state laws. The vested interests—usually represented by the states— not only insisted that they had a right to the water but were very arrogant about it. They tried to kick the U.S. Government off its own land and prevent it from using its own water. The Supreme Court threw out their contentions. But over the years, the stockmen, miners, and lumber interests have filed claims on public water in thousands of instances and have attempted to have their filing legalized. They contended, in other words, that state laws were paramount and that Congress should enact legislation overriding the Supreme Court. Admitting that discussion of the Implied Reservation Doctrine had become academic, the PLLRC didn't challenge the Supreme Court's rulings. But it maintains that owners of pretended water rights should be compensated for them—that they should be paid for water that they had no right to in the first place! No one has ever tried to calculate what these "rights" would be worth if they were legal. I suspect that the amount would come to many billions of dollars. Paying the water filers for something they didn't own would constitute a gigantic raid on the Treasury.

Corporate Interests

When I appeared before the National Water Commission in November 1969, I talked about a part of reclamation law commonly referred to as the 160-acre limitation. The PLLRC wants this limitation repealed, along with the Homestead Acts. It also favors the repeal of residency requirements for homesteaders and the ban on corporate homesteading. Here again the Public Land Law Review Commission is representing large corporate interests instead of the interests of small farmers and landholders. It wants to make it easy for the Kern County Land Company, which owns and controls several million acres, to do a little homesteading along with railroads, oil companies, and other giant corporations.

Proposals to sell or give away public lands and their resources were terrible years ago, when they were made by Wesley D'Ewart and then-Congressman Richard Nixon. But they are worse now, far worse. Because then, we didn't have much of an environmental problem, or pollution problem, or big-city crowding problem. And we didn't have a population problem. The solution to problems of congested cities is population control and the return of people to smaller cities and towns that still have some space and air left. The solution is *not* a bankruptcy sale of the whole nation's western lands and resources to greedy absentee landlords and corporate giants who, in the past, have just about ruined this country.

A CRITIQUE OF THE PUBLIC LAND LAW REPORT [5]

The dominant-use principle of land management simply will not work. It cannot work because it is ecologically unsound. It has not worked, as one may observe from the severe deterioration of millions of acres where this principle has been in force for generations. It is a wholly negative idea, intended to spur and sanction the exploitation of natural resources. It is frightening.

Yet the American people are now being told this is the way their public lands should be run. It seems absurd, almost unbelievable, that such a proposal should come at this hour of crisis, when the future of the nation, perhaps of all mankind, hangs in the balance of ecological respect. Yet here we have a body of nineteen men, including thirteen members of Congress, a former forestry dean, and a professor of law, seriously and soberly suggesting that we move backward, instead of forward, into the future.

What's more, the people paid over $7 million out of the Federal treasury to sustain the body of nineteen, together with assorted staff, consultants, and contractors, in deliberations that produced this lurid concoction. I refer, if you haven't guessed, to the report of the Public Land Law Review Commission, the PLLRC, or, as they say in the Washington jargon, "Plerk." However you cut it, the substance is that vast portions of public lands be set aside solely for private and industrial use. It would be utterly tragic for the environment and for sportsmen if much of the report is ever approved by Congress.

The motivation behind the study is plainly not scientific. It is not ethical. It is economic and political, reflecting the peculiar biases of Representative Wayne N. Aspinall [Democrat, Colorado], the ringmaster of the circus, and the pressures of special economic interests of the West. . . .

[5] From "A Powerful Congressional Group Moves Backward into the Future," by Michael Frome, conservation editor. *Field & Stream*. 75:38+. O. '70. Reprinted by permission.

Strong points? Yes, even the tough but fair-minded critic will recognize the report contains a number of significantly constructive proposals. These must not be lost, but rather be incorporated into a program of political action. . . . It is encouraging, for example, to read proposals that greater emphasis be placed on fish and wildlife values in public lands; that game and nongame species be given equal attention; that agencies institute positive programs to control hunter and fishermen density; and that nefarious predator control programs of the Interior Department be eliminated or reduced.

The report further recommends that Federal policy be designed to enhance and maintain a quality environment both on and off public lands. This concept is valid and urgent. After all, what value are national parks, forests, and wildlife refuges in the total thrust if they are encircled by adverse ecological influences? The PLLRC has the right approach when it says that public land agencies should grant privileges to commercial users based on adherence to the highest environmental standards in their own operations. This means that public timber would be denied to companies spreading pesticides, causing air and water pollution, and wasting natural resources.

The challenge before the people is to ferret out such useful and desirable features of the Plerk report and build on them. This cannot easily be done, unfortunately, because the report is composed of many disconnected and disjointed sections, lacking unity and cohesion. For every excellent idea, there is one that is equally awful, as for example perpetuation of the 1872 Mining Law and the promotion of strip-mining in the land. . . .

The Dominant Use Principle

Dominant use is the underlying principle, which we find proposed for the national forests and the areas administered by the Bureau of Land Management. Although these areas belong to all the people, the Commission's design would divide them into zones to serve specific functions, such as recreation, grazing, mining, timber, to the total or partial exclusion of all other uses.

"The agencies in fact use primary-use designation as a matter of course now," the Aspinall report declares in justification of its proposal. True enough, as a result of law, the mining interests exercise first call over the public lands, without consideration of other resources. As a result of precedent and influence, grazing alone has prevailed over millions of acres and utterly destroyed them for other purposes.

The dominant-use principle as concocted by Plerk is used to promote the same goal as the National Timber Supply Bill, which a wrathful outcry of public protest has thus far prevented from being considered in Congress. It strikes me as another way to promote surrender of public woodlands for private profit. . . .

According to . . . [Representative Aspinall], there should be "dominant-use production units" managed by a separate Federal timber corporation on the basis of receipts from timber sales—an equivalent to the high-yield timber fund of the Timber Supply Bill. This agency would control all the productive forests administered both by the Forest Service and BLM not already set aside as wilderness or as special recreation areas. How much would this cover? Up to one fourth the total area of the national forests and one half the total forest land now in Federal ownership.

Sure, the timber section declares, "The diversity and intensity of use dictates that great care be taken on forest lands to assure that environmental values are not lost through poor forestry practices." But these are just so many words when accompanied by the proposal that Federal timber be managed "primarily on the basis of economic factors so as to maximize net dollar return." The land mechanism cannot be worked to give economic production and environmental protection equal priority.

The dominant-use theory is irreconcilable with genuine multiple use, which dictates that commodity values be balanced with protection of soil, water, wildlife, scenery and, in the case of wood and forage, renewal of the resources. It is lacking in ecological foundation or framework. It fails to recognize the impossibility of managing a biological community by statute or formula. Certainly most forms of wildlife are unable to distinguish between dominant-use production units and other areas of public lands—nor should they be expected to. Think of the wolves, a rich part of our heritage, which might still survive in the wilderness areas of the West were it not for the dominant-use accorded to the grazing industry down through the years. We can only look forward to more of the same if Congress and the people accept the suggestions of the PLLRC report. This is plainly evident on reading that "Mining operations should not be unreasonably impeded by regulations pertaining to wilderness areas."

Dissent on the Committee

The Public Land Law Review Commission was inadequately constituted at best. The Congressional members were chosen only from the Senate and House Interior Committees, eliminating the talents of such others as Senators Philip Hart [Democrat, Michigan], Edmund Muskie [Democrat, Maine], and George Aiken [Republican, Vermont], and Representatives John D. Dingell [Democrat, Michigan] and Henry S. Reuss [Democrat, Wisconsin]. With due deference to the six public members, not one derives from the biological or ecological communities. It is interesting to note that three members, Senator Henry Jackson [Democrat, Washington], Representative John P. Saylor [Republican, Pennsylvania], and Philip H. Hoff, the former Governor of Vermont, absented themselves from the official photograph appearing in the report, and by so doing expressed their dissent. So I take it.

Public lands are mostly in the West, but they belong to all Americans, everywhere. Every member of Congress must be encouraged to feel that he is part of the action. Eastern sportsmen and other conservationists now have their opportunity to be heard. Sometimes I think the anwer to it all is the magical appearance of a new Theodore Roosevelt, Gifford

Pinchot, or George Bird Grinnell, but the real need is not for a single messiah, but for a thousand spread across the grass roots. Here is the chance to be heard.

NEW GOALS FOR PUBLIC LAND POLICY [6]

I think it would be most useful to define fitting goals in public land policy, as a basis for measuring the PLLRC report and the need for action. [See "Public Land Law Review Commission Recommendations on Public Land Use," in this section above.—Ed.]

First and foremost, all land policy must henceforth be based on the foundation of environmental respect. To insure the prosperity of the nation, the goals must be to provide a continuing supply of clean air, clear water, stable soil, natural beauty, and open space. These must be recognized as the rights of all people sharing a common environment in this generation and generations hence. The only alternative will be the continuing decline in natural resources and ultimate national collapse.

Thus we need to break with the past, when land values were determined in narrow economic terms. The public interest must be superior to the forces of commodity production which have spurred exploitation of the public lands. They have contributed to the growth of the nation . . . , but in a manner that has sometimes been ruthless, anarchic, and destructive. Now we need to shape a new image of responsibility and respect for the total land resource.

From this point of broad national policy we can proceed to the resolution of specific critical issues. The two big ones are as follows:

A New Policy on Mining

1. *A modern system of mineral leasing based on multiple use of public lands must replace the Mining Law of 1872.*

[6] From "Moment of Truth for the Public Lands," by Michael Frome, conservation editor. *Field & Stream.* 75:18+. Jl. '70. Reprinted by permission.

The public cannot settle for less. The American Mining Congress, which fought for years to protect and perpetuate the archaic system, at last has recognized the need for change. "In 1872," as it declared in a statement to the PLLRC, "90 per cent of the land in the eleven western states was unsurveyed and there was no real competing demand for use of the public domain. Today, less than 17 per cent of the land in these states remains unsurveyed, and there are stronger competing demands for use of the public domain."

Yet the old law continues in many ways to serve as a mechanism for the giveaway of national resources. It encourages anyone who may call himself a miner to rove the public estate and to stake a claim on any land not specifically set aside. He is permitted to file notice of his claim in the handiest county court house—without notifying the Federal agency administering the land involved, without even specifying the mineral he has found. By meeting simple requirements and paying a nominal sum, he can receive title to the land as his private property. The system permits uncontrolled exploitation of public lands with irreparable damage to other resources. It has stimulated notorious abuses and land frauds.

In 1920 Congress excepted coal, phosphates, oil and gas, oil shale, and sodium from the 1872 law and made those minerals available only by leasing from the Government. Title to the land, control of the surface and its resources, continues to belong to the United States—as it should in all cases.

Moreover, extraction of minerals must be weighed against the values of other resources. The Wilderness Law of 1964, to be specific, should be amended to eliminate the provision that permits prospecting in the slender remaining vestiges of the original America. In its proper place, mining must be better planned in the future to avoid the devastations of the past. The Government must be assured sufficient authority to prevent pollution, control erosion, provide for reclamation and restoration, and to fit mining into the wise and proper management of renewable resources.

Retaining Ownership

2. *There should be affirmation of the need to retain ownership of Federal lands, which become more precious in the context of modern times.* The 700 million acres need to be retained in order to insure the quality of life by providing for a continuous supply of timber and forage, by protecting the watersheds, and by providing habitat for wildlife, including rare and endangered species. But also, the Federal lands comprise open spaces available to all.

This is especially true of the public domain of the West, the "leftover lands" which nobody wanted in the course of settlement. Now they constitute the last great roving room, a recreational and scientific resource, a sanctuary for man. In such ways they serve the entire country, and especially the communities immediately adjacent to them. They should serve further as models of land use planning.

Old laws need to be updated. The Homestead Act and Desert Land Entry Act have long lost their original meaning and intent. They are utilized now largely by land boomers and speculators and need to be revoked.

Retention, of course, opens other questions of protection and management. Millions upon millions of acres of public domain have gone steadily downhill because they have been restricted to a single use—livestock grazing—without adequate protection. In this area I . . . [favor] the following proposals:

(a) *Bureau of Land Management lands should henceforth be truly managed lands, on the multiple use principle, based upon a new organic act and Congressional mandate.* The Taylor Grazing Act of 1934 authorized the Secretary of the Interior to do certain things "in order to promote the highest use of the public lands pending its final disposal." That was the first step to management, but it dealt almost exclusively with grazing values and lacked a commitment to permanence. Then came the Classification and Multiple Use Act of 1964, which has demonstrated the value and public desire for retention and protection of the land. Beyond a doubt, if Government had been truly progressive, classification would have taken place years ago.

[Former] Secretary of the Interior Walter J. Hickel took positive action in March [1970] by proposing the designation of a 10.5-million-acre National Scenic Area in the Wrangell Mountains in south-central Alaska, . . . a new category of land use under his Department, designed for balanced recreation and commodity production. It represents a step in the right direction, but the real answer is for Congress to authorize and fund the management of what could be called National Resource Areas, units comparable to the national forests and parks, for administration by BLM.

(b) *Fees for grazing on public lands need to be raised from the ridiculously low levels, compared to fair market value, presently enjoyed by a small minority of privileged livestock growers.* The importance of such action has been recognized and recommended by the Bureau of the Budget since Dwight Eisenhower was President. Through political pressure, the livestock lobby has blocked the increase and the assertion of public management of public lands.

Livestock interests have proposed these areas be dispensed to private ownership, or "returned to the states" (though the states never owned them), or that they be given "long term, assured and preferential tenure." Through domination of BLM advisory boards, they have kept administration weak. Grazing is important, but not necessarily the primary use of western public range lands. All "publics" need to be involved in developing a balanced program for restoration of soil, water, and wildlife values, as well as improvement of the livestock forage resource. There needs to be guarantee of public access and an end to the practice of landowners setting up barriers and charging gate fees to hunters to come on the public land.

(c) *The principle of multiple use should be clearly re-affirmed as the fundamental management system governing national forests and BLM areas.* The recent defeat of the National Timber Supply Bill in the House of Representatives demonstrated the desire of the people that uses of public lands not be decided on the basis of the greatest dollar return or the maximum production of a single commodity.

If public lands were managed to secure the greatest dollar return from commodities such as timber or forage, as some have proposed, rather than the best combination of environmental, social, and economic uses, the latter would be the obvious losers. All resources must be regarded as interrelated. In fact, for improved multiple use management of the National Forest System, Congress should provide for accelerated acquisition of private in-holdings.

(d) *Fishermen and hunters should be expected to pay a fair fee for use of national forests and BLM areas, with their funds applied to improvement of facilities.* Appropriated funds for wildlife habitat improvement are terribly inadequate, in many places virtually nonexistent. A new program under which sportsmen pay their way can assure them of better recreation and make their investment worthwhile. This system has worked well in two eastern national forests, where the state imposes a stamp of $1 for habitat improvement.

(e) *New attention should be paid by Congress to management concepts in national parks and national wildlife refuges.* The former should not continually be regarded as playgrounds with space unlimited. The National Park Service should be directed to strive for optimum appreciation and understanding of the natural scene, rather than for maximum numbers of visitors. The time may be at hand in some parks to institute a reservation system and to restrict, or reduce, the space available to trailers and large luxury vehicles. The national wildlife refuges should be carefully reviewed for such uses as farming, grazing, and timber cutting, which seem at variance with restoration of the native wilderness tableau.

(f) *The antiquities resource is in desperate need of care and protection.* Throngs of Americans journey overseas to view and photograph the vestiges of ancient civilizations, while the very things they adore abroad they are inclined to overlook, even to destroy, at home. The Antiquities Act of

1906 was designed to protect ancient Indian ruins from vandalism, but little has been done in recent years to weigh the cultural value of antiquities against other resources. Thus we are squandering the story of Man in America—possibly because it offers no demonstrable immediate economic value.

THE PRESIDENT SPEAKS OUT [7]

The use of our land not only affects the natural environment but shapes the pattern of our daily lives. Unfortunately, the sensible use of our land is often thwarted by the inability of the many competing and overlapping local units of government to control land use decisions which have regional significance.

While most land use decisions will continue to be made at the local level, we must draw upon the basic authority of state government to deal with land use issues which spill over local jurisdictional boundaries. The states are uniquely qualified to effect the institutional reform that is so badly needed, for they are closer to the local problems than is the Federal Government and yet removed enough from local tax and other pressures to represent the broader regional interests of the public. Federal programs which influence major land use decisions can thereby fit into a coherent pattern. In addition, we must begin to restructure economic incentives bearing upon land use to encourage wise and orderly decisions for preservation and development of the land.

I am calling upon the Congress to adopt a national land use policy. In addition, I am proposing other major initiatives on land use to bring "parks to the people," to expand our wilderness system, to restore and preserve historic and older buildings, to provide an orderly system for power plant siting, and to prevent environmental degradation from mining.

[7] "Promoting Environmental Quality in Our Land Use Decisions," excerpts from President Richard M. Nixon's second environmental message to Congress. *Congressional Record*. 117:509-11. F. 8, '71.

A National Land Use Policy

We must reform the institutional framework in which land use decisions are made.

I propose legislation to establish a National Land Use Policy which will encourage the states, in cooperation with local government, to plan for and regulate major developments affecting growth and the use of critical land areas. This should be done by establishing methods for protecting lands of critical environmental concern, methods for controlling large-scale developments, and improving use of lands around key facilities and new communities.

One hundred million dollars in new funds would be authorized to assist the states in this effort—$20 million in each of the next five years—with priority given to the states of the coastal zone. Accordingly, this proposal will replace and expand my proposal submitted to the last Congress for coastal zone management, while still giving priority attention to this area of the country which is especially sensitive to development pressures. Steps will be taken to assure that federally assisted programs are consistent with the approved state land use programs.

Public Lands Management

The Federal public lands comprise approximately one third of the nation's land area. This vast domain contains land with spectacular scenery, mineral and timber resources, major wildlife habitat, ecological significance, and tremendous recreational importance. In a sense, it is the "breathing space" of the nation.

The public lands belong to all Americans. They are part of the heritage and the birthright of every citizen. It is important, therefore, that these lands be managed wisely, that their environmental values be carefully safeguarded, and that we deal with these lands as trustees for the future. They have an important place in national land use considerations. . . .

The largest single block of Federal public land lies in the State of Alaska. Recent major oil discoveries suggest that the state is on the threshold of a major economic development. Such development can bring great benefits both to the state and to the nation. It could also—if unplanned and unguided —despoil the last and greatest American wilderness.

We should act now, in close cooperation with the State of Alaska, to develop a comprehensive land use plan for the Federal lands in Alaska, giving priority to those north of the Yukon River. Such a plan should take account of the needs and aspirations of the native peoples, the importance of balanced economic development, and the special need for maintaining and protecting the unique natural heritage of Alaska. This can be accomplished through a system of parks, wilderness, recreation, and wildlife areas and through wise management of the Federal lands generally. I am asking the Secretary of the Interior to take the lead in this task, calling upon other Federal agencies as appropriate. ...

Preserving Our Legacy

Merely acquiring land for open space and recreation is not enough. We must bring parks to where the people are so that everyone has access to nearby recreational areas. In my budget for 1972, I have proposed a new "Legacy of Parks" program which will help states and local governments provide parks and recreation areas, not just for today's Americans but for tomorrow's as well. Only if we set aside and develop such recreation areas now can we ensure that they will be available for future generations.

As part of this legacy, I have requested a $200 million appropriation to begin a new program for the acquisition and development of additional park lands in urban areas. To be administered by the Department of Housing and Urban Development, this would include provision for facilities such as swimming pools to add to the use and enjoyment of these parks.

Also, I have recommended in my 1972 budget that the appropriation for the Land and Water Conservation Fund be increased to $380 million, permitting the continued acquisition of Federal parks and recreation areas as well as an expanded state grant program. However, because of the way in which these state grant funds were allocated over the past five years, a relatively small percentage has been used for the purchase and development of recreational facilities in and near urban areas. The allocation formula should be changed to ensure that more parks will be developed in and near our urban areas.

I am submitting legislation to reform the state grant program so that Federal grants for the purchase and development of recreation lands bear a closer relationship to the population distribution. I am also proposing amendments to the Internal Revenue Code which should greatly expand the use of charitable land transfers for conservation purposes and thereby enlarge the role of private citizens in preserving the best of America's landscape.

Additional public parks will be created as a result of my program for examining the need for retention of real property owned by the Government. The Property Review Board, which I established last year, is continuing its review of individual properties as well as its evaluation of the Government's overall Federal real property program. Properties identified as suitable for park use and determined to be surplus can be conveyed to states and political subdivisions for park purposes without cost. The state or other political subdivision must prepare an acceptable park use plan and must agree to use the property as a park in perpetuity. More than forty properties with high potential for park use have already been identified.

Five such properties are now available for conversion to public park use. One, Border Field, California, will be developed as a recreation area with the assistance of the Department of the Interior. The other four will be conveyed to states or local units of government as soon as adequate guarantees can be obtained for their proper maintenance and operation. These four are: (1) part of the former Naval Training Devices Center on Long Island Sound, New York; (2) land at a Clinical Research Center in Fort Worth, Texas; (3) about ten miles of sand dunes and beach along the Atlantic Coast and Sandy Hook Bay, a part of Fort Hancock, New Jersey; and (4) a portion of Fort Lawton, Washington, a wooded, hilly area near the heart of Seattle. In addition, efforts are underway to open a significant stretch of Pacific Ocean Beach Front and Coastal Bluffs at Camp Pendleton, California.

Many parcels of Federal real property are currently underutilized because of the budgetary and procedural difficulties that are involved in transferring a Federal operation from the current site to a more suitable location.

I am again proposing legislation to simplify relocation of Federal installations that occupy properties that could better be used for other purposes.

This will allow conversion of many additional Federal real properties to a more beneficial public use. Lands now used for Federal operations but more suited to park and recreational uses will be given priority consideration for relocation procedures. The program will be self-financing and will provide new opportunities for improving the utilization of Federal lands.

Wilderness Areas

While there is clearly a need for greater efforts to provide neighborhood parks and other public recreation areas, there must still be places where nature thrives and man enters only as a visitor. These wilderness areas are an important part of a comprehensive open space system. We must continue to expand our wilderness preservation system, in order to save for all time those magnificent areas of America where nature still predominates. . . .

I will soon be recommending to the Congress a number of specific proposals for a major enlargement of our wilderness preservation system by the addition of a wide spectrum of natural areas spread across the entire continent.

National Parks

While placing much greater emphasis on parks in urban areas and the designation of new wilderness areas, we must continue to expand our national park system. We are currently obligating substantial sums to acquire the privately owned lands in units of the National Park System which have already been authorized by the Congress.

Last year, joint efforts of the administration and the Congress resulted in authorization of ten areas in the National Park System, including such outstanding sites as Voyageurs National Park in Minnesota, Apostle Islands National Lakeshore in Wisconsin, Sleeping Bear Dunes National Lakeshore in Michigan, Gulf Islands National Seashore in Mississippi and Florida, and the Chesapeake and Ohio Canal National Historical Park in the District of Columbia, Maryland and West Virginia.

However, the job of filling out the National Park System is not complete. Other unique areas must still be preserved. Despite all our wealth and scientific knowledge, we cannot recreate these unspoiled areas once they are lost to the onrush of development. I am directing the Secretary of the Interior to review the outstanding opportunities for setting aside nationally significant natural and historic areas, and to develop priorities for their possible addition to the National Park System.

Power-Plant Siting

The power shortage last summer and continuing disputes across the country over the siting of power plants and the routing of transmission lines highlight the need for longer-range planning by the producers of electric power to project their future needs and identify environmental concerns well in advance of construction deadlines. . . . Only through involving the environmental protection agencies early in the planning of future power facilities can we avoid disputes which delay construction timetables. . . .

I propose a power-plant siting law to provide for establishment within each state or region of a single agency with responsibility for assuring that environmental concerns are properly considered in the certification of specific power-plant sites and transmission-line routes.

Under this law, utilities would be required to identify needed power supply facilities ten years prior to construction of the required facilities. They would be required to identify the power-plant sites and general transmission routes under consideration five years before construction and apply for certification for specific sites, facilities, and routes two years in advance of construction. Public hearings at which all interested parties could be heard without delaying construction timetables would be required.

Mined Area Protection

Surface and underground mining have scarred millions of acres of land and have caused environmental damages such as air and water pollution. Burning coal fires, subsidence, acid mine drainage which pollutes our streams and rivers and the destruction of esthetic and recreational values frequently but unnecessarily accompany mining activities. These problems will worsen as the demand for fossil fuels and other raw materials continues to grow, unless such mining is subject to regulation requiring both preventive and restorative measures.

I propose a Mined Area Protection Act to establish Federal requirements and guidelines for state programs to regulate the environmental consequences of surface and underground mining. In any state which does not enact the necessary regulations or enforce them properly, the Federal Government would be authorized to do so.

BIBLIOGRAPHY

An asterisk (*) preceding a reference indicates that the article or a part of it has been reprinted in this book.

BOOKS, PAMPHLETS, AND DOCUMENTS

Banfield, E. C. The unheavenly city: the nature and future of our urban crisis. Little. '70.

Banz, George. Elements of urban form. McGraw. '70.

Boyle, R. H. The Hudson river: a natural and unnatural history. Norton. '69.

Carson, Rachel. The sea around us. rev. ed. Oxford University Press. '61.

Carson, Rachel. Silent Spring. Houghton. '62.

Clawson, Marion. The Federal lands since 1956: recent trends in use and management. Resources for the Future, Inc. 1755 Massachusetts Ave. N.W. Washington, D.C. 20036. '67.

Dansereau, P. M. and Weadcock, V. A. eds. Challenge for survival: land, air and water for man in megalopolis. Columbia University Press. '70.

De Bell, Garrett. The environmental handbook. Ballantine. '70.

Dober, R. P. Environmental design. Van Nostrand-Reinhold. '69.

Douglas, W. O. My wilderness: the Pacific West. Doubleday. '60.

Edwards, Gordon. Land, people and policy. Chandler-Davis. '69.

Ehrlich, P. R. The population bomb. Ballantine. '68.

Ehrlich, P. R. and Ehrlich, A. H. Population resources environment: issues in human ecology. Freeman. '70.

Foss, P. O. ed. Public land policy: proceedings of the 1968 Western Resources Conference. Colorado Associated University Press. '70.

Graham, Frank, Jr. Since Silent Spring. Houghton. '70.
      Review. Environment. 12:30-1. My. '70. Prophet without honor. K. P. Shea.

Grava, Sigurd. Urban planning aspects of water pollution control. Columbia University Press. '69.

Grossman, M. L. and others. Our vanishing wilderness. Grosset. '69.

Helfrich, H. W. Jr. ed. The environmental crisis; man's struggle to live with himself. Yale University Press. '70.

Holland, L. B. ed. Who designs America? Doubleday. '66.

*Jackson, H. M. A view from Capitol hill. (Policy Memorandum no 37: Ecology and Politics in America's Environmental Crisis) Princeton University. Center of International Studies. Corwin Hall. Princeton, N.J. 08540. '70.

Landsberg, H. H. and others. Resources in America's future. Resources for the Future, Inc. 1755 Massachusetts Ave. N.W. Washington, D.C. 20036. '63.

*League of Women Voters of the United States. Local zoning ordinances and housing for lower income families—goals in conflict? (Current Review no 8: Human resources) The League. 1730 M St. N.W. Washington, D.C. 20036. '69.

*Leavitt, Helen. Superhighway—superhoax. Doubleday. '68.
        Condensed version: Reader's Digest. 98:61-5. F. '71. The folly of our superhighway system.

Leinwand, Gerald and Popkin, Gerald. Air and water pollution. (Problems of American Society) Washington Square Press. '69.

Little, C. E. Challenge of the land: open space preservation at the local level. Pergamon. '69.

McClellan, G. S. ed. Protecting our environment. (Reference Shelf. v 42, no 1) Wilson. '70.

McHarg, I. L. Design with nature. Natural History Press. '69.

Marine, Gene. America the raped: the engineering mentality and the devastation of a continent. Simon & Schuster. '69.

Mishan, E. J. Technology and growth: the price we pay. Praeger. '70.

Mitchell, J. G. and Stallings, C. L. eds. Ecotactics: the Sierra Club handbook for environmental activists. Pocket Books. '70.

Moss, F. E. The water crisis. Praeger. '67.

Nash, Roderick. Wilderness and the American mind. Yale University Press. '67.

National Committee on Urban Growth Policy. The new city. Praeger. '69.

Nicholson, Max. The environmental revolution. McGraw. '70.

Nikolaieff, G. A. ed. The water crisis. (Reference Shelf. v 38, no 6) Wilson. '67.

Novick, Sheldon. The careless atom. Houghton. '69; paper ed. Dell. '70.

Ogden, S. R. ed. America the vanishing: rural life and the price of progress. Stephen Greene Press. '69.

Perloff, H. S. ed. The quality of the urban environment. Resources for the Future, Inc. 1755 Massachusetts Ave. N.W. Washington, D.C. 20036. '69.

Porter, Eliot. Appalachian wilderness: the Great Smoky Mountains; natural and human history, by Edward Abbey. Dutton. '70.

Revelle, Roger and Landsberg, H. H. eds. America's changing environment. Houghton. '70.

Rienow, Robert and Rienow, L. T. Moment in the sun: a report on the deteriorating quality of the American environment. Dial. '67.

Rogers, G. W. ed. Change in Alaska: people, politics & petroleum. University of Washington Press. '70.

Seymour, W. N. Jr. Small urban spaces. New York University Press. '69.

Smith, F. E. The politics of conservation. Pantheon. '66.

Teal, John and Teal, Mildred. Life and death of the salt marsh. (Atlantic Monthly Press Book) Little. '69.

Tilden, Freeman. The national parks. Knopf. '68.

United States. Advisory Commission on Intergovernmental Relations. Urban and rural America: policies for future growth. Supt. of Docs. Washington, D.C. 20402. '68.

United States. Congress. House of Representatives. Committee on Government Operations. Our waters and wetlands: how the Corps of Engineers can help prevent their destruction and pollution. 91st Congress, 2d session. Supt. of Docs. Washington, D.C. 20402. '70.

United States. Congress. Senate. Committee on Interior and Insular Affairs. First environmental quality report; hearing, Aug. 13, 1970. 91st Congress, 2d session. U.S. Gov. Ptg. Office. Washington, D.C. 20401. '70.

United States. Congress. Senate. Committee on Interior and Insular Affairs. National land use policy; hearings. 91st Congress, 2d session. U.S. Gov. Ptg. Office. Washington, D.C. 20401. '70.

United States. Council on Environmental Quality. Environmental quality, first annual report of Council together with President's message to Congress, transmitted Aug. 1970. Supt. of Docs. Washington, D.C. 20402. '70.

United States. Department of Health, Education and Welfare. Task Force on Environmental Health and Related Problems. A strategy for a livable environment; report. Supt. of Docs. Washington, D.C. 20402. '67.

United States. National Advisory Commission on Rural Poverty. The people left behind; a report. Supt. of Docs. Washington, D.C. 20402. '67.
  Condensed transcript, by C. E. Bishop. U.S. Department of Labor. Manpower Administration. 14th St. and Constitution Ave. N.W. Washington, D.C. 20210. '68.

United States. National Commission on Urban Problems. Building the American city; report to the Congress and to the President of the United States. Supt. of Docs. Washington, D.C. 20402. '69.

United States. National Commission on Urban Problems. Problems of zoning and land-use regulation. U.S. Gov. Ptg. Office. Washington, D.C. 20401. '68.

United States. National Goals Research Staff. Toward balanced growth: quantity with quality; report. Supt. of Docs. Washington, D.C. 20402. '70.

United States. President's Council on Recreation and Natural Beauty. From sea to shining sea: a report on the American environment, our natural heritage. Supt. of Docs. Washington, D.C. 20402. '68.

*United States. Public Land Law Review Commission. One third of the nation's land; a report to the President and to the Congress. Supt. of Docs. Washington, D.C. 20402. '70.
  A digest of this report appears in the New York *Times*. p 22. Je. 24, '70.

Welles, Christopher. The elusive bonanza: the story of oil shale. Dutton. '70.

*Whyte, W. H. The last landscape. Doubleday. '68.

Zurhorst, Charles. The conservation fraud. Cowles. '70.

PERIODICALS

American Federationist. 77:15-19. D. '70. The fight for water. P. S. Taylor.

American Forests. 76:11. N. '70. Go or no go for the trans-Alaskan pipeline? W. E. Towell.

American Forests. 76:28-31. N. '70. The corps and the environment. J. T. Starr.

American Forests. 77:7. Ja. '71. Seven gut issues on public lands. W. E. Towell.

American Forests. 77:11. Ja. '71. The forest service in the seventies. E. P. Cliff.

Architectural Forum. 132:62-5. My. '70. Zoning: the new battleground. Clarence Funnyé.

Atlantic. 227:45-56. F. '71. "Precautions are being taken by those who know": an inquiry into the power and responsibilities of the AEC [Atomic Energy Commission]. Paul Jacobs.

Christian Science Monitor. p 11. Ja. 7, '71. Reds, whites, and Blue Lake. Jack Waugh.

Christian Science Monitor. p 1+. Ja. 13, '71. Ecology council: year one. P. C. Stuart.

City. 5:1-96. Ja.-F. '71. Suburban America [entire issue].

*Congressional Record. 117:506-11. F. 8, '71. First annual report on the state of the nation's environment [President's second environmental message to Congress]. R. M. Nixon.
    Excerpts. U.S. News & World Report. 70:72-7. F. 22, '71.

Cry California. 4:18-40. Fall '69. Our 19th-century state lands commission. Michael Harris.

Cry California. 6:18-40. Winter '70-71. Irvine: the case for a new kind of planning. David Curry.

*Current Biography. 31:18-20. Jl. '70. Hartzog, George B (enjamin), Jr.
    Also available in Current Biography Yearbook 1970. p 173-5.

*Current History. 58:321-69. Je. '70. U.S. resources: a tally sheet.
    Included in this volume: Forest lands and wilderness. Michael Frome. p 343-8+.

Current History. 59:1-54. Jl. '70. America's polluted environment; symposium.

*Current History. 59:65-116. Ag. '70. Options for a cleaner America.
    Included in this volume: Wilderness and forests tomorrow. K. P. Davis. p 91-4+; Coastal areas and seashores. W. S. Beller. p 100-4+.

Daedalus. Fall '67. America's changing environment [entire issue].

Environment. 12:2-13. Ja. '70. Earthquake at Giza. Sheldon Novick.

Environment. 12:36-41 Ja. '70. A new river; an Environment staff report.

Environment. 12:28-30. My. '70. Reviews: Ecopublishing [a bibliography of recent books on environmental issues, with reviews]. Sheldon Novick.

*Environment. 12:16-18. N. '70. Problems underfoot. Terri Aaronson.

*Field & Stream. 75:18+. Jl. '70. Moment of truth for the public lands. Michael Frome.

*Field & Stream. 75:38+. O. '70. A powerful congressional group moves backward into the future. Michael Frome.

Fortune. 82:112-15+. O. '70. The long, littered path to clean air and water. Gene Bylinsky.

Fortune. 82:116. O. '70. States join the pollution battle. Ernest Holsendolph.

*Harper's Magazine. 239:21-5. N. '69. The easy chair—planning for the second America. John Fischer.

Interplay. 3:37-41. N. '70. The freeway tug of war. Richard Karp.

*Journal of Housing. 27:527-9. N. 23, '70. Cemeteries becoming critical factor in land-use planning as urban areas grow. Martha Fisher.

Life. 67:33-43. Ag. 1, '69. Threatened America. Donald Jackson.

*Life. 70:32-43. Ja. 8, '71. This land is our land. Donald Jackson.

Look. 33:44-50+. S. 9, '69. The assault on the Everglades. Anthony Wolff.

Look. 33:25-7. N. 4, '69. America the beautiful? David Perlman.

Los Angeles Times. p G 1. D. 27, '70. Do we really need the channel's oil? H. A. Wilcox.

*Minnesota Law Review. 53:1163-78. Je. '69. Towards a national policy on balanced communities. O. L. Freeman.

*Nation. 208:275-6. Mr. 3, '69. A tip from the Conqueror. J. T. Younger.
       Same abridged. Current. 107:48-51. My. '69. Land to live in.

Nation. 209:729-32. D. 29, '69. Vandal ideology. Scott Paradise.

Nation. 211:684-7. D. 28, '70. The gray woman of Appalachia. H. S. Arnow.

*Nation. 212:110-13. Ja. 25, '71. "Mining" the national forests. D.A. Burk.

National Geographic. 138:738-83. D. '70. Our ecological crisis [includes map supplement].

*National Observer. p 1+. D. 28, '70. A storm roils the Mississippi. D. W. Hacker.

National Observer. p 4. Ja. 11, '71. Park vs. highway: high court will hear key dispute.

National Observer. p 6. F. 1, '71. Power needs jolt a western scene. D. W. Hacker.

Nation's Cities. 8:15+. D. '70. The New Town idea is vastly over-rated. A. L. Otten.

New Republic. 163:10-11. Jl. 11, '70. This land is whose land? W. K. Wyant, Jr.

New Republic. 164:18-21. Ja. 23; 20-3. F. 6; 17-21. F 27, '71. The nuclear plant controversy. R. E. Lapp.

New South. 25:63-9. Fall '70. Improving the southern environment. F. E. Smith.

*New York Times. p 1+. Je. 24, '70. Revised policy for U.S. lands asked in study. Gladwin Hill.

New York Times. p 26. Je. 25, '70. Focus on public land. Gladwin Hill.

New York Times. p 22. Je. 26, '70. Nixon accused of bypassing Congress to spur timber cutting. E. W. Kenworthy.

New York Times. p 34M. Jl. 29, '70. Too much for highways . . .

New York Times. p 30M. Ag. 11, '70. To rescue the environment.

New York Times. p 72. Ag. 20, '70. Lands acquired for preservation. J. C. Devlin.

New York Times. p 1+. Ag. 23, '70. Alaskans fear boom in oil perils the land. S. V. Roberts.

*New York Times. p 1+. O. 18, '70. Prairie partisans move to save grasslands. J. N. Wilford.

New York Times. p 25. N. 19, '70. Forestry Service scored on timber conservation.

New York Times. p 43. D. 14, '70. Woodman—chop that tree! F. C. Simmons.

New York Times. p 1+. D. 15, '70. Strip-mining boom leaves wasteland in its wake. B. A. Franklin.

*New York Times. p 32. D. 22, '70. The great soil swindle.

*New York Times. p 1+. Ja. 14, '71. Alaska pipeline is upheld by Interior agency study. D. E. Rosenbaum.

New York Times. p 1+. Ja. 25, '71. Urban population pressures spur new land rush in the West. Anthony Ripley.

New York Times. p 1+. Ja. 29, '71. U.A.W. maintains a Jersey suburb keeps out poor. Ronald Sullivan.

New York Times. p 15. Ja. 10; p 35. Mr. 4, '71. The highway juggernaut. Tom Wicker.

New York Times. p 30. Mr. 8, '71. Counterattack by cities. Richard Reeves.

New York Times. p 1+. Mr. 15, '71. Ruckelshaus asks a delay on Alaska pipeline permit. E. W. Kenworthy.

New York Times. p 19. Ap. 6, '71. Forest Service assailed for "clear-cutting" as Senate panel opens hearings. E. W. Kenworthy.

New York Times. p 85. Ap. 7, '71. Clear-cutting defended by timber men. E. W. Kenworthy.

New York Times. p 1+. Ap. 11, '71. Coast desert a vast, littered playground for millions. S. V. Roberts.

New York Times Magazine. p 16-17+. F. 7, '71. The four big fears about nuclear power. R. E. Lapp.

New Yorker. 47:42-8+. Mr. 20; 42-8+. Mr. 27; 41-4+. Ap. 3, '71. Encounters with the archdruid. John McPhee.
    Profiles of David Brower, Charles Park, Charles Fraser, and Floyd Dominy.

Newsweek. 76:68-73. N. 2, '70. Dirty flows the Delaware. George Alexander.

Newsweek. 76:49-51. D. 28, '70. Pollution: puffery or progress?

*Not Man Apart. 1:18-19. Ja. '71. The Public Land Law Review Commission report. Angus McDonald.

Oceans Magazine. 3:34-41. S.-O. '70. How to rescue a bay in distress. Wesley Marx.

*Playboy. 18:147+. Ja. '71. Cleansing the environment. Gaylord Nelson.

Progressive. 35:21-5. Mr. '71. The plunder of Alaska. Richard Pollak.

*Reader's Digest. 97:78-83. D. '70. Crisis on our rivers. J. N. Miller and Robert Simmons.

Saturday Review. 52:19-21+. S. 20, '69. Life on a dying lake. Peter Schrag.

Saturday Review. 53:53-61. D. 5, '70. Clean power from inside the earth. John Lear.

Saturday Review. 54:45-8. Mr. 6, '71. Land: making room for tomorrow. John Lear.

*Science. 169:1003-4. S. 4, '70. Land-use problems in Illinois; AAAS [American Association for the Advancement of Science] symposium, December 30, 1970. R. E. Bergstrom.

*Science. 170:718-19. N. 13, '70. Land use: congress taking up conflict over power plants. L. J. Carter.

Science. 170:1387-90. D. 25, '70. Timber management: improvement implies new land-use policies. L. J. Carter.

Social Education. 35:5-120. Ja. '71. The environmental crisis; symposium.

State Government. 44:2-11. Winter '71. Toward a state land-use policy. R. H. Slavin.

Time. 96:44-50. Jl. 27, '70. The great land: boom or doom?

U.S. News & World Report. 68:39-40. Je. 22, '70. Battle to open the suburbs: new attack on zoning laws.

U.S. News & World Report. 70:20-1. Ja. 11, '71. Stepped-up war on pollution.

United States Naval Institute Proceedings. 95:63-75. My. '69. Oil pollution: no solution? T. A. Clingan, Jr.

Vital Speeches of the Day. 37:177-81. Ja. 1, '71. National policy for coastal management; address, Oct. 19, 1970. Edward Wenk, Jr.

Wall Street Journal. p 14, S. 23, '70. Meet a prime polluter: Uncle Sam. Dennis Farney.

*Wall Street Journal. p 1+. O. 27, '70. Saving the scenery. Burt Schore.

*Wall Street Journal. p 1+. O. 30, '70. Nature's nurseries. W. E. Burrows.

Wall Steet Journal. p 1+. Ja. 25, '71. Atom-age trash. Dennis Farney.

*Washington Post. p B 3. N. 8, '70. The future of American cities: two views. F. L. Hope, Jr.; Wolf Von Eckardt.

*Washington Post. p A 6. Ap. 11, '71. Oil refinery: jobs vs. environment. Maxwell Wiesenthal.

Washington Post. p A 4. Ap. 12, '71. McGee plans bill to curb logging. E. W. Lammi.

Wilson Library Bulletin. bibliog 44:158-77. O. '69. Nature and conservation. R. G. Lillard.